The Language of Empire
Abu Ghraib and the American Media

Lila Rajiva

MONTHLY REVIEW PRESS
New York

Library of Congress Cataloging-in-Publication Data

Rajiva, Lila.
The language of empire: Abu Ghraib and the American media / by Lila Rajiva.
p. cm.
ISBN 1-58367-119-6 (pbk.) — ISBN 1-58367-120-X (cloth)

1. Abu Ghraib Prison. 2. Iraq War, 2003—Mass media and the war. 3. Iraq War, 2003—Prisoners and prisons, American. 4. Iraq War, 2003—Atrocities. 5. Prisoners of war—Abuse of—United States. I. Title.
DS79.76.R353 2005
070.4'49956704437—dc22
2005024611

MONTHLY REVIEW PRESS
122 West 27th Street
New York, NY 10001
www.monthlyreview.org

Printed in Canada

10 9 8 7 6 5 4 3 2 1

To my parents, Dr. Adolf Walter and Dr. Sylvia Walter of Christian Medical College & Hospital, Vellore, South India, whose dedicated service to the health of the poor and the education of generations of doctors is my constant inspiration. Their unfailing love and support through difficult times made this book possible. And to my brothers, Dr. Noel and Dr. David Walter, for help and encouragement whenever I needed it.

Acknowledgments

I would like to thank Sunil Sharma of Dissident Voice, who first published some of the essays on which this book is based and Counterpunch magazine which published Chapter 10 in an earlier version. Thanks also to my parents, to Michael Neumann for commenting on individual chapters, and to Andrew Nash and Erin Clermont for helping to make the final version ready.

Contents

Prologue

There are five compounds, each separately walled, and everywhere there are jagged watchtowers, twenty-four in all, set in a crooked gray fortress. This is Baghdad Central Correctional Facility, known after May 2004 as Camp Redemption. It is a town inside a town, 112 hectares of land, a 4-kilometer security wall of concrete block topped with wire, high-security jails mixed with tent cities, all in a small, dusty town about twenty miles west of Baghdad, just off the main highway that runs between Baghdad and Fallujah in the center of Iraq. Before the Gulf wars, the surrounding farmland was much greener than the desert. There were date palms everywhere, and the gardens in the town were watered freely from the rivers and filled with the red *al juri* flowers and a species of white magnolia, *narjis*.

Abu Ghraib town itself is really part of Baghdad's sprawling suburbs and lies only a little to the north of Baghdad (formerly Saddam) International Airport. Abu Ghraib market is about 12 miles west of the city limits on the old road to Jordan. People liked to shop here, because the region was known for its cucumbers, onions, potatoes, broad beans, oranges, and lamb. For everything else, the looters' bazaar next door was preferable.

In the 1920s, when Iraq was a mandate of the League of Nations under British stewardship, the Agriculture Department initiated a program of research, founding the first experimental station at Abu Ghraib and Neinevah. In the 1940s, a decade after Iraq became independent, the headquarters of agricultural research was still at Abu Ghraib. In 1944, the Iraqi government created the Abi-Gharib district, 15 kilometers west of Baghdad, in order to make consultation easier for farmers whose homes were in the town.

In the 1960s British and Western contractors built the prison that was to become notorious under Saddam Hussein first, and then under the Americans.

Although accurate figures are unavailable, as many as fifty thousand men and women were jammed into Abu Ghraib at one time, penned inside twelve-by twelve-foot cells. After the American invasion in April 2003, the abandoned prison was stripped to its scaffolding by looters. Since then it has been cleaned and repaired and turned into an American military prison, which by late 2003 held thousands of civilians, including women and children, swept up by the military in house raids and at checkpoints. Some of them were classified as common criminals, others as security risks, and a small number as high-value detainees, that is, individuals highly placed in the former Iraqi regime.

1
Graphic Evidence I: Photographs

The photos on the CBS News program *Sixty Minutes II*, on Wednesday, April 28, 2004, were riveting—a hooded figure in a ragged black poncho balanced uneasily on a box, an off-kilter Halloween Christ with bare feet and palms plaintively open, electric wires running from the hands like the strings of a marionette; an American girl with a cigarette dangling from the corner of her mouth in one photo and an impish grin in another as she points derisively at the genitals of a naked, hooded Iraqi man and signals thumbs up; smiling soldiers behind naked men posed in a tangled human pyramid; hooded, stripped prisoners simulating fellatio and sodomy; an unmuzzled dog snarling at a cowering, naked prisoner.[1] CBS News claimed it had dozens more, even worse.

The Americans in the pictures were soldiers of the 800th Military Police Brigade. The Iraqis were prisoners in their custody at Abu Ghraib, near Baghdad, once Iraq's most notorious prison under the deposed dictator Saddam Hussein. Suddenly, the name Abu Ghraib was again a synonym for torture, only this time, American torture.

The images set the national and international media on fire. On newspapers and magazines, television channels, news broadcasts, the radio waves, and most of all, the Internet, other pictures that CBS had chosen to withhold began circulating. On Friday, April 30, they were broadcast on the Arab satellite TV channels, Al-Jazeera and Al-Arabiya, although no images, not even of death or mutilation, could have been more offensive to Muslims. The Baghdad papers did not show them, out of deference to the birthday celebration of the prophet Mohammed in the lunar month of Muharram, which falls at the end of April, but also because in Iraq newspapers are not published on Friday.[2] The editors were understandably hesitant about the impact of such graphic pictures on Muslim culture, in which nudity is shameful and public displays of sexuality, particularly homosexuality, are fiercely condemned and proscribed.

A Reuters article described the worldwide revulsion to the pictures: Abdel-Bari Atwan, editor of the Arab newspaper *Al Quds Al Arabi* claimed that the liberators were worse than the dictators. "They have not just lost the hearts and minds of Iraqis but all the Third World and the Arab countries." The left-wing *L'Unita* in Italy pronounced that what had taken place was "classic" and "irrefutable" torture; "forced public sodomy" was "one of the gravest offenses"; the torture was "not an isolated incident" but routine.[3] Calling for an independent inquiry, Amnesty International said, "There is a real crisis of leadership in Iraq with double standards and double speak on human rights."[4] In the U.S. *Newsday*, Mohammed Bazzi described the enraged reactions of Iraqis.[5] In Britain, after the *Daily Mirror* announced on Friday that it had pictures of British soldiers involved in abuse, the government announced that it would launch its own investigation into the charges.[6] And President Bush added his voice, "Their treatment does not reflect the nature of the American people. That's not the way we do things in America."[7]

On May 1, the Saturday edition of the *Mirror* carried new pictures that included one showing a hooded man being attacked. "The prisoner, aged 18–20, begged for mercy as he was battered with rifle butts and batons in the head and groin, was kicked, stamped and urinated on, and had a gun barrel forced into his mouth." Barely conscious after eight hours of assaults, he was thrown out of a moving truck. It was not known if he had survived. The *Mirror* claimed it had been given the photos by two anonymous soldiers upset over the abuse. The following day the *Sunday Telegraph* claimed that six soldiers from the Queen's Lancashire Regiment were to be arrested over it.[8] By then the images had been sen around the world and even the U.N. Secretary General had issued a condemnation.[9]

But the story had only begun. Over the weekend and into the next week it became apparent that the photos on CBS were only a small sample of what investigators had collected and that hundreds, some said thousands, more were circulating on computer discs and in e-mails sent home to parents or stored on hard drives. The floodgates were threatening to open. The *Washington Post* reported that it had new pictures.[10] Then, the brigadier-general in charge of the prison charged that military intelligence and senior officers were involved.[11] Meanwhile, human rights organizations brought up earlier reports that had been ignored. In 2003 Amnesty International had recorded four deaths of Iraqi prisoners in British custody among a catalog of complaints, and one after the other, victims came forward with harrowing stories.[12] Lawyers for the families of at least eighteen Iraqis allegedly killed by British soldiers prepared to go to the high court in the first week of May.[13]

***Case*:** Abdullah Mohammed Abdulrazzaq was tortured with electricity for three days in Adhamiya palace. He was tied naked to a chair and deprived of food and water until he collapsed.

***Case*:** Saif Mahmoud Shakir was beaten so badly that his kidneys were damaged and he urinated blood.[14]

***Case*:** Sami Abbas was forced to do kneebends until he collapsed. Black marks still ring his wrists from the pinch of plastic handcuffs. Rest was made impossible by loudspeakers blaring, over and over, the Beastie Boys' rap anthem, "No Sleep Till Brooklyn."[15]

Prisoners were maintained on one meal a day and a liter of water a week supplemented once a week with an army MRE. Unruly prisoners were shut inside filthy shipping containers in which prison dogs were kept.

A State Department review of international reactions cited both a British commentary that called the treatment at Abu Ghraib "barbaric idiocy" and an Italian commentary warning that the abuse reflected a failure of leadership that would multiply recruits for Al Qaeda. Britain and Italy are two of the key European contributors to coalition forces in Iraq and officials immediately sensed the potential that what international support remained for the occupation could collapse. In Brazil, a commentator called for world condemnation and described the abuse as "the bastard daughter" of the Guantanamo Bay detention center.[16]

Anticipating the outrage, CBS had actually sat on the story for two weeks at the Pentagon's request and ran with it only when it became clear that a report of the army's secret internal investigation by Major General Taguba had been leaked to Seymour Hersh, the Pulitzer Prize–winning journalist best known for breaking the story of the My Lai massacre in Vietnam. In a piece in the *New Yorker,* Hersh described the "sadistic, blatant, and wanton acts of abuse" in Taguba's report.[17] In one telling paragraph, he sighted the tip of what was soon to prove an iceberg ready to sink domestic support for the war:

> Breaking chemical lights and pouring the phosphoric liquid on detainees; pouring cold water on naked detainees; beating detainees with a broom handle and a chair; threatening male detainees with rape; allowing a military police

> guard to stitch the wound of a detainee who was injured after being slammed against the wall in his cell; sodomizing a detainee with a chemical light and perhaps a broomstick, and using military working dogs to frighten and intimidate detainees with threats of attack, and in one instance actually biting a detainee.

It was the anticipated publication of Hersh's May 10 article, "Torture at Abu Ghraib," the first of a series of three, that forced CBS to go public with the photos. As Hersh noted, an earlier report by Major General Donald Ryder had already concluded that serious deficiencies in training and manpower had made the detention system ripe for human rights abuse and in need of immediate attention, especially to separate military intelligence personnel from military policemen. The Taguba report was thus not the first time that the role of MI had been raised by someone at a high level, although Ryder's conclusion that no MP units were "purposely applying inappropriate confinement practices," was a blatant whitewash. Taguba, on the contrary, refused to mince words. He recommended that Colonel Thomas Pappas, an MI commander, be reprimanded and receive nonjudicial punishment, that Lieutenant-Colonel Steven Jordan, the former director of the Joint Interrogation and Debriefing Center (the site of the collaboration between MIs and MPs) be relieved of duty and reprimanded; that a civilian contractor, Steven Stephanowicz of Consolidated Analysis Centers Inc. (CACI) be fired from his army job; that John Israel, another contractor from CACI, be disciplined; and that Brigadier General Janis Karpinski, the commanding officer of Abu Ghraib, as well as seven brigade MPs be reprimanded. His report presented a picture of "a virtual collapse of the command structure" in which army reservists, instigated by MI and by CIA employees, "set physical and mental conditions for favorable interrogation of witnesses."

Hersh's stunning account implied that Abu Ghraib was no aberration. Powerful people had known, powerful people had looked away, and there was every reason to believe that powerful people had encouraged what had occurred. As the lawyer of one of the main defendants asked, "Do you really believe the army relieved a general officer because of six soldiers? Not a chance."[18] What was at stake was not the careers of a handful of reservists but the entire command structure of the Iraq operation.

The army's reaction to the CBS exposé was quite instructive. The weekend following, General Myers, chairman of the Joint Chiefs of Staff and the highest-ranked military leader, appeared on the prominent Sunday talk show *Face the*

Nation to field questions.[19] Asked why Taguba's investigation, begun at the end of January, was only seeing the light of day in May, Myers faltered, "It's just working its way up—up the chain. The—but the action we took as soon as we heard about this—we were deeply involved in that." Asked about the statement made by Karpinsky that military intelligence personnel had instigated the guards' behavior, the faltering became incoherence, "We had a—besides looking at how we treat detainees by those folks responsible for the day to day caring and feeding of the detainees, we're looking at that aspect of it."

When Schieffer asked about Amnesty International's request for an independent investigation, Myers hesitated once again, hinting that the investigation might fall directly under the purview of Rumsfeld. Why the actions of a handful of soldiers warranted the personal scrutiny of the secretary of defense was a question he neither raised nor answered, but his confusion over the mere suggestion of an independent review implied awareness that the scandal reached higher.

While Myers prevaricated and newspapers wondered, the Pentagon knew just what was involved. The same Sunday, the *Post* reported a widening of the investigation to the CIA and intelligence. But a CIA spokesman who was quoted was careful to make a subtle distinction, "We have found no *direct* evidence connecting CIA personnel."[20]

This, of course, had already become apparent from Karpinski's *Newsweek* interview on Saturday night during which she claimed that the MPs were being made to take the fall. She charged that a month before the abuse, a military intelligence team from Guantanamo had come over with the "main and specific mission" to "give them new techniques to get more information from detainees." The cellblock involved—IA—was controlled by military intelligence throughout the day.[21]

Of course, it's possible that Myers had not read the Karpinsky interview before the show, but even so, he had known for two weeks that CBS had the pictures and wanted to run them. It was he who made Dan Rather postpone the show to avoid endangering the military situation. It's impossible that he was unaware of the nature of the charges or of the type of defense the accused was using. Both indicated that the abuse was widespread and had been carried out not only without censure but with encouragement. There were other clues. For example, the Taguba report described the rape of an underage male prisoner by a civilian contractor outside military jurisdiction. Given the extent of the army's reliance on contractors to perform all sorts of security and intelligence functions, that one incident alone should have indicated the existence of a widespread problem. But there were also the statements of Staff Sergeant "Chip" Frederick, who had had his Article 32 hearing (the equivalent of a grand jury proceeding) and had been keeping a journal ever since investigators approached him on January 14. He said that commanders had ignored his request for operating procedures and that when he complained that prisoners were being confined naked in damp, unventilated three- by three-foot cells, without toilets or running water, they had told him, "I don't care if they have to sleep standing up." Frederick's civilian lawyer even stated, "I can assure you Chip Frederick had no idea how to humiliate an Arab until he met up with higher-ranking people who told him how."[22] Frederick is no innocent. A witness recounted how this six-year veteran of the Virginia Department of Corrections "punched a detainee in the chest so hard that the detainee almost went into cardiac arrest." But his account is substantiated by witnesses with their own mute stories—the battered face of prisoner No. 153399, the bloodied body of another prisoner wrapped in cellophane and packed in ice, a photograph of an empty room splattered with blood.[23]

In fact, Myers did not have to have read Taguba's or the news reports to know that something was horribly wrong with the system of detention and interrogation. The incidents that surfaced in April had been under investigation since January, and even before that, in the fall of 2003, two generals, Ryder and Miller, had criticized the detention process throughout Iraq. Myers and Rumsfeld could not have been ignorant of all this. If they were, their negligence made them just as culpable.

Who Knew What and When

There was considerable circumstantial evidence that responsibility went high. A paper trail of news reports and complaints had been issuing from Amnesty International, the Red Cross, and Human Rights Watch for well over a year. Reed Brody, an HRW lawyer, pointed out that the bold poses of the soldiers with the prisoners "suggests they had nothing to hide from their superiors." He noted that the United States had "failed to provide clear information on its treatment of 10,000 civilians held in Iraq" and in Afghanistan the United States was holding civilians in a "legal black hole at a number of off-limits detention facilities with no tribunals, no legal counsel and no family visits."[24]

In August 2003, Amnesty International reported on abuse in Afghanistan at the main site, Bagram, as well as at others scattered across the country in which about a thousand detainees were being held.[25] That report was stonewalled even after two deaths were reported in December and after the Washington head of

Human Rights First said Bush, Rice, and Rumsfeld had been informed that a crisis was in the making.[26] The military announced investigations but kept the details and outcomes secret. On May 4 they acknowledged that as many as twenty investigations were under way.[27] In a letter to Rumsfeld on February 10, 2004, HRW complained that prisoners were being held without access to family or lawyers, without good cause or legal review, and that most had committed no crimes. The letter was left unanswered by the DOD.[28] Richard Dicker, director of HRW's International Justice program, stated in April that no information was available for at least two hundred "high-security detainees" as well as prisoners being interrogated before transfer.[29]

Besides these reports, there were direct complaints to the Coalition Provisional Authority about specific cases. Former Iraqi human rights minister Abdul Basset Turki said that then-ambassador Paul Bremer, the highest American civilian official in Iraq, had known that Iraqi prisoners were being abused.[30] Turki complained to him as early as November 2003 and again in December about the suffering of women detainees and prisoners beaten and left out for hours in the sun. Bremer reportedly did not show any interest and denied his request to visit Abu Ghraib. Turki then made weekly complaints to the CPA, reported to the Arab League, and then again in March made another complaint to the CPA about the rape of an Iraqi woman.[31] At a human rights meeting under UN auspices he demanded the continuation of monitoring in Iraq, a practice that had been discontinued in April 2003. According to him, the Americans refused.

The worst case he told Bremer about occurred in Mosul during a house raid when occupation forces threw a grenade into a room and closed the door. A woman, her four children, and her brother-in-law were killed before the soldiers found that they were at the wrong address.[32]

There was another report eerily prescient of Abu Ghraib. Christian Peacemaker Teams (CPT), a church-backed group, described how, in November 2003, GIs loosed a military dog on civilians during a raid on Ramadi, thirty miles west of Fallujah. Soldiers arrested thirty people including Saad al-Khashab, an attorney with Organization for Human Rights in Iraq, who told CPT that thirty detainees were handcuffed, laid on the ground, and then pushed into a house where the soldiers let the dog loose to bite several people.[33] An Austalian barrister, Richard Bourke, who had been investigating abuse at Guantanamo and Afghanistan since 2001, testified in 2003 that it went beyond the Geneva Conventions and amounted to medieval torture.[34]

The Scandal Widens

The media, however, seemed reluctant to apply the word *torture* to what was happening, still preferring to call it abuse. This may partly have been caution following a case of apparent fraud when photos published by the *Mirror* were alleged by the British government to be doctored and the editor was forced to resign.[35] Nonetheless, it was quickly becoming obvious that the CBS exposé had only touched the surface of a larger problem. New pictures were coming to light, including over a thousand acquired by the *Washington Post*. In one, a soldier is seen holding a leash tied around the neck of a naked Iraqi, who is grimacing and squirming on the floor. In another, naked men sprawl on top of one another while soldiers stand around. A naked man, a dark hood over his head, is handcuffed to a cell door; another man, also naked, is handcuffed to a bunk bed, arms splayed so wide that his back is arched. His face is covered with a pair of women's underwear. A *Post* article describes pictures of "soldiers simulating sexually explicit acts with one another," "a cow being skinned and gutted and soldiers posing with its severed head," "dozens of pictures of a cat's severed head," "wounded men and corpses," "a dead man ... covered in blood," "a body, gray and decomposing" next to a soldier "smiling broadly and giving the "thumbs-up sign," and a photo in which "a young woman lifts her shirt, exposing her breasts ... but it is unclear whether she is a prisoner." Unclear, it seems, even though she is "wearing a white band with numbers on her wrist."

The charges went beyond the merely bizarre.

Abbas Hassan told his mother that Americans were electrocuting prisoners and raping Iraqi men.

Suhaib al-Baz, a cameraman for Al-Jazeera, said he was stripped, beaten, spat upon, and kept awake during his 74 days in custody. Soldiers photographed him with personal cameras and he saw a computer screensaver with a picture of a hooded, handcuffed prisoner being attacked by a dog. A twelve- or thirteen-year-old girl was brought in at night in front of the prison cells, naked and screaming for her brother, who was in an upper cell. Another time he saw a sick fifteen-year-old boy forced to carry two heavy cans of water and run up and down a corridor while being beaten by a soldier. When the boy collapsed, he was stripped, doused with cold water, and then confronted with a naked, hooded man who turned out to be his father. Laughing soldiers forced the father to wear a bra and knickers.[36]

Unknown to the public and most journalists, the child abuse charges were not new. Earlier, in April 2004, the *Denver Post* had already unearthed evidence of rape and sodomy including an assault by MI personnel against an Iraqi woman and by a soldier against an Iraqi boy.[37]

In other accounts, one inmate, Abu Salem, described how prisoners were kept naked constantly and then, just before Red Cross visits, handed a few clothes and warned that they would never be let out if they talked, hardly a practice that could have taken place without the knowledge of superiors. At least once, the 320th MP Battalion moved around a handful of "ghost detainees" to hide them from a visiting International Committee of the Red Cross team. This too was clearly something that could not have occurred without high-level clearance.

Torin Nelson, who worked in MI at Guantanamo before shifting to Abu Ghraib as a private contractor in 2003, placed the blame on the MI command structure and private contractors. He alleged that private companies were so eager to meet the demand for their services that they even sent cooks and truck drivers to work as interrogators. There was intense pressure to crack high-level detainees rather than sift tediously through information provided by less important prisoners. "All it takes is the signature of a low-ranking NCO to send someone right around the world and have them locked up indefinitely, but it takes the signature of the secretary of defense to let them go."[38]

"Ghosts," special forces involvement, child abuse, clear signals of a systemic lawless practice—the threat to the administration was palpable enough for President Bush to take the unusual step of going on Arab television to apologize, giving two interviews on Al Hurra and Al Arabiya on May 5, 2004.[39] At home there were calls for higher-level inquiries as well as resignations. The cover of *The Economist* carried the picture of the hooded prisoner on a box beneath the headline: "Resign, Rumsfeld!"[40] Citing what it called "the botched handling" of the abuse investigation and the war, the *St. Louis Post-Dispatch* suggested that the exiting Rumsfeld should "take his top deputies with him."[41] The stakes were getting higher by the day.

2
Framing a Narrative I: Politics as the Personal

The View from the Right

Antiwar newspapers from the beginning insisted that torture in the American prison camps was a common, flagrant, and systemic practice. The *Guardian* was one of the few British papers that seemed to grasp almost immediately that Abu Ghraib was not simply something that could be patched over. "This is not just a colossal blunder by the U.S.—it inaugurates a whole new level of fears and dangers, both in Iraq and among many Muslims throughout the world."[1] But in the liberal American papers—the *New York Times* or the *Washington Post*, for example—there was a different reaction. There was an intense focus on the story, as though reporters were bent on redeeming themselves after their docility during the invasion and occupation. Yet there was also hesitation in drawing any broad conclusions. As for domestic conservatives, they were more concerned with the American image. In a strategy familiar from partisan politics, they carefully distanced themselves from the abuse while simultaneously expressing skepticism over whether anything much had actually happened. The abuse was "alleged," the reports were "hearsay," and more investigation was needed. Meanwhile, they argued, people would be held accountable and the American system vindicated.

Well into the first week of May, the coverage of the scandal held to this predictable trajectory among the more conservative news outlets, right-wing pundits, and government spokesmen. For all of them, no matter the evidence, the abuse was alleged, limited, and un-American.

The *Wall Street Journal*, for instance, highlighted the 24-page report of the International Committee of the Red Cross that described prisoner maltreatment in Iraq as "beyond exceptional cases" and "a practice tolerated by coalition forces." Yet, on the very same day the paper ran an op-ed piece by Newt Gingrich, one of the architects of the conservative resurgence, that insisted that "any effort by the anti-American left or the Arab media to generalize the acts of a few into an attack on America, or on America's armed forces, should be repudiated and condemned." [2]

This was a view very much in keeping with the *Journal*'s own editorial position, "Like reporters at a free buffet," it claimed sourly, "members of Congress are swarming to the TV cameras to declare their outrage and demand someone's head, usually Donald Rumsfeld's. The goal seems to be less to punish the offenders then to grab one more reason to discredit the war."[3] But the *Journal* protested too loudly, especially when it attacked Congress's belief that the Pentagon decision to degrade the legal status of "enemy combatants" might have had something to do with Abu Ghraib. Congress's "bizarre notion" was increasingly becoming everyone's and the *Journal*'s vituperative reaction was only a grudging admission of this.

Of course, conservatives were well aware of the danger that Abu Ghraib posed to the war effort. When Jed Babbin in the *National Review* claimed that the real story of Abu Ghraib was the systematic problem in gathering military intelligence and not the actions of a few "dirt bags," he was unwittingly using precisely the argument that had led the military into the position in which it now found itself, as well as precisely the defense to which it now resorted.[4] There was actually a remarkable consonance between the explanations of movement conservatives and those of the government. More remarkably, the media's supposedly liberal exposés seemed ultimately to reinforce rather than question that position.

From the start, the way in which the story was reframed provides an example of how news outlets, while seeming to critique the official line, actually reinforced it. *Face the Nation*, for instance, sandwiched its interview with General Myers between a story about Thomas Hamill, an American hostage who had just escaped from his captors and a fiftieth-anniversary remembrance of the boxer Mohammed Ali. Bob Schieffer's interview of Myers was replete with examples of the PR strategy of repackaging, in which elements of a story are downplayed or highlighted to alter the appearance of the "package" being sold. The story of Hamill, which led the show, set the tone, subtly transforming revulsion from the abuse to patriotic solidarity with the war effort, replacing ugly pictures of pain with warm ones of a family reunited, and allowing Iraqis to subside into the faceless anonymity of the "enemy" as viewers celebrated a fellow American's courage.

As the CBS transcript shows, the reservists are quickly winnowed out as a handful of deviants through a convenient distinction between "American" and "un-American" soldiers and then Myers asserts, "You . . . you. . . . All you have to do is look at the photographs and know that's not how we do business. We don't torture people."

That is, we are not to trust our own eyes but allow government to put the picture into the bigger context in which Americans "don't torture." Myers continues: "If you look at our adversaries and the way they celebrate the deaths of innocent men, women, and children after 9/11, after Riyadh, after Madrid, in Iraq after the Baghdad bombings and so forth, they celebrate deaths of innocent men, and children. … We don't celebrate this."

If one look at the glee on the faces of the soldiers in the photos, it's clear that some Americans *are* celebrating, but while the Arabs who celebrated 9/11 (and Palestinians are conflated with Iraqis) are representative, those who torture with grins are aberrations, because for Myers it is a tale of two very different groups, *we* and *they*, whose intentions cannot be read aright from outside. We, the "good guys," do exactly the same as the "bad guys," but our acts are not the same because we are not the same. The American military is never the "bad guy," but even as a "good guy," it never errs.

These techniques are consistently applied, whether by government officials, paid "expert opinion" in the journals, or by conservative editorial writers. Events are retold to diffuse any cognitive dissonance between the official version of events and what the public sees for itself in the photos, and attention is deflected elsewhere. The story is refocused on the personalities of the abusers, on the human interest angle. In part, this springs from the nature of the commercial news business in which a story about individual wrongdoing is seen as more likely to keep viewers tuned in. The commercial nature of the news also drives the focus on graphic images that are highly sexual but in American culture not immediately recognizable as depicting the worst pain. News is shaped by and in turn shapes public demand for the lurid. But there is also another reason. Personalizing and sensationalizing the story prevents analysis that might lead to dangerous conclusions about what constitutes abuse, whether it might be taking place elsewhere, and why.

The distortion extends to historical facts. The elegant propaganda of Victor Hansen, a classics professor and columnist for Benador Associates, a public relations group that promotes neoconservative experts, owes more to his studies in mythology, it seems, than to history. Hansen blames antiwar activists for the "Western disease" of reflexive self-hatred and assures us in essay after essay in the run-up to the war that Americans are in Iraq for the most selfless of motives.

Alone among all countries, America has never acted lawlessly. He cites the Chinese conquest of Tibet but not the much bloodier American invasion of the Philippines. In Soviet style, American conquest is always about liberation, freedom, and democracy. We are in Iraq to establish "consensual democracy" even if Iraqi newspapers have to be shut down and threatened and Iraqi leaders appointed by America.[5]

In an article in the *Wall Street Journal* on May 3 Hansen begins with the usual qualification that the pictures of military police "in some cases, allegedly torturing prisoners" while "seemingly inhuman" have to be seen in the context of Saddam and his "fascist and Islamicist successors" who "do it all the time." He concedes that as "emissaries of human rights" Americans have to be held to higher standards, but he warns readers of the dangers of rushing to judgment on the basis of "lurid pictures, hearsay and leaked accounts to the *New Yorker* magazine" and is incensed that the "apparent transgressions" of a "few renegade correctional officers" has provoked more outrage than the dismemberment of four American contractors at Fallujah. Forgotten is the evidence provided by the army's own internal investigation, as well as the fact that the contractors were professional security personnel, mercenaries, who were killed by civilians in retaliation against escalating American violence against the population.

Not only are Hansen's assertions shorn of such context, what history he uses is tendentious. In the familiar neoconservative style, he solders fascism and Islamism together and treats regime change in the Middle East as a replay of D-Day. He invokes Daniel Pearl, the *Wall Street Journal* reporter beheaded in Pakistan in 2002, preemptively hijacking the language of religious persecution on behalf of his argument. This gambit, like the coinage Islamo-fascist, automatically tars as anti-Semitic any resistance by Muslim and Arab societies, even when that resistance is explicitly directed against Israeli and American policies. The implication is that there can never be reasonable grounds to object to American or Israeli actions. There can never be racism among Americans or Israelis but there is always racism among Arabs.

Hansen passes over pictures of beaten bodies, a corpse, and group masturbation to focus on the picture of naked men making a human pyramid before a smiling female because is it the easiest to gloss over and the one most likely to play to the gallery in America where Islamic paternalism is fair game to be targeted on behalf of women. A smiling female guard in the utero-topia of the army acting out the desires of her superiors in the fatuous belief that her equality is now complete allows Hansen to posture subliminally as a feminist striking a blow against the patriarchy while defending acts of grotesque sexual degradation, although the postures of the victimized men nevertheless convey all the sublime dignity of human beings *in extremis*. The homoeroticism of the image adds to its choiceness, with Muslim culture, which taboos male homosexual contact, being publicly chastised and enlightened by the "emissaries of human rights."[6]

Hansen is not alone in distorting the record. Conservative columnist James Taranto writes derisively, "Here are the horrors to which America subjected him [Dhia al-Shweiri]: During his stay at Abu Ghraib, he said [he] was asked to take off his clothes only once and for about 15 minutes."[7]

Since Taranto writes this when the assault, rape, and sodomy at Abu Ghraib were well-known, this is surely disingenuous. By May 6, even he has to concede that "they [the soldiers involved] sound like a bunch of losers." Still, for him, the torture remains a by-product of the sixties to be blamed on left-leaning universities like Harvard that, by banning military recruiters from their campuses, have prevented the best and brightest from being inducted into the army. Taranto's Abu Ghraib is nothing more than a brief skirmish in the domestic culture wars.[8]

Other commentators were also intent on making a molehill out of a mountain. Midge Decter, doyenne of neoconservative polemicists and author of a flattering biography of Rumsfeld, pronounced the scandal "ersatz."[9] Fox News columnist Ann Coulter blamed the abuse on "girl soldiers," although she otherwise pointedly ignored it.[10] Coulter, never at a loss for inflammatory words, has in the past urged that "we should invade their [Muslim] countries, kill their leaders and convert them to Christianity." She would certainly have had more to say had the prisoners been American.[11] For Linda Chavez and Peggy Noonan as well, the fault lay with the culture wars, with "girly boys" and feminism.[12] Kate O'Beirne scolded "the Republican leadership in the House, who never got around to condemning the savage videotaped execution of Daniel Pearl," evidently forgetting that Congress does not have oversight authority over terrorists but does over the occupation.[13] In fact, conservative fingers pointed everywhere except back home.

Pulitzer Prize–winning *Washington Post* columnist Charles Krauthammer, a subtler intellect, concedes that the guilty need to be judged by American's self-professed standards and not by Saddam's. But for him, too, the story turns into a morality play about why the United States is not what it looks like while Islamic societies are whatever Krauthammer says they are. He writes,

> There is one fundamental issue at stake that dares not speak its name. This war is also about—deeply about—sex. For the jihadists, at stake in the war against the infidels is the control of women. Western freedom means the end of women's mastery by men. They prize their traditional prerogatives that allow them to keep their women barefoot in the kitchen as illiterate economic and sexual slaves.

Krauthammer fails to specify who his jihadists are. Is this a selective portrait of the Taliban, a group midwifed by the CIA? Or of theocratic Iran, where officials point out that there are more female members in the parliament than in the U.S. Senate? In Iraq, a secular state, women are educated and have held high-ranking positions in government. Saddam's top weapons expert was a woman. Yet, on behalf of gender feminism of a kind rejected by much of conservative America, Krauthammer is prepared to characterize jihadists as motivated by a desire for the "dictatorial clerical control of sexuality," surely a desire that could just as easily attributed to conservative Christianity or Judaism. And even if Krauthammer were right in his characterization, the imposition of Western sexual mores on another society can hardly be said to be a traditional goal of foreign policy. Arabs, he argues, are only too happy to capitalize on the scandal,

> the case the jihadists make against freedom is that wherever it goes, especially the United States and Europe, it brings sexual license and corruption, decadence and depravity. Through this lens, Abu Ghraib is an "I told you so" played out in an Arab capital recorded on film … a pictorial representation of precisely the lunatic fantasies that the jihadists believe.[14]

Perhaps Krauthammer should be less concerned with what jihadists think and more concerned that conservatives from Rush Limbaugh to Oliver North apparently share the "lunatic fantasies" of an iron link between sexual freedom and pornographic torture.

In conservative reactions in May the abuse is "alleged," the actions of a few, and un-American, and its prompt investigation and correction will eventually vindicate the system. The torture is not about "us" but about "them," those few rotten apples souring the American pie. Alternating between denial and distortion, the writers never attach blame to government policy, the general political culture, mass opinion or anything reflecting mainstream thought and behavior.

In a democracy that would be unthinkable. The result is that their moral self-satisfaction is invigorated and their faith in the official version of events remains unshaken.

But there were more muscular defenses of Abu Ghraib. One that made the rounds of the right-wing talk shows was that it was nothing more than a kind of crude fraternity hazing. This came not from libertarians but from cultural conservatives who until then had made careers out of skewering Hollywood and the counterculture of the campuses, from Fox News's *Hannity & Colmes*, the *Weekly Standard*, and CNBC.

On *Hannity*, a former U.S. Army sergeant and interrogation instructor started the meme that was picked up by *Weekly Standard* online editor Jonathan Last.[15] Rush Limbaugh, who in the nineties rode the juggernaut of radio talk to stardom as the plain-speaking thinker of the Republican backlash added his part on his May 4 show, "It's Not About Us, This Is War":

> This is no different than what happens at the Skull and Bones initiation. ... I'm talking about people having a good time. ... You ever heard of need [sic] to blow some steam off?[16]

Oliver North, the maverick colonel who became notorious for his role in the Iran-Contra affair, added his agreement.[17] More significantly, Scott McClellan, President Bush's press secretary, declined to distance himself from or condemn Limbaugh's remarks.[18] Later, refusing to back down despite strong criticism from public interest groups, Limbaugh offered an analysis that undercuts any argument that the abuse was not directed specifically against Muslim culture:

> And we hear that the most humiliating thing you can do is make one Arab male disrobe in front of another ... and especially if you put a woman in front of them and then spread those pictures around the Arab world. Maybe the people who executed this pulled off a brilliant maneuver. ... Nobody got hurt. ... Sounds pretty effective to me if you look at us [sic] in the right context.[19]

What is the right context, one wonders, in which sexual and physical assault are welcome? Even though Christian (or post- Christian) societies tolerate high levels of sexuality and nudity, one can only imagine the outrage if a Christian soldier had had his genitals wired by taunting Muslims with digital cameras.

Torture is feminist, he argued on his May 3 show: "Have you noticed who the tortures are? Women! The babes! ... It looks just like anything you'd see Madonna, or Britney Spears do on stage." It's also a display of gay sexuality: "We have these pictures of homoeroticism that look like standard good-old American pornography."

So much for the new cultural conservatives. The most prominent media personality of the movement is not arguing that the abuse was an aberration of a deviant culture but a legitimate expression of homosexuality and feminism not different from that displayed in American entertainment and campus life. Yet he also blames public outrage over the photos on "the feminization of this country."[20] Apparently, feminization is all-American when it yields sadism but anti-American when it leads to moral outrage over sadism.

Here Limbaugh moves out of the range of respectable opinion altogether. Hansen and Taranto both equivocated about the abuse but eventually condemned it. But when Limbaugh was claiming that no one got injured, the *Post* was reporting assault under which prisoners had collapsed.[21] While Rumsfeld was vehemently denying accusations that the abuse was driven by a policy, Limbaugh was delighting in the brilliance of that policy and reveling in the ingenious way it had targeted Islam.[22]

Others didn't even pretend that "nobody got hurt." Popular Christian columnist Cal Thomas pointed out that fighting Muslims has a bottom line before which objections to torture have to yield: "It is good and right to have such a high standard, but not good if that standard is one-sided and undermines what we are trying to achieve in Iraq. ... All that matters is victory."[23]

Meanwhile, in *Front Page*, the online magazine whose editor, former Trotskyite David Horowitz, campaigns to dismantle Islamic studies on campuses, a media myth is revived by Don Feder: "Remember Jessica Lynch, the American private who was captured by the Iraqi army?... Apparently, the rape of a female POW doesn't offend the Arabs' exquisite sensibilities."[24]

Both Lynch and her family have stated that she was treated well by Iraqi doctors and contemporary medical reports do not show rape. That claim was made only after she was flown out of the country to Germany and the United States and has never been verified by her.[25] There is ample evidence that her story was manipulated by the media and the government to the point that whatever happened originally may be impossible to fully reconstruct. But such nuance is beside the point when a diatribe makes a better case against "Muhammad's mob."

Krauthammer has to find Islamic societies ethically deficient in order to attack Islam credibly. Feder, like Limbaugh, does not even need that rationale. Difference, not inferiority, is what he attacks. Difference is inferiority: "Do you recall protestations of outrage in the Arab world? But then, Lynch was an infidel Crusader and a defiler of the sacred sand of Islam, and—as such—probably had it coming, from the humane perspective of enlightened Arab opinion. (She was also out of burqa)."

Consider that at least one detainee was tortured in prison "for Jessica" and Feder's hyperbole becomes hard to dismiss as words uttered in the heat of the moment.[26] The heat is created by such moments. His technique of attacking straw men is consonant with his former profession which, as with so many right-wing commentators, is public relations. The language is intemperate—the Palestinian Authority is a group of "thugs" and Arafat would have "chortled with glee" at bullet-ridden bodies if he had seen them. He conflates Muslim and Arab and attacks on Pakistani churches with slavery in the Sudan, even inviting Hinduism into his vision of a universe besieged by Islam. But the sugar of multiculturalism cannot hide the deadly confection of racial and religious bigotry. It is only too clear that the aggregation of the Taliban today with the Caliphates of the past is ultimately intended to justify mass murder and ethnic cleansing of Palestinians in the present. In prominent conservative forums this is the norm—selective history as an apology for collective punishment, or if one prefers, collective history as a rationale for selective punishment.

The Forensic Drama

Of course, these are right-wing polemicists and their bias is to be expected. What is more surprising is to find the same bias in the major media. An article in the *Christian Science Monitor* is typical. "Regardless of the outcome" of the investigations into the abuse, it begins, "the United States' image has suffered a serious blow."[27] The unspoken implication of this, that the facts are still in dispute, is typical of the way in which the story is from the outset framed as a case under investigation. Actually, the particular incidents depicted in the photographs were well documented. What was left to investigate was only the extent of the abuse and the responsibility for it, not whether it had occurred or not. Yet the typical narrative frame in the media was that the incidents were alleged, the racism unproved, and the main damage one of perceptions not deeds. The language in these accounts is controlled throughout by a legal paradigm that sets the parameters of what can be debated in a manner crucial for understanding how the story played out over the next few months. Just as the language of personalities and sensationalism is used effectively to renarrate the story at one level, a quasi-juristic style of argument, one focused on procedure, documentation, and rule-following is employed in the press at another level to limit the extent of the debate and shape it in advance.

An instance of this occurred on CBS's *The Early Show* when Arizona Republican Senator John McCain was asked whether Rumsfeld should go. He replied, "It's obvious that there's a lot of explaining that Secretary Rumsfeld and others have to do, including why Congress was never informed as to this."[28] While apparently denouncing the abuse, McCain deftly shifts the emphasis to procedure, implying that the real damage at Abu Ghraib was done to the American system of government and its high standards.

Likewise, the *Monitor* article quoted a *Chicago Tribune* report in which experts expressed their agreement that the main damage was one of perception. The *Financial Times* noted that the American PR campaign in the Middle East was "floundering." Stephen Walt, a professor of international affairs at Harvard pointed out, "This is only going to reinforce the belief that the United States is anti-Arab and anti-Muslim, *whether it's true or not*" (my emphasis).

Georgetown professor Robert Leibar added, "We must keep in mind that ... it pales in comparison to what Saddam (Hussein) did to his own people over thirty years." The remark is both typical and suggestive. Is Saddam more culpable because he did it to his "own people"? Is one year of torture an improvement over thirty? The artificial neutrality betrays a highly tendentious position.

In editorial after editorial, the pictures displaced the hard evidence of assault and murder. Right-wing commentators expressed perfunctory disgust at the antics of the "six morons who lost the war," but then quickly pointed out that the pictures did not display "real" torture. Quietly forgotten was the Red Cross estimate that 70 to 90 percent of detainees were innocent, had been seized in their homes and kept for months without charges or access to lawyers and families.[29] Mass internment without due process alone qualifies as a contravention of the Geneva Conventions, to which the U.S. is a signatory. Yet by defining the scandal as narrowly as the administration did, commentators managed to deflect attention from this enormous but barely-noticed crime to the lurid antics on film, reducing the entire debate to a legal quibble over the exact status of the detainees, as though the violation of Geneva stood and fell alone on that, and as though the patent immorality of the war itself needed to be proved from Geneva. Neither proposition was true. Yet since the scandal was almost from the start discussed within the framework of the Conventions, it is vital to look at them.

The Geneva Conventions

Signed in 1949, the Geneva Conventions are the most popular regulations concerning the laws of war and are actually far broader in scope than the arguments about the status of terrorists under them suggests. There are four conventions: Convention I on the treatment of wounded and sick soldiers in the battlefield, Convention II on their treatment at sea, Convention III on the treatment of prisoners of war, and Convention IV on the treatment of citizens in times of war.[30]

The Convention most invoked over Iraq as well as over Afghanistan and Guantanamo was the Third, specifically Article 3, which stipulates that POWs should he treated "humanely, without any adverse distinction founded on race, color, religion or faith, sex, birth or wealth, or any other similar criteria" and forbids "outrages upon personal dignity, in particular murders of all kinds, mutilation, cruel treatment and torture." Article 4 defines POWs as " having a fixed distinctive sign recognizable at a distance ... carrying arms openly ... conducting their operations in accordance with the laws and customs of war."

The Bush administration's initially plausible position was that by these criteria, terrorists as non-state actors do not fall under Convention III. But what this argument overlooks is that the Convention also has hundreds of other articles far broader and more flexible in their definition of protected persons; for instance, Article 5—"Should any doubt arise as to whether persons, having committed a belligerent act and having fallen into the hands of the enemy, belong to any of the cases enumerated in Article 4, such persons shall enjoy the protection of the present Convention until such time as their status has been determined by a competent tribunal." Even if there were a doubt about the status of Iraqis arrested in house raids and on the battlefield, the Third Convention would thus have covered them. Under it, prisoners held for security reasons have to be released as soon as those reasons expire, or their detention constitutes a war crime.

However, Convention III applies, as I have noted, to POWs, that is, enemy combatants who have laid down their arms or been rendered *hors-de-combat*. But by the army's own account as well as that of the Red Cross, up to 90 percent of the Iraqis detained had never attacked the coalition at all but were either bystanders or criminals. They should have fallen under the specifications of Convention IV. But that also does not improve matters for the administration, because under that convention, denial of access to family and lawyers constitutes a war crime. Whichever way one looks at the detentions, the inescapable conclusion is that they flout Geneva's standards. It thus becomes clear why in the years after 9/11, the administration was frantic to find ways to undermine the conventions or to find loopholes to exploit. Top White House lawyer Alberto Gonzales wrote, "In my judgment, this new paradigm renders obsolete Geneva's strict limitations on questioning of enemy prisoners and renders quaint some of its provisions."[31] Cofer Black, onetime director of the CIA's counterterrorist unit, put it more combatively in testimony to Congress in 2002, "There was a before-9/11 and an after-9/11. After 9/11 the gloves came off."[32]

Behind the scramble for a legal fig leaf was a well-founded fear of the War Crimes Act, a rather obscure piece of legislation passed by Congress in 1996 that prohibits grave breaches of Geneva, such as "outrages against personal dignity." In order to escape prosecution under this act, it was vital for the Bush team to prove legally that Geneva did not apply to terrorists in order to give themselves enough room to look for intelligence as aggressively as they wanted. The surfacing of the pictures forced them, at least in public statements, to backpedal on their earlier enthusiasm for torture and present the abuse as aberrations in a setting still strictly regulated by Geneva. The pictures reduced innumerable incidents from 24 internment camps imprisoning a minimum of 30–40,000 people (some reports are as high as 50,000) over the year to a few felonies by half a dozen reservists.[33] Yet the truth is that the army's own investigation had already revealed systemic mistreatment in the Iraq theater paralleling what critics had decried for three years in Afghanistan and Guantanamo. Abu Ghraib was a restrained glimpse into an American gulag. That it took digital photos for the media to see this is consistent with the silence or complicity of American journalism in an unparalleled campaign of disinformation before the war and its continued servility after it.

The Pulp Drama

The strategy of personalizing and sensationalizing by which the story was removed from the realm of the political and reinstated as a narrative about individual morality parallels that by which the war crimes issue was narrowed and then reframed as a debate on the status of individual detainees under Geneva and therefore of the paper trail left by the administration in undermining their status.

In both these narrative genres, what we might call the *pulp drama* surrounding the low-level reservists and the *forensic drama* focused on the higher ranks, significant aspects of the scandal are simply ignored or displaced by less significant ones and the script is tightly controlled by the expectations elicited by the two genres. In the pulp drama, personal character and motivations, racial and religious identity, cultural and sexual elements are emphasized and institutional factors are pushed into the background. In the forensic drama, procedural and institutional analysis is foregrounded and the individual personalities are ignored.

Both strategies have their uses. The pulp drama, which by its nature limits culpability to the protagonists, is the natural form for a narrative that focuses on the misdeeds of a few. Institutional analysis would lead too far afield for comfort. Even focusing on personalities, though, has its discomfiting side—the ethnic and religious identities of two of the most prominent actors, Charles Graner and Lynndie England, are Caucasian and Christian. Consequently, the immediate question of personal responsibility, "Who did this?" yields the unacceptable answer, "Americans and Christians." Unless, of course, it is rewritten subtly to run, "Who among us did this?" Then the answer is more reassuring, "Americans of a marginal variety. In fact, this abuse is un-American and these people are really not Americans. They are criminals, perverts, trailer trash."

And that precisely is how the facts are represented. We are repeatedly told about England's roots in rural Virginia, her work on the night shift at a chicken processing plant, how she enjoyed running out into storms as a child, loved the movie *Twister*, and wanted to be a meteorologist when she grew up.[34] Both she and Graner had failed marriages behind them, we are told. Graner's home, Uniontown, a former mining town, is only 75 miles from Fort Ashby, where England's parents live in a trailer park at the end of the dirt road off the highway. Graner, a one-time marine, worked as a guard at the maximum-security state prison in Greene County, Pennsylvania, and in his spare time remodeled his house and played with his children. We learn that in 2001 Graner was accused by his then wife of grabbing her by the hair, dragging her out of a bedroom, and trying to throw her down the stairs. We hear that his idea of a joke was spraying mace into the coffee of a new guard at Fayette County Prison.[35] Such details satisfy popular tastes and there is no need to question the motivation of the reporter who looks for them or to ascribe it to bias against the rural poor since Jessica Lynch, from a similar background, a Sunday School teacher from a small town in Virginia, was transformed into a national heroine.

But consider also how the pulp drama played up the religious beliefs of the perpetrators. Specialist Darby, the soldier who reported the abuse anonymously in January, said that Graner told him: "The Christian in me knows it's wrong, but the corrections officer in me can't help but love making a grown man piss himself."[36] Graner and England are described as regulars at a Pentecostal tabernacle and we are given a picture of Graner's half-finished porch in Uniontown with a flag in the window and scripture on a stone in his front yard. The scripture is from the Old Testament prophet Hosea, who used his own ill-fated marriage to warn others of the bitter fruits of infidelity: "Reap the fruit of unfailing love … for it is time to seek the Lord until he comes and showers righteousness on you."[37]

The personal or professional histories of senior officials were not publicized in the same way. The professional histories of Donald Rumsfeld, Paul Wolfowitz, "Jerry" Boykin, Steven Bucci, Douglas Feith, and Stephen Cambone ought to have warranted at least as much scrutiny as the résumé of a low-level correctional officer. But none of them were questioned about any of their affiliations or views that might have adversely affected the formulation of American policies. Instead, they were allowed to defend themselves with the bureaucratic jargon and semantic hair-splitting characteristic of the forensic drama. The reason is obvious. Discounting personalities and emphasizing procedures works well as a strategy if one's objective is to escape personal culpability and lay the blame on institutional factors, on failure in communication, lack of oversight and coordination, or on improper follow-through, and this was precisely how the most dangerous charges facing the administration were finally neutralized.

That happened at the appropriate forum, a meeting of the Senate Armed Services Committee on May 7.

3
Framing a Narrative II: Politics as Law

The Senate Armed Services Committee Hearings, May 7, 2004
Witnesses: Donald Rumsfeld, Richard Myers, Les Brownlee, Peter Schoomaker, Lance Smith, and Steve Cambone

Despite the furor, the Senate Armed Services Committee hearings were focused rather arcanely on the system's corrective mechanism—whether or not it had kicked in and why Congress had had to learn about the story from the media.[1] On one level, given the enormous damage to the country's international standing, this emphasis was quite understandable, but on another it steered the debate toward analyzing the process by which the abuse came to light rather than considering the substantive changes needed to correct it. This emphasis on procedure only added to an inherent tendency in American public debate for issues to be rewritten as legal argumentation. The chaotic irrationality of political reality is forced into the straitjacket of statutory law and documentary evidence, while mastery of political reality—political skill—is superseded by adherence to laws. Of course, the forensic model is not at all exceptional in American political discourse. It is actually written into the founding of the country by those who framed the constitution to create "a nation of laws not men."

In this sense, Abu Ghraib was not caused by the abandonment of the rule of law, as many argue, as much as by an excessive regard for the rule of law, a regard that fails to take into account the men under the laws and the political reality in which laws operate. That reality was one to which the founders themselves were acutely sensitive and the constitutional framework they created was meant only to *guide* not substitute for it. The founders were well aware that when political reality—in other words, men—change, the law becomes not simply redundant but actually counterproductive. Like the softly-lit mirror in which an aging beauty finds the reassurance that harsh daylight cannot give her, the law and the courts dangerously encourage a polity's illusions about its own impeccable nature when reality suggests otherwise. The forensic drama conveys the same moral self-satisfaction as the narrative of the pulp drama, except that where the pulp drama allows us to admire our own probity against the villainy of some select targets, the forensic drama allows us to admire the rule of law against the infraction of some specific regulation. In both cases, the debate itself is constrained by the language of morality and becomes a self-referential system that does not allow its users the awareness that the use of moral language is not the same thing as either the capacity for moral intuition or the practice of moral action. By reducing the complexity and ambiguity of a political disaster to specific cases of legal wrongdoing, both parties accepted the premise that Abu Ghraib was an infraction of law, whereas in Talleyrand's memorable phrase, it was far worse than a crime, it was a blunder.

The chairman of the committee, Republican Senator John Warner of Virginia, took the party line, which was, predictably, that the breakdown in military discipline was "an extremely rare—and I repeat, rare—chapter in the otherwise proud history of the armed forces of the United States." He also succinctly stated the essence of the Committee's interest in the matter, which was, *who knew what and when?* What was done about it and why wasn't Congress properly informed?

The Democrats were equally predictable, trying with considerable success to show that Rumsfeld and Myers were not credible when they denied a cover-up. Senator Levin suggested that Taguba's findings were proof that what happened was part of a plan for extracting intelligence and that the planners were at least as guilty as the soldiers involved. Levin "expressed deep dismay" that when Rumsfeld and Myers briefed senators in a classified session on Iraq on April 28 just hours before the story came out on television, they made no reference to the story. "Executive branch consultation with Congress is not supposed to be an option," he pointed out, "but a long-standing and fundamental responsibility."

These two charges—that responsibility went much higher than the DOD was revealing and that the administration had failed to keep Congress informed—were at the heart of the questioning. Both questions are crucial to the debate. But the manner in which they were asked, as part of a legal investigation, narrowed what counted as evidence to the paper trail left by the administration rather than the military culture from which Abu Ghraib arose. From a broader perspective, such documentation would be only secondary evidence, for is it credible that the secretary would ever have put on paper directions to commit war crimes? The parameters of the legal model thus gave Rumsfeld an easy opening and allowed him to take the usual "full responsibility" for what happened. He indicated that he had appointed several former officials to examine the ongoing investigations and to determine whether additional studies were needed; he admitted to failing to inform the president and Congress; and he stated his intention to compensate the victims of the abuse because it was "the right thing to do."

This was simply window-dressing. Appointing a committee of his own colleagues in government and lobbying simply protected the administration and allowed it both to monitor the official investigation and control access to incriminating documents; admitting an error was pointless when neither blame nor punishment was attached; compensating a few vocal victims was pure public relations next to the number and extent of the crimes. Instead of correcting the situation, Rumsfeld's strategy simply provided effective cover to continue it. Thus his argument was still that the abuse was aberrant and that in correcting its mistakes, the American government was displaying an example that would reassure the world and reiterate the difference between America and its enemies. America was not Saddam.

Having said that, however, Rumsfeld did not give any indication that a genuinely independent investigation was going to be pursued. He was noticeably evasive when asked about the chain of command and failed to explain the unintelligible gaps in the way knowledge about the abuse had been transmitted through the hierarchy. The government's strategic emphasis on the timeline adroitly moved the focus to procedural questions, as though if only there had been a better way to have information channeled up or down the chain of command, there would have been no abuse. This is the classic strategy of the forensic drama—to admit to an infraction in the legal realm that has already been established and cannot damage one further and then deploy that admission into a gain in the moral realm in which the admission of guilt *per se* becomes the proof of moral responsibility. From that elision of the discourse of the legal with the discourse of the moral it is a mere step to a whole plethora of largely irrelevant posturing ("mistakes happen," "no one is perfect," "we should have known") that can now be reintroduced into the legal debate as the language of innocence or exculpation.

Asked by the doyen of the Senate, eighty-year-old Robert Byrd of West Virginia, why there had not been "a peep" out of the administration about the abuse until the photos were aired on CBS, Rumsfeld claimed that he had not read the "two-feet high" report but had read a summary of 50 to 75 pages. It was only the photos, he claimed, that gave "these incidents a vividness, indeed a horror, in the eyes of the world." Again, the emphasis on perception is suggestive and quite extraordinary when one considers that even the short Taguba extract includes incidents such as the sodomizing of a detainee with a lightbulb and possibly a broom handle.

Even though the bearings were interrupted by cries of "Fire Rumsfeld!" from protesters, the secretary made it plain that he had no intention of falling on the sword in response to critics whom he believed were politically motivated. Yet aside from the question of culpability, what are we to make of his competence? Not only did he claim not to have fully read a report that was requested at the highest level, but he was unable to explain who exactly was in change of Abu Ghraib. McCain, a decorated veteran of Vietcong torture and a strong critic of President Bush on Iraq, had a memorable exchange with him in which McCain asks the question, "Who was in command?" in one form or another at least ten times before he elicits the completely confused answer that they were under some kind of changing authority according to the Geneva Conventions. Rumsfeld tries to give the impression that the military "told the world" about the investigation while General Myers suggests that spokesman Brigadier General Mark Kimmitt had briefed reporters about the pictures.

But in the DOD archives for January 16, 2004, the brief is notably bland and uninformative[2]:

> Release Number: 04-01-43
> BAGHDAD, Iraq—An investigation has been initiated into reported incidents of detainee abuse at a Coalition Forces detention facility. The release of specific information concerning the incidents could hinder the investigation, which is in its early stages. The investigation will be conducted in a thorough and professional manner.

There are other contradictions. While Rumsfeld learned of the abuse through the briefing, Myers claims to have heard it *prior* to the briefing. Rumsfeld, Abizaid, Sanchez, and Myers spoke to each other every day, according to Rumsfeld, several times. Rumsfeld briefed the president with Myers present every other day and somewhere in late January or early February at a meeting at which General Pace, Myers' deputy, was sitting in for him, the president was also informed. Rumsfeld then asks us to believe that between this briefing and the airing of the photos on April 28, no further information was given to the president, not even a heads-up on the CBS airing of the photographs. Bush had expressed a strong interest in a new approach to torture from 2002 onward.[3] That makes it unlikely that he would not have been briefed at least once in a period of three months during which he and his defense chiefs met at least 30–40 times. If, in Myers's words, people "inside our building" discussed the photographs, why was the president unaware? Myers knew in January that the press wanted the photos. Wouldn't graphic evidence be overwhelmingly important to a commander-in-chief in an election year? It certainly was to Myers, who while claiming not to have read the report or seen the photographs, still knew they were too explosive for *60 Minutes II* to release.

We know that the criminal investigation uncovered something important enough to lead to Karpinski's suspension only three days later and to Abizaid himself tasking Sanchez to investigate further. On January 31, Taguba began his inquiry. In early February, two more investigations were opened, one into the training of reservists in detention and the other into detention practices at other sites in Iraq and in Afghanistan. A fifth was opened in April to look into the gathering of military intelligence. Obviously Taguba's concerns had had an effect. Yet with five investigations going on, Rumsfeld claims he had no idea of the importance of the matter.

Hillary Clinton addressed that issue when she brought up the case of the Muslim army chaplain from Guantanamo, Captain James Yee, who was arrested on charges of spying in September 2003 and kept in solitary confinement for more than a month at the Navy brig at Charleston, South Carolina. The charges against him were eventually dropped but the case was given enormous publicity as a front line of the war on terror.[4] How, asked Clinton, was it possible for a trumped-up case to be so publicized while the outrages at Abu Ghraib were shrouded in secrecy until the photos came out?

Was the silence, as Myers and Rumsfeld insisted, simply to protect the integrity of due process?

At a Pentagon news conference a week before the hearings, Rumsfeld and Pace insisted that the investigation had moved routinely, if slowly, through the command, because of built-in safeguards. In interviews, however, officials charged that the system had failed. In his second *New Yorker* piece, Hersh quotes one as saying, "Everybody I've talked to said, 'We just didn't know'—not even in the JCS." The source said he was informed by Pentagon employees that senior army generals had been in the dark on the story.[5]

Rumsfeld suggests that it would have been wrong to reach down into the process because of the danger of "command influence." Yet he states that he alerted the president and other senior officials as early as late January. But if they already knew, what further harm could have been done by alerting them about the upcoming broadcast? A senior defense official stated that the president was shown a "representative sample" of hundreds of photographs not yet seen by the public on May 10, that is, well after the first public exposé.[6] Rumsfeld's excuse for this is that he failed to appreciate the impact of the raw quality of the contents. But is this credible when Myers squashed it at CBS precisely because of its rawness?

Secrecy would be a secondary issue if the administration had tried to correct the situation. But even that is in doubt. Taguba submitted his report on February 26. Yet, his report was only approved by the army on May 1.Why? The timeline of events suggests strongly that contrary to the impression that Myers and Rumsfeld were assiduously fostering in public, in private, the army had not been so happy about the report:

February 26: Taguba submits report.

March 3-9: Taguba presents report to commanders. Strongly criticizes Miller for advocating use of MI.

March 20: Kimmitt tells reporters six military personnel have been charged with criminal offenses.

Late March: Miller brought from Guantanamo to head Abu Ghraib.

May l: Taguba report approved.

Notice that Miller was named head of prisons in April *after* Karpinski was suspended, even though it is Miller's Gitmoization strategy that appears to be the "missing link" between the lower-level perpetrators and the commanders. Is it possible that the Taguba report was only approved hastily after the photos went public to give the appearance that the army was ready to investigate itself fairly? The timing of the approval is certainly suspicious. And there is other evidence. Hersh reports that among many army officers Taguba is not seen as a hero but as a troublemaker. Myers explains the long delay in approval of the report as simply caused by the vetting process. But by January 18 the 320th MP Brigade had already been suspended—"pretty dramatic action to take," as Senator Sessions noted. It's hard to see what the vetting could have been about if the personnel involved had already been charged or suspended by March 20, shortly after Taguba's presentation.

Rumsfeld is also rather strikingly focused on the perception of the abuse rather than the substance as though, absent the photos, the incidents did not warrant the highest priority:

> The problem at that stage was one-dimensional. It wasn't three-dimensional. … It's my failure for not understanding and knowing that hundreds or however many there are of these things that could eventually end up in the public and do the damage they've done.

The extent to which Rumsfeld and Myers are sensitive to the imagery of the photos and public perception at first seems to contradict the logic of the forensic model in which political reality and perceptions of it are frequently displaced by legalism. But Rumsfeld's concern is only that a change in perception might alter domestic support for the administration; perception itself is still seen as something to be manipulated by the discourse of law, not altered by a change in policy.

Reality only counts when it threatens to become so obviously messy that legal niceties can no longer hold it at bay. Very little is said, for instance, about the Iraqi or international perception of Abu Ghraib. I do not mean the international impact of the photographs, but the impact of the abuse itself. Even without the documented evidence of abuse, it should not have escaped notice that tens of thousands of prisoners in detention were likely to have spread a dark picture of the occupation. Yet it does not seem to have occurred to anyone that apart from the PR issue of the photographs, or the legal issue of contravening Geneva, or the moral issue of the torture of noncombatants, the brutalization of a population is *bad policy*. Furthermore, it does not seem to have occurred to anyone that even if Geneva had been observed to the letter, the imprisonment of so large a part of a population, the usurpation of its government, the seizure of natural resources, and the massive repression of all popular resistance, even if conducted with the chivalry of Saladin, could not have been seen by most of the world—which is also the postcolonial world—in any manner except as a neocolonial occupation. And it does not seem to have occurred to Rumsfeld that this perception is not only a perception but a precisely accurate assessment of political reality.

The Senate Armed Services Committee Hearings, May 11

The committee received Taguba's report on Tuesday, May 4, and its classified annexes—classified records—on Monday, May 10. It met on May 11.[7] Originally, Taguba was supposed to be on the morning panel and Under Secretary Steven Cambone and General Smith were supposed to speak in the afternoon. For some reason, this was altered and Taguba ended up being preceded by Cambone.[8] If it was intentional, there was good reason. Since Cambone's testimony flatly contradicted Taguba's on the question of the policy directive that put MI personnel in control at Abu Ghraib, it materially undercut the effect Taguba's unaccompanied testimony would have otherwise had.

In his opening remarks, Chairman Warner pointed to a general breakdown in discipline as the cause of the abuse, but Senator Levin made it clear that he was determined to look for reasons at the highest level. Cambone, making his first appearance before the Committee, was equally determined to find no reasons there. He immediately declared that the Geneva Conventions applied to Iraq, no question, a position quite different from Rumsfeld's, and he connected this declaration to General Sanchez, the highest officer in Iraq. Sanchez has now quietly retired and it is Miller who is in charge of Iraq, a notable advancement for the man apparently responsible for policies at Abu Ghraib.

Cambone quickly tried to erect a firewall between the Al Qaeda or Taliban detainees at Guantanamo and those in Iraq. He did this in a series of tightly connected assertions. First, he insisted against the evidence that the Geneva Conventions had applied at Guantanamo although "not precisely." Next, he insisted that even if they had not applied, the strategy of "Gitmoizing" Iraq did not imply contravening Geneva. Then, he suggested that "Gitmoizing" was only a recommendation, not a directive, and that the directive placing MIs in command only *followed* the adoption of the Gitmoizing strategy but did not result from it. He also insisted that being in command did not mean that MIs were in charge of MPs. Finally, even if MPs had been ordered to contravene Geneva, they had enough training to know that they ought to have disobeyed.

There was a clear purpose in erecting a firewall between the two theaters. Bush and Rumsfeld had both publicly questioned the application of Geneva to Guantanamo and any indication that Guantanamo policies had affected Iraq would establish a line from the civilian leadership to the torture at Abu Ghraib. Establishing the direct responsibility of civilian leadership for policies under which torture was inflicted would open American leaders, at least theoretically, to prosecution as war criminals. At the highest level, therefore, Cambone had to show that neither the president nor the secretary of defense knew of the abuse.

At the next level, to protect both under secretaries for defense (Feith for policy and Cambone for intelligence), Cambone had to show that neither had heard complaints about the abuse in 2003 and that official directives had been issued by underlings. It was impossible, at that point, to deny that the February International Committee of the Red Cross (ICRC) report had been read, but Cambone was able to fudge the issue. He was also able to minimize or ignore the role of special forces and military intelligence, both of which had strong ties to the two under secretaries.

General Myers had managed to limit his own exposure by claiming to have known little about the torture until just before *60 Minutes II*, but Miller, his subordinate, was in the fire with his Gitmoizing report. In order to protect Miller, Cambone used the tactic of diluting the Miller report into a suggestion rather than a directive. Although less protective of Sanchez, Cambone also downplayed the importance of Sanchez's Fragmentary Order (FRAGO) that had put military intelligence in charge. He did this by placing blame at every turn on Karpinski and suggesting that her incompetence or negligence was responsible for the breakdown in communication and procedure. He located the responsibility for Abu Ghraib at her command level or lower, but certainly no higher.

***The Bush-Rumsfeld Torture Doctrine*:** Cambone's first move was to protect Bush and Rumsfeld. He began by citing Bush's determination that since Al Qaeda and Taliban prisoners targeted civilians in contravention of the Conventions they were ineligible for its protections. Cambone noted that Bush had nonetheless ordered that they be held "humanely" and in a manner "consistent with the Geneva Conventions," a very flexible description that can include a wide variety of behaviors. Actually, by classifying them as detainees with no enforceable rights, Bush was creating a distinction supported neither by the International Law on Land Warfare nor the Conventions.

Cambone's argument was extremely convoluted—Guantanamo prisoners were not worthy of Geneva's protection, but had still been given them; Miller had been tasked by the secretary to improve intelligence in Iraq, but he had given suggestions not directives; Sanchez had put MIs in charge, but not in charge of MPs. Elsewhere, he suggested that Gitmoizing Abu Ghraib was simply an attempt to restore order. Levin was quick to pounce on these semantic calisthenics.

MR. CAMBONE: I think what the secretary—I—let me tell you what the facts are. The Geneva Convention applies in Iraq.

SEN. LEVIN: Precisely?

MR. CAMBONE: Precisely.

MP CAMBONE: They do not apply in the precise way that the secretary was talking about—Guantanamo and the unlawful combatants—

SEN. LEVIN: Well, he was talking about Iraq—let me cut you right off there. This—the whole interview here was about Iraq and the conditions at that prison. ... And the secretary said something he said elsewhere, and I've heard this with my own ears recently—that—he said that the Geneva Conventions apply not precisely; that prisoners are treated consistent with but not pursuant to.

There was only one reason for Cambone's parsing: the public statements of his own boss were directly at odds with his own position.

***The Miller Report: Gitmoization*:** The debate about the responsibility for torture hinged on whether bringing Miller over to "Gitmoize" Abu Ghraib had led to torture. If Guantanamo was not under Geneva III for POWs—the most protected standard—then a request to Gitmoize was obviously a request to loosen restraint that would lead to abuse.

Cambone thus had to revise the significance of the Miller report. He admitted that he had encouraged Miller, because of his successful Guantanamo record, to visit Iraq in late August under "Joint Staff auspices" to see if he could improve the intelligence flow, but he insisted that the visit had resulted only in a "series of recommendations." This motif was taken up by General Lance Smith, whose unintelligible position was that although Miller had introduced more stringent interrogation methods to Abu Ghraib, he did not want them used because they violated Geneva. Smith later retracted this and suggested that just *one* of the new techniques (prolonged isolation) was introduced, with Sanchez's permission. Smith apparently wanted to disassociate Miller from the use of dogs. But if Miller wasn't recommending dogs as well as prolonged isolation, why did Sanchez recommend them on October 12, shortly after Miller's report? Smith's testimony that the use of dogs needed Sanchez's approval seems to conflict with Cambone's earlier statement as well as documents that imply that special interrogation techniques at Guantauamo had needed *Rumsfeld's* approval, as Kennedy and Levin pointed out to Cambone.[9] Cambone eventually promised to produce the relevant manual.

***The International Red Cross Report*:** If one strategy was to distance policymakers from the actions of the soldiers by proving a breakdown in command, the other was to show that the information flow from bottom to top had also failed. That required denying that earlier human rights reports had reached senior levels, and when that wasn't possible, as in the case of the February Red Cross report where there was public documentation that it had reached, watering down the significance of the complaint. Bremer hadn't known until February, Cambone told Byrd. Then, after first stating that he "was not aware of the complaints" to Ambassador Bremer and Secretary Powell, he suggests that Bremer's worries were general, not specific, to the prisoners:

> CAMBONE: Until the pictures began appearing in the press, Sir, I had no sense of that scope and scale. I knew of the problem, that there was abuse, that there was a criminal investigation, that there was an investigation being done by General Taguba, but I had no sense of it, Sir.

So although Cambone admits that he informed Rumsfeld, he claims he did not convey the importance of the problem and Rumsfeld in turn chose to say nothing to 35 to 40 senators who met with him on April 28, hours before the CBS exposé, surely an incredible chain of circumstances. Cambone also denies having seen the Red Cross reports issued on November 12, 2003, until "well after they were issued." He says that they were addressed to Karpinski, who replied on December 23; that they were delivered at the command level; and that they never reached Rumsfeld. These assertions, however, are hedged with phrases like "to my knowledge" and "as far as I understand them," which in Washington have frequently signaled strategic rather than accurate information. Words are orchestrated with a fine ear—Carbone refers to the November report as "working papers" delivered and worked out at the command level in order to avoid a higher-level confrontation and to encourage collaborative effort on problems, somewhat, one supposes, like the collaborative efforts he also finds between MIs and MPs. Cambone does admit that the Red Cross's February Report, which the *Wall Street Journal* had published on May 6, was delivered to the CPA, the highest authority in Iraq, but that, he claims, is because it was a "historical paper" reviewing incidents of abuse and torture—he calls them "activity"—from March to January 2004. As a matter of fact, the ICRC report covers March to November 2003 and is a detailed analysis of cases in that period, which in its own words, "have been thoroughly revised in order to present this report as factually as possible."

Dismissing the report as historical also contradicts the repeated oral and written complaints by the Red Cross to the CPA from March 2003 onward, including one made to "the highest level of the Coalition Forces in August 2003," to quote the report. Presumably, this refers to Sanchez, who we know from Rumsfeld's own testimony on May 7 spoke every day both to Rumsfeld and to Myers. Yet we are asked to believe that DOD only became familiar with the incidents when an anonymous soldier slipped a disk under the door in January. Since the issue is ultimately what Bremer, Myers, Cambone, Feith, Rumsfeld, and thus also Wolfowitz, Rice, and Bush knew and when they knew it, it is worth examining the ICRC report itself to test how credible the Department of Defense is in claiming to be unaware of the abuse.

The February report, which even Cambone admits reached the CPA, covers a wide swathe of illegal and inhumane actions committed by coalition forces. As far as civilian oversight goes, its purview certainly falls squarely within the scope of both the under secretaries—intelligence (Cambone) and policy (Feith, who is referred to only briefly). Cambone states that the report came through the Coalition to the Department of State in February, which means that he and Feith must have known about the abuse, at the very least, since February.

> CAMBONE: With respect to the 2004 report, I can only tell you again what I know, and that is that there was a meeting in that time frame of February at which senior members of the CPA staff met with members of the ICRC and this report was made available. And from that, there were some communications from CPA to the State Department and elsewhere with respect to these concerns.

Cambone's assertion that he was not aware of the "scale or scope" of the abuse might be true if the only information Defense had had in front of it until April ended had been the findings from the criminal investigation. But in fact the February report had also gone to Sanchez who would have been duty-bound to have said something about it to Myers and Rumsfeld, with whom he claimed to meet daily.

In any case, long before the ICRC report, Human Rights Watch had written to Bush on December 27, 2002; the directors of several rights groups had written to Wolfowitz on January 14, 2003, to Bush on January 31, and to White House counsel Haynes on Feb 5; to Condoleeza Rice on June 24; to Haynes again on November 17; to Rumsfeld on January 12 and February 10; and to Rice again on May 3; the HRW report on Abu Ghraib had come out on March 8, 2004.[10] Before 2003, the CPA had also heard complaints from Iraqi officials and reporters and a case of abuse in May 2003 at Bucca had been investigated and disposed of on December 29, 2003.[11]

It is simply not credible that Cambone or Rumsfeld were ignorant of a matter that attracted such extensive attention.

The ICRC report describes a "consistent pattern" of brutality in arrest, with MIs themselves reporting that about 70 to 90 percent of those arrested were innocent. It confirms that regular procedure entailed holding people "completely naked in totally empty concrete cells and in total darkness, allegedly for several consecutive days" and that military intelligence was primarily culpable. It includes a memo from May 2003 citing over two hundred charges of abuse substantiated by marks on the victims' bodies observed by the ICRC medical delegate. Victims were burned, beaten, and exposed to the sun in temperatures of up to 50 degrees Celsius (122 degrees Fahrenheit). The report states that notification of the family was absent "in almost all instances" and that soldiers routinely confiscated private property worth thousands of dollars without receipt. The report also describes killing and wounding of unarmed prisoners and orders to guards to go immediately to lethal rather than nonlethal methods of control.

Furthermore, contrary to Cambone's claim, the ICRC report itself claimed that its objective was more than documentation:

> The ICRC has regularly brought its concerns to the attention of the CF. The observations in the present report are consistent with those made earlier on several occasions orally and in writing to the CF throughout 2003. In spite of some improvements ... [ill-treatment of prisoners] might be considered as a practice tolerated by the CF.

On April 1, an ICRC oral complaint to Central Command in Doha, Kuwait, had the immediate effect of stopping the systematic use of hoods and flexi-cuffs at Umm Qasr in Iraq. The report also admits to being far from complete as a record:

> The ICRC report does not aim to be exhaustive. ... Rather, it illustrates priority areas that warrant attention and corrective action. ... This report is part of the bilateral and confidential dialogue undertaken by the ICRC with the CF.

These statements undercut three claims made in defense of the government: they make it impossible for Cambone as Under Secretary of Defense for Intelligence to claim ignorance of extensive abuse by military intelligence; they undercut Cambone's tendentious description of the report as a historical paper by demonstrating ongoing monitoring and intervention; and they destroy the argument made by Senator Inhofe, in one of the most widely quoted segments of the hearing, that the prisoners had "American blood" on their hands. While the prisoners photographed at cell blocks IA and B may have been labeled "security threats" or criminals, the truth is many were suspects rounded up arbitrarily.

> ALLARD: Okay. Now, did we have terrorists in the population at this prison?
> TAGUBA: Sir, none that we were made aware of.

Sanchez: The November 19 FRAGO and the Role of MI: Cambone's next goal was to shift responsibility from Sanchez to Karpinski. On November 19, Sanchez issued a fragmentary order placing Abu Ghraib under the tactical control of the 205th MI Brigade, but Cambone denied that this meant control over the MPs, citing an interview to that effect by Karpinski on May 10. Miller, he said, was just emphasizing the need for MPs and MIs to work together and not "undermine" each other. In this, Cambone directly contradicted Taguba. He also cited Miller's statement on May 8 that procedures in Iraq had been "sanctioned under the Geneva Conventions and authorized in U.S. Army manuals" as proof that the policy change was not to blame.

Having severed MI leadership (that ultimately led to his own office) from any connection to the abuse, Cambone proceeded to separate the MI contractors from it as well, claiming that they operated under the same rules of interrogation governing the CIA and the military. This was a way of fobbing off responsibility for Abu Ghraib to the MPs, a peculiar move for a Defense official who might be expected to protect his own. Cambone instead seems more interested in protecting the nonmilitary parties. He was unable to state categorically that contractors had always performed interrogations under the supervision of the military, the question before the investigation under Generals Fay and Kern.

But though contractors were not culpable under military law, he insisted they were not operating without constraints—they could not give orders to the military and unlawful conduct could lead to suspension from contracts, as well as federal criminal prosecution. Cambone did not mention, but Taguba did, that MI contractors were in fact under the brigade commander of MI who was answerable to Cambone. Instead, Cambone insisted that his office was only responsible for the information flow from detainees. The responsibility for the detainees themselves lay with the Under Secretary of Defense for Policy, Douglas Feith. And did the blame for Abu Ghraib lie also with Feith? Apparently not. Cambone pinned it on Karpinski, who had 8 MP brigades under her and was "not frequently present at Abu Ghraib." Unable to cope with the difficulties of moving prisoners from temporary to permanent facilities, Karpinski had looked for help to Pappas, commander of the 205th MI Brigade. It was at Karpinski's command level that the orders from above had been misconstrued or ignored.

While Taguba confined himself to the role of the MPs, his 6,000-page report based on extensive research by a team of MPs, corrections and detentions experts, judge advocates, public relations experts, and psychiatrists revealed enough to call the truthfulness of Cambone's version of events into question.

Take the dogs:

> TAGUBA: No, sir. The dogs were invited in there, according to witness statements, and collaborated (*sic*) by interviews by the two MP guards.

But Cambone himself indicates that the use of dogs was a command-level decision taken in the theater.

> SEN. LEVIN: Secretary Cambone, were you personally aware that permissible interrogation techniques in the Iraqi theater included sleep management, sensory deprivation, isolation longer than thirty days, and dogs?
> MR. CAMBONE: No, sir. That list, both in terms of its detail and its exceptions, were approved at the command level in the theater.

General Smith meanwhile asserted that the use of dogs was actually a technique whose approval required the authorization of General Sanchez. Only two months later, *USA Today* cited classified documents showing that Sanchez issued orders approving the use of dogs and leaving their use to the interrogators' discretion.

***Karpinski's Leadership*:** Janis Karpinski has been depicted as completely incompetent and some have even implied she benefited from the political correctness of the nineties. But if so, why was there no abuse at the two other camps she ran, Cropper and Ashraf? There was certainly overcrowding at Abu Ghraib and an MP-detainee ratio of 80 to 1 (against the normal ratio of 10 to 1). The annexes of the Taguba report paint a horrific picture: "Detainees walked around in knee-deep mud, defecating and urinating all over the compounds," said James Jones, commander of the 229th MP Battalion.[12]

In e-mails in October and November, Major Dinenna of the 320th MP Battalion complained to his superior, with copies to senior command, that the private contractor supplying food was falling short by hundreds of meals a day and that meals containing bugs, rats, and dirt were making prisoners vomit. But his superior scoffed at the complaint. While this particular contract was not renewed, the contractors still hold others with the military.

The documented chaos at Abu Ghraib supports Karpinski's claim that it had been turned into an all-purpose pen for every type of detainee, convenient to Baghdad but also somewhat outside the scrutiny of international observers in the capital city. Furthermore, Karpinski comes off in the interview as someone likely to handle Iraqis more sympathetically than other generals. An Arabic speaker and familiar with Saudi Arabia, she seems an unlikely source of policies of racial humiliation, although detainees claim to have observed her present at some of the incidents.

The annexes also seem to back her suggestion that one of the reasons why soldiers felt free to act as they did at Abu Ghraib was that after an incident at Bucca where MPs savagely attacked prisoners, smashing in the face of one, no one was prosecuted, although four received less-than-honorable discharges. At the hearings, Taguba emphatically asserted that the May incident, investigated in December, could not have influenced events that took place in October–November. But in the annexes, one of the officers involved confirms Karpinski's assessment.

The Taguba report also asserts that MPs at Abu Ghraib were not well trained in handling detainees or familiar with Iraqi or Muslim culture, making it unlikely that they would have had the sophistication to wire prisoners in simulated electrocution or break them down with religious and sexual taunting. When interrogations were not photographed anywhere else, why would MPs take such explicit pictures at Abu Ghraib if they had not felt the practice was sanctioned? Karpinski's claim that MPs were confused about the chain of command also seems supported by the annexes. For Taguba, the MPs and Karpinski were in charge of force protection at the base. But the files describe the MIs dispatched to Iraq by Sanchez as in charge of interrogation techniques.

***Private Contractors, Special Forces, Third-Party Nationals*:** Taguba mentioned two "third-party nationals" working as translators in interrogations, both of them civilian contractors, and also another private contractor working as an interrogator. He describes the third-party nationals as having free access to the detainees, which considerably undermines his earlier assertion that the MPs were in charge. If private contractors not required to report to the MP command were freely interviewing detainees, it is hard to see how they could have been restrained by MPs who were *not* supposed to participate in interrogations. The contractors working at the Joint Interrogation and Debriefing Center (JIDC) apparently answered to the MI commander Pappas, which means that, as Karpinski alleges, MIs were indeed in conflict with the MP chain of command.

Senator Reed pointed out the chronology:

> General Miller came to Iraq in August. ... He also recommended the establishment of a theater joint interrogation and detention center ... . That's August, and then October we start seeing a series of abusive behaviors, which the accused suggest were a result of encouragement or direction from these intelligence people in this theater joint interrogation and detention center.

As Reed notes, Taguba's investigation did not extend to the MIs or the JIDC where the most obvious conflicts in command took place, so he really was not in a position to contradict Karpinski. He also did not interview Karpinski's boss, Sanchez, whom she berated in classified testimony for his indifference to the welfare of soldiers and detainees and even for sexism. Counter-allegations are to be expected in such cases, but given the indifference of superiors to simple requests for food, it is quite credible that Karpinski met with a similar response when she complained. Taguba's main evidence for refuting Karpinki is the fact that she did not bring up the November 19 Fragmentary Order until the second time he interviewed her. But if Miller in his August report had already decided that Gitmoization required that MIs be in charge and had recommended this to Sanchez, Karpinski was probably already aware of it, and not referencing the FRAGO might only mean that the shift in policy was well-known even without it. Since the abuse supposedly took place in the fall, the issue is not really if the order itself directly instigated the abuse but if the strategy brought in that August did so.

What was amply established by testimony was that MIs were widely involved in interrogation in a freewheeling and unaccountable manner immediately after an important directive. The most plausible explanation is that the directive changed the manner of interrogation. That the civilian officials responsible—Cambone and Feith—should have been unaware of so significant a change is not only implausible, it is downright incredible. Yet this is what Cambone insisted:

> REED: But General Miller didn't think it [getting guards to condition detainees] was important enough to brief you, Mr. Secretary?
> CAMBONE: That's right, I was not briefed by General Miller.
> REED: Who were you briefed by?
> CAMBONE: My deputy general, Boykin, briefed me on the report.
> REED: And he ... so General Boykin didn't think it was important enough to brief you on that?

The General Boykin referred to is William "Jerry" Boykin, a high-ranking official with strongly negative and well-publicized views of Islam. There was criticism from the press and a few public interest and Arab-American groups about Boykin's involvement. It seemed willfully provocative that a man with his outspoken past should have had a hand in giving the green light to such sensitive policies. Bush quickly distanced himself from Boykin's remarks, but Rumsfeld, also a fundamentalist Christian, defended him as an officer with an "outstanding" military record. Even less attention was given to something that should have been far more alarming—Boykin's long history of involvement in deadly and unaccountable special forces missions, an involvement typical of many of the policymakers on the Rumsfeld team, including Cambone himself and Stephen Bucci, Rumsfeld's military assistant.

The increasing presence of special forces in the Iraq war was tied to still another development of enormous significance, the use of private contractors as security forces and in MI. Like special forces, the military contractors introduced a greater element of unpredictability and secrecy. Boykin, like Feith, was at the confluence of these explosive developments and should properly have been brought before the committee and questioned. Yet after this brief mention, his name is not brought up again in the hearing.

On other issues like rendering—turning prisoners over to countries that practice torture—Cambone slid back into traditional Washington speak: "I am not aware," "as best I know," and "that's about the extent of my knowledge." On the involvement of the CIA in interrogation, he was also evasive and, like Smith, professed ignorance on the number of intelligence contractors. Again, his paramount desire seemed to be to minimize the involvement of intelligence, CIA, and private contractors regardless of the evidence to the contrary:

> CAMBONE: I did not know the nature of that implication [of MIs], the extent or scope of the abuse that had taken place, so I didn't make a connection in the sense that there was a significant issue here. ... Furthermore, I still don't know that there is a significant issue here.

While Cambone didn't find MI involved, both the Red Cross and Taguba did. While Cambone did not find the role of MIs to be in contradiction of army policy, Taguba did. While Cambone was sure that the private MIs were not part of the MI chain of command, Taguba was certain they were. While Cambone, Rumsfeld, and Smith thought the soldiers were well trained, Taguba insisted they were not.

Cambone's entire performance was calculated to obscure what was clearly evident. It was also calculated to buy more time for the administration, now under pressure to clean house. In *Chain of Command*, Seymour Hersh cites one officer as saying he discovered the abuse in November 2003 and took that information to two of his superiors, General Abizaid, the CENTCOM commander, and his deputy, General Smith:

> Abizaid just didn't say a thing. He looked at me—beyond me, as if to say, "Move on. I don't want to touch this." Smith also said nothing. "They knew last year," the officer said.[13]

With CNN reporting that there were three hundred more photos waiting to be leaked out through the media, there was serious dissension at the White House and Pentagon over whether to come clean or risk the damage of further bad news dripping out daily into the press. But as a piece in the *Guardian* that Thursday was to reveal, the number of photographs to which the government was privy was actually much larger—1,800 —and included images even more graphic: dogs terrorizing cowering prisoners, women baring their breasts, and even genitals at gunpoint.[14] Coming clean had the potential to provoke a public backlash that would topple senior military and civilian leaders and even threaten the White House.

Rumsfeld's performance at the first hearing, the president's unprecedented public apology on TV, Cambone's insistent denial of key segments of the report, all showed the extent of the administration's concern. There was a paper trail from the prison camps to the Pentagon that could not convincingly be argued away, and an imminent and real danger that public support for the war would be entirely derailed. But to withhold the rest of the pictures from the public was equally dangerous. Accusations were being made, the complaints were piling up, victims were talking to the newspapers, and worst of all, there were many more pictures unaccounted for. If we are to believe the word of a soldier who committed suicide after returning from Iraq, there were other atrocities, all too many—incidents where civilians had been shot deliberately, ambulances sniped, women and children blown away. There was no telling what might show up if the lid was taken off. There was no knowing who might come forward to shatter even the tightest conspiracy of silence.

4
Graphic Evidence II: Video

Although the hearings put considerable pressure on the administration to release the rest of the photographs, there was also every reason for the government to keep matters quiet.

But then, late in the evening when senators and officials were locked in debate, a video was posted on an Islamic website. It showed the beheading of an American contractor named Nicholas Berg by a group claiming to retaliate for Abu Ghraib. The hour-long recording claimed that their offer to American authorities to release Berg had been refused. "For the mothers and wives of American soldiers, we tell you that we asked the U.S. administration to exchange this hostage with some of the detainees in Abu Ghraib, and they refused. ... So we tell you that the dignity of the Muslim men and women in Abu Ghraib and others is not redeemed except by blood and souls," a voice intoned. "You will receive nothing from us but coffin after coffin slaughtered in this way."[1]

American authorities claimed that Berg's body had been found over the weekend outside Baghdad near a highway overpass. In some reports, officials claimed that the body had been found on Saturday, May 8, which was also the same day of the beheading, according to the recording.[2] The video showed a pallid young man in an orange jumpsuit, arms tied behind his back, seated in front of hooded and armed captors who are later shown hacking off the head of what seems to be the same figure.

For the next few days, the national and international media were flooded with the images. The uncensored video was posted on scores of websites, allowing viewers to watch the gruesome details of the decapitation, and a deluge of letters to *National Review*'s weblog demanded more photos.[3] The beheading immediately deflected attention from the burgeoning torture scandal and allowed apologists for the administration to claim that Abu Ghraib was fully justified by the barbarism of the enemy. On Capitol Hill, senators ceased criticizing the government and the administration claimed the right, indeed the duty, to withhold the remaining pictures in case they incited further revenge killings. The major papers took up the cry, the *New York Post* kicking off an article on the killing with the line "What cruel sick bastards" and calling for a resumption of major combat.[4] The twenty-six-year-old Nicholas Berg was portrayed in media accounts as an idealistic young man who had gone to help the Iraqis with his technological know-how. The grieving father, especially, drew nationwide sympathy.

However, in a war where so much, from the rescue of Private Lynch to the fall of Saddam's statue, has been staged, a story this opportune always warrants a closer look. The theatrical appearance of Abu Musab al-Zarqawi, a Jordanian operative, was itself odd. Earlier in the year, a letter that the FBI claimed was from Zarqawi had turned out to be a forgery. Fortuitously, it had perpetuated the notion that civil war would ensue if America were to withdraw from Iraq.[5] So, when the FBI began dusting off the fingerprints of Zarqawi again, a second look seemed in order to a small army of international Internet vigilantes, this time antiwar in sympathies, who swarmed over the story. No sooner had the video gone public on Tuesday evening than they began asking questions.

Who was Nicholas Berg? What was he doing in Iraq traveling alone? Why had he stayed on? Berg's own parents blamed the administration for his death, claiming that he would have returned earlier had it not been for the detention. Whether or not this was the case, there were troubling questions about the young man. Before long, bloggers like the Romanian Soj (whose blog catapulted the following week to the top of the heap) were claiming that the beheading was a staged event, a psychological operation manufactured by the covert arm of the American government to deflect attention from the prison scandal and save Rumsfeld and his senior colleagues from the fire.[6]

A timeline was easily roughed out from the official press releases and it showed holes.[7] Berg went to Iraq on December 21, made contacts that indicated he could get work, and returned on February 1. He then flew back to Iraq on March 14 to begin work. On March 24, he spoke to his parents and told them he would return on March 30 to attend a wedding, but on the same day he was detained by Iraqi police at a checkpoint at Mosul and turned over to the Americans. When his father, Michael Berg, went to meet him at the airport, he was not on the flight. Accustomed to receiving daily e-mails from him, his family claimed that he was being held without due process and demanded his release. The government refused. On March 31, FBI agents visited the Bergs in West Chester, Pennsylvania, to confirm their son's identity. On April 5, the family filed a habeas corpus suit in federal court in Philadelphia, contending that Nick was being held illegally by the U.S. military. According to the FBI, he was released the next day and told his parents he hadn't been mistreated. The Bergs last heard from their son on April 9, when he said he would come home by way of Jordan. Soldiers on a routine patrol found his headless body at 5:30 P.M. on Saturday, May 8. It was hanging from a highway overpass a few miles east of Baghdad International Airport, his severed head lying nearby. On Monday Berg was identified and the parents informed and then the next day, Tuesday May 11, while the Senate deliberated on whether to make public even more graphic evidence of torture at Abu Ghraib, Muntada Al-Ansar—a website known for running militant Islamist messages from Al Qaeda—carried a video in which a bearded man seated in front of five masked men in black identified himself as Nicholas Berg. One of the captors read a long speech in Arabic from papers in his hand and performed the beheading. The killers signed off on the tape with the name of Abu Musab al-Zarqawi. The execution closely resembled the beheading of *Wall Street Journal* reporter, Daniel Pearl, also Jewish, in February 2002.[8] The date on the video was May 11.

This was the official account, and it bristled with problems, as the left-wing bloggers noted almost immediately.

First, there was the authenticity of the video. The decapitation looked extremely suspicious, for while a pool of blood was clearly visible on tape, none seemed to stain the executioner's hands or body and none seemed to spurt from the head during the act of beheading. "I would have thought that all the people in the vicinity would have been covered in blood, in a matter of seconds … if it was genuine," said Dr. John Simpson, executive director for surgical affairs at the Royal Australasian College of Surgeons in a report in *Asia Times.* The body also did not move or jerk as it should have or show appropriate facial expressions. Jon Nordby, fellow of the American Board of Medicolegal Death Investigators, agreed. Both thought it highly probable that Berg had died prior to his decapitation, which they felt had been staged, and they thought that in the scenes where he was shown alive, he looked drugged. Both also raised questions about the time when the footage was taken and the lapse between the shooting of the segments.[9]

In addition, there was some confusion about who the killers were. Initially, CNN staffers, including an Arabic analyst familiar with Zarqawi's voice, Octavia Nasr, said that the voice of the executioner did not match Zarqawi's Jordanian accent. Nasr also pointed out that the government had inserted the phrase "*al qaeda*"—the base—into its official translation where the original statement reads "*al qaed,*" that is, the one who sits or who does nothing.[10] But on May 14, CIA officials claimed that according to its own technical analysis, Berg's masked killer was Zarqawi after all.[11] However convenient this identification was for the official story, the truth was that Zarqawi's whereabouts had been murky for quite some time. In January, a letter purported by the CIA to be from Zarqawi had proved to be a forgery.[12] In March, at least twelve militant groups asserted that he was not behind bombings attributed to him and that he had been killed earlier by coalition fire.[13] Even according to the military, Zarqawi has typically been disinclined to claim responsibility for violent acts in the way in which Berg's killers had.[14] As late as March, Brigadier General David Rodriguez confessed "There is no direct evidence of whether he's alive or dead at this point."

Now, suddenly, U.S. experts insisted that the beheading, like five earlier tapes and letters, did indeed belong to the shadowy Jordanian whom they claimed was trying to raise his profile within Al Qaeda.[15] This insistence that Zarqawi was the culprit responsible for the increased violence after March seemed to many antiwar bloggers simply military "spin" on the amorphous growth of the Iraqi insurgency that was undermining coalition claims about the broad popularity of the invasion. Besides, bloggers wanted to know why Zarqawi, whose appearance was well-known, had hidden his face on the tape with a scarf and ski mask while simultaneously announcing his identity and claiming responsibility for the beheading.

That was only one problem with the video. Others abounded.[16] Why did Zarqawi wear a large ring—whose flashing was quite visible on the video —in contradiction of orthodox Muslim practice? Why was Berg wearing an outfit similar to that worn by Al Qaeda suspects at Guantanamo an entire month after he was detained at Mosul? How believable was it that terrorists on the run in a war-torn and impoverished country should look as burly as the five men in the video and should all display noticeably fair skin? Why was the video so heavily spliced, edited, and dubbed that the continuity of the beheading was impossible to establish at crucial points? Why did the video use military time? The resemblance of the white chair on which Berg sat to those in American prisons might simply have indicated that it was a common model easily available, but it added to other oddities in the tape, such as the voice at the conclusion muttering what sounded like Russian words. Could it be that the executioners taped over an old American video and used an American video camera, jumpsuit, and chair? Or were they Muslim militants from Russia?

There were more problems. The video seemed to show a lapse between the time the masked men read their statement and the time of the beheading.[17] This discrepancy was explained by a claim that two cameras were used and that the time gaps were really much smaller.[18] Still, there did seem to be an obvious lack of synchronization between the audio and video. The video's style was also remarkably similar to the taped beheading of Daniel Pearl, as though it were a deliberate attempt to mimic the handiwork of the Pakistani nationalists who killed Pearl. The pronouncements about Abu Ghraib seemed calculated to play to an American audience for whom the prison abuse was new. In Iraq, after all, it had been known for some time. Why would a real terrorist target an American audience in this way? Was Al Qaeda reacting to CNN?

While the video clock on the camera appeared to date the decapitation to Tuesday, May 11, between 13:46 and 13:47, the decapitated body was found on May 8. An early report on Al-Jazeera spoke of the body being found "on Monday" and then a little later "over the weekend," although this might simply be a confusion over the dates when the body was found and when it was identified. Yet Matt Drudge had pictures of the beheading on his site as early as Monday, May 10.[19] Was the video dating, therefore, entirely faulty and not to be taken seriously? Could this have been accidental? While the killers explicitly stated that the execution was revenge for the abuse of Iraqi prisoners and claimed that their offers to exchange Berg for Abu Ghraib prisoners had been turned down by the U.S. administration, the administration itself denied that any such offer was made, a denial that embittered the Berg family.[20]

A Reuters journalist in Dubai first named the Muntada al-Ansar al-Islami website as the source for the video—at www.al-ansar.biz and www.al-asnar.net—and the Malaysian host claimed that the sites were shut down shortly after the initial posting by "authorities" because of the surge in traffic.[21] But the circumstances of the video release were strange. Al-Jazeera looked at the site within 90 minutes of the story breaking on May 11, Tuesday evening, and could not find it, but Fox News, CNN, and the BBC were all able to download the footage from the Arabic-only website and report the story within the hour.[22] While the Internet server was in Malaysia, the publishers were in London and Nurnberg, Denmark.

The video's grainy visuals and poor sound quality all make it possible that there may be innocuous answers for some of these troubling questions. Still, there is no explanation that makes sense of all of them. The fact remains that no government agency was prepared to certify on record that the video was authentic or that the audio was the voice of Zarqawi. Under oath in front of a Senate panel on May 19, General John Abizaid side-stepped questions about al Qaeda and al-Zarqawi's involvement in the murder of Nicholas Berg.

Invitation to a Beheading

Just as curious as the video was the narrative of a young idealist struck down on a mission for humanity. A CNN report on May 11 described Berg as someone quick with a laugh, who liked to work out, and who knew a little bit about everything. He was an idealist in love with adventure and was said to have returned from a trip to Ghana emaciated after having given away most of his food to the poor.[23]

A science prodigy, he cobbled together his varied interests in technology into a system he called Bergology which he enjoyed introducing to his students at high school. A former teacher claims that the Iraqis would have had a friend in the young man had he lived.[24]

But some haphazard facts don't fit this tidy picture of an innocent abroad. While Berg's parents were part of the left-wing antiwar movement, it seems that their son was strongly in favor of the war. A passionate supporter of President Bush, Nick Berg was active enough in partisan politics to provide technical support for the Republican convention in 2000.[25] There is no reason to think he was not the idealist friends have described, but he was also certainly looking for lucrative construction contracts when, on a trip to Iraq in December 2003 he set up a company with an Iraqi associate under the name, Babylon Towers.

Even for a young adventurer, Berg's behavior in Iraq was odd. He traveled alone, a very dangerous practice for an American and one he insisted on despite robbery and arrest.[26] He was even held in prison for two weeks. Michael Berg claimed that it was the American government who detained him and that, if Nick hadn't been held for so long, he might have been able to leave the country before the violence worsened.[27] But after the video aired, the spokesman for the Coalition Provisional Authority (CPA) denied flat-out that the United States had ever held Nick and claimed that it was the Iraqis who had detained him, a story quickly disproved by the reports of people who spoke to Nick at the time as well as by the American Consul. After several such contradictions, the FBI finally admitted to having known where he was from the outset, and also that they had actually requested his detention. E-mails sent by Berg to his family just after he was released on April 6 confirm that he was picked up at Mosul by the American military police who lost interest in him after a background check with the Criminal Investigation Division (CID).[28] Subsequently, the FBI paid him the first of three visits, apparently curious about the Farsi literature he was carrying with him. Around March 28, after he had been interviewed twice by the FBI, he was transferred to a cellblock with seventy petty offenders and "war criminals," to use the words in an e-mail he sent home, although friends who spoke to him about it described them as freedom fighters. In prison, word spread that Jewish items had been found among his things and the other prisoners began shouting, "Yehudien!" and "Israelein!" at him, prompting the police to remove him to a separate cell, which he describes as a toilet. He claims that once it was known that he spoke a little Arabic, he got on better with the others, many of whom were foreign fighters from India, Pakistan, Afghanistan, and Iran.

Several reasons have been offered for Berg's detention. Some say it was his Jewish identity and the Israeli stamp in his passport, others that it was his father's membership in the antiwar group, A.N.S.W.E.R. Perhaps the most intriguing explanation is that he was detained because of a mysterious episode in his past—FBI questioning in 2002 on how his college e-mail account had ended up being used by Zacarias Moussaoui, one of the suspects in the 9/11 attacks, the only suspect to be apprehended on U.S. soil. The FBI apparently concluded that he had lent out his e-mail accidentally while he was briefly a student at Oklahoma University, a story that few bloggers right or left seem to believe. Another possibility is that Berg's electronic equipment, which he often lugged around with him, might have attracted the attention of the police.[29]

The Berg story is riddled throughout with these sorts of peculiarities. For instance, what are we to make of the innumerable contradictions between the explanations by the State Department (represented by the consular office), the military (represented by the military police in Mosul), the CPA, and the intelligence agencies (FBI and CID)? How much of a coincidence is it that Berg, an ardent Republican, inadvertently ran into Al Qaeda twice in his short life, once in the United States and once fatally in Iraq? If the FBI had a valid reason to question and detain him, why was it not forthcoming about it? If he was released to freedom on April 6 and was seen on April 9, why was he wearing the orange jumpsuit typical of U.S. custody, if indeed that was what it was, a month later on May 8 on the so-called Al Qaeda video? What was he really doing in Iraq?

Berg's first trip in December had apparently been an exploratory one to make contacts. In colorful e-mails in January, he describes working on towers at various locations, including, strangely, Abu Ghraib. He mentions having contacted a relative in Mosul and being arrested south of Baghdad on January 18. Iraq was rife with rumors of Iranian infiltration, and in the dark Berg was apparently mistaken for an Iranian spy.[30] Also in the January e-mail he writes that his company had been announced as an approved subcontractor for a broadcast consortium awarded a contract for the U.S.-controlled Iraq media. "Practically, this means we should be involved with quite a bit of tower work as part of the reconstruction, repair, and new construction of the Iraqi Media Network," he writes, and adds that the network was "something like NPR in the U.S."[31]

By his own account, then, Nick Berg was working in one of the most sensitive fields—telecommunications for the coalition. But his business partner, Aziz Al-Taee, states that the young man couldn't find work and eventually returned to America, leaving some of his tools behind. By other accounts, he set up a preliminary contact on his first trip and returned in March to start the job. Michael Berg first claimed that his son was unable to find work as expected and had planned on returning but later contradicts this and claims that although his initial contact had not worked out, Nick had found himself a job elsewhere and planned on returning on March 30, though only for a friend's wedding.[32] According to Michael Berg, it was only after Nick was detained that he decided he was through with being a contractor and ready to return permanently.[33] There is a problem with this account. If the January contract fell through, why does Berg's own e-mail of April 6 state that he intended to start work with the Iraq Media Network (IMN, known in Iraq as al-Iraqiya) contractor after his visit to Mosul in the last week of March? Before he left for Mosul, he also arranged to call Al-Fawares, the IMN contractor, on his return, and on April 8 he sent an e-mail to Taee apologizing for not having been in contact with him as he had promised. Finally, although he told his family that his business was struggling, a friend stated that he appeared to be reaping the benefits of a golden age for contractors in Iraq.[34]

Berg's family business, Prometheus Methods Towers, is equally mysterious. According to Michael Berg, Nick was not in Iraq for money and the family business "was very profitable before he went to Iraq," but he adds that he will "make good on anything the company owes anybody, but it's pretty much going to be defunct." Pennsylvania state officials have gone on record that Prometheus Towers does not advertise, and it cannot be found in the Yellow Pages online.[35]

It gets curiouser. An AP report reveals that Michael's sister, now dead, married an Iraqi man named Mudafer who became close to Nicholas. In the e-mails from his first trip, Berg describes going to Mosul, introducing himself to Mudafer's brother and setting up an e-mail account for him.[36] It was Mudafer whom Berg was visiting in Mosul when he was arrested. So here is a young American businessman who insists on traveling alone in Iraq; who has apparently made money working on telecommunications for a prison once notorious for torture under Saddam Hussein and now again at the center of a torture scandal, this time under the Americans; who has had some problems with the law; whose family business and father have been listed on a right-wing hit list; who travels with Iranian literature and currency on his person and an Israeli stamp in his passport; who also has an Iraqi uncle and a Jewish last name as well as a coincidental connection with Zacarias Moussaoui.[37]

In the interim period between Berg's release from detention and his disappearance, the FBI narrative again diverges from eyewitness accounts. Berg's own e-mails suggest that U.S. authorities held him incommunicado until a lawsuit was filed by his parents.[38] Responding to the Bergs' habeas corpus petition against Rumsfeld, the FBI and State Department insisted that since Berg had been turned over to U.S. Army MPs, they had no control over his release. This seems peculiar to say the least. A written statement by the FBI, however, blames Berg for refusing help in contacting his family and leaving the country.[39] Yet in the three days after his release, Berg did contact family members, which calls into question the FBI's version of the story.

The State Department claims that again on April 10 he was offered a flight out to Jordan but that he refused, claiming the road to the airport was unsafe. He intended instead to go overland through Kuwait.[40] On April 14, alerted by the Berg family, the U.S. consul's office sent a contractor to the Al Fanar Hotel where he was believed to be, but hotel administrators could not remember him. The Berg family then sent a private investigator to the Al Fanar who found other hotel guests who did remember him, even though, strangely, the administrators still did not. Muscular, redheaded, gregarious, and with a smattering of Arabic at his command, Berg was a striking figure. In his T-shirt, baseball cap, and work belt he was not easy to forget in Iraq. However, the accounts by those who remembered him are again contradictory. A businessman who had a drink with him on the evening of April 9 got the impression that he was planning to go home overland through Turkey, yet some of his belongings were left in storage when he left at 7 A.M. on April 10. Another guest claims that Berg told him he was leaving on the flight to Jordan. But according to the State Department, he had just turned down their offer to fly him out to Jordan. Taee claims that at nine on the morning he left, Berg made a call to him to say that he had met people he was going to travel with to Jordan. On April 19, again according to Taee, calls were made from Nick's cell phone to Jordan, the U.A.E., and a local number, although it is not known who made them and Taee is the only one who seems to know about them. But Taee himself is suspicious. Although Berg refers to him casually as someone he met in Iraq and set up as an office manager, Taee was actually a rather prominent figure in the Iraq reconstruction effort. He ran the Iraq-American Council in Virginia, a pro-war group, and it was he who had signed Berg on in December at a three-day conference there touting business opportunities with the reconstruction. Taee was a presence in Republican pro-war circles and appeared at numerous war rallies on Fox News and CBS, even after he pleaded guilty to selling crack vials in 1994.[41] He ran into even more legal trouble later over stolen computers and bootlegged CDs and was reportedly tied to a criminal network of immigrants from Russia or the former Eastern bloc. He left for Baghdad in 2003 apparently to avoid deportation proceedings. Bloggers did not fail to connect Taee to the "Islamists" on the video with their noticeably fair skin and who seemed to be muttering words in Russian. No leap of faith was needed to see how Taee's legal problems might have made him especially vulnerable to recruitment by U.S. intelligence.

Whether or not this was the case, it was still obvious that there was more to the strange life and times of Nicholas Berg than officials were prepared to disclose. Agent, counteragent, blundering naif, or government patsy? He could have been any of these. But more important than the mystery surrounding his savage end is where and when it took place, in the vortex of currents seething in the aftermath of war, in a nebulous world of private contractors, covert intelligence operations, foreign fighters, electronic espionage, and psychological operations. It is in this world that we find clues to the real nature of the occupation behind the propaganda of democracy and human rights, and from its dark intrigues the torture at Abu Ghraib erupts.

5
Context I: The Violence of Virtue

Media Reaction

The beheading of Nick Berg swept Abu Ghraib off the air. While the video itself was not played on network television, in the 24-hour news cycle on cable or on front pages, there was overwhelming exposure on the Internet, where a number of sites became disabled by the heavy traffic it caused that week. On Friday, search strings like "nick berg video," "nick berg beheading," and "beheading video" topped the Google charts. Nick Berg beat all other searches, even of pop culture leaders on *The Lycos 50* for the week following the beheading.[1]

The response on the Net was divided into two camps—one represented by the activist right-wing website, Free Republic, that initially accepted the video uncritically and the other, more diverse in its response, that found too many unanswered questions to leave it satisfied with the official story. On Liberty Forum, a libertarian site, a blogger noted the earliest online mention of Nick Berg on September 15, 2001: "I called many of my friends to make sure their femiliers (*sic*) were ok. The first one I called was Nick Berg, whose grandfather helped build the Towers."[2]

One blogger was anxious that photos of Aziz Taee with Wolfowitz or Taee at a Free Republic rally might be deleted from the Net.[3] Another claimed that an Oklahoma University library employee had told him she was present at an FBI interview where she learned that a library computer terminal had been used for the purchase of an airline ticket for a 9/11 hijacker who was on the plane that crashed in Pennsylvania. The person who made the purchase had not been a hijacker but a white American male who knew he was assisting the hijacking. The blogger claimed to have obtained a document confirming that Berg was arrested twice for trespassing on the Oklahoma University campus during the spring of 2000 when he had been living as a vagrant. Some wondered how a vagrant in spring 2000 had made the transition to independent telecommunications businessman in Iraq in 2004.

Meanwhile, most of the right-wing blogs were more interested in denouncing what seemed to them a double standard in the coverage of the Berg story by mainstream TV. Their primary objection was that in mainstream media the story was being presented with reference to the killers' motivations and to the unanswered questions surrounding the story rather than as an illustration of depraved terrorism.

CBS ran a picture of the grieving family alongside a smaller inset on the prison abuse story on May 11. When it ran a picture of the captured American the next day, its story focused on the denial by coalition authorities that they had ever held him in custody. "Video on Islamic militant website appears to show beheading of American," said MSNBC. Fox News was more forthright: "Militants Behead American Hostage in Iraq." *NBC Nightly News with Tom Brokaw* led with the title, "Barbaric murder: An American civilian in Iraq is beheaded. His executioners could be tied to bin Laden and they were citing the prison abuse scandal." Peter Jennings's commentary on *World News Tonight* was the only one that referred to the questions about the tape and did not immediately buy the administration's Zarqawi–Al Qaeda tie, for which Jennings was widely criticized as "spiking" the story.[4] In fact, he was quite right to approach the story skeptically. Even Rumsfeld later backed off the claim that Zarqawi was Bin Laden's right-hand man.[5] Arab intelligence sources have since told *Newsweek* that he is a rival and not nearly as powerful as he as well as the United States would like people to believe.[6]

Otherwise the media by no means muted the story, as the right-wing bloggers claimed. While none of the networks showed the actual killing, *CBS Evening News* did run the tape through to the frame in which Berg was pushed over and a knife put to his throat. It then held the still frame as it played the audio of him screaming as his head was being hacked off. The *Philadelphia Daily News* printed a full-page picture of the seated Berg with a single word in a massive font above: "Bastards." "Vengeance on Video," declaimed the *Arizona Republic*. New York's *Daily News* trumpeted the words "Pure Evil" in huge white lettering against a black backdrop of Berg and his captors. Under the caption "Terrorists Behead American" the *New York Sun* referred to the "grisly video" on the "Al Qaeda–linked website."

Still, a greater number of American newspapers chose to run a picture of the grieving family as their lead rather than a clip from the video, whereas on foreign front pages the video capture was more popular. Only a few of the major U.S. newspapers ran the video images alongside front-page stories in the immediate aftermath. Among those who did, were the *Los Angeles Times, Chicago Tribune*, and *Washington Post.* The *New York Times, Miami Herald*, and *Baltimore Sun* opted for inside pages. A German paper, one of four foreign papers that did so, ran a picture of the actual beheading, something no American paper chose to do. Journalists who avoided the pictures said they did so because the explicit imagery violated standards of decency. Those who opted to show them argued that the photos allowed the public to understand the nature of the threat confronting America.

In the blogosphere, the frenetic cyberspace where conservative media watchers, amateur sleuths, and private pundits circulated meta-critical commentary on blogs like Glen Reynold's massively popular Instapundit, the conservatives cried foul almost immediately.[7] The verdict was in—the official gatekeeper, the Dan Rathers, the Peter Jenningses, the Tom Brokaws, did not "get it." They were out of touch with the American pulse, bleating endlessly about a few naked Iraqi men while "animals," "savages," and "barbarians" were hacking off a young American's head. *New Republic*'s Andrew Sullivan argued that the media was guilty of a double standard. Neil Boortz, a talk-show host, believed the slant was aimed at causing damage to President Bush.[8] Tim Graham of the conservative Media Research Center accused the press of treating the Berg beheading like a one-day story while playing up Abu Ghraib because it fit the "Vietnam quagmire syndrome."[9] The *Washington Times* took the *Washington Post* to task for running two prison abuse stories on the front page on May 13 and three related stories elsewhere in the A-section but only a single story on Berg inside. Meanwhile, the *New York Times* had three prison abuse stories on the front page to only one story on Berg, and even that emphasized that "federal officials" had failed to protect him. Three more prison abuse stories ran in the A-section.[10]

Brent Bozell, a noted Christian conservative, found the news magazines wanting as well:

> *U.S. News & World Report*'s cover read "Inside the Iraq Prison Scandal. The Ghosts of Abu Ghraib. Why the System Broke. The Psychology of Torture." Inside the magazine carried 10 pages of Abu Ghraib coverage but gave just about three-fourths of a page to the Berg killing. *Time* carried a Bush/Iraq cover with no mention of Berg. It carried five different Abu Ghraib articles

> and one sidebar on Berg. *Newsweek* was the worst of all. The cover carried the hot authors of the evangelical "Left Behind" novel series on the cover, with a top-of-cover plug for "The Truth About (U.S.) Torture." Inside the magazine, there was no Berg article. *None.* [11]

Bozell cited a CBS poll that showed that by 57 to 37 percent, Americans surveyed didn't want any more prison abuse pictures to be released. Forty-nine percent said the media had spent too much time on the prison abuse story, compared to only 6 percent who thought it had been undercovered.

There is no question that the Abu Ghraib story was covered far more widely than any other, especially in the early part of the summer. According to the Tyndall Report, a media analysis site, the abuse story led every newscast on each network. It was the year's second-biggest Story of the Week (122 minutes vs. 134 minutes) behind only the August 2003 electricity blackout. A "Media Reality Check" by Tim Graham claimed that NBC devoted ten times more airtime to Abu Ghraib than to Saddam's mass murders and accused ABC's Jennings of playing down Zarqawi's ties to Al Qaeda.[12] Telephone polls conducted May 18–19, 2004, of a sample of 900 registered voters also seemed to indicate that the public felt the beheading story deserved more attention than it got. The beheading was a much more upsetting story to Americans than the abuse scandal (60 percent and 8 percent respectively), with 29 percent saying both news reports were equally upsetting. Some Americans (34 percent) believed the abuse scandal was covered "excessively," compared to only 9 percent who thought the beheading received too much coverage. Over 35 percent thought both stories received excessive coverage and 15 percent said neither.[13]

While Abu Ghraib may have run far more than the Berg killing in the major media, what are we to say of Bozell's equation of the two except that it is deeply partisan? The stories are clearly in entirely different classes of newsworthiness and political importance. The Berg story was a single killing while the prison story involved the detention and ill treatment of tens of thousands, not just a thousand or so, as he asserts, as well as the torture or killing of several hundreds of civilians in a country ravaged by the most powerful state in history. The United States is not just any political actor but in many senses the indispensable one, the underwriter of international law and the bulwark of the international economy. It ought without dispute to be held to the highest standards and cannot get away with claiming symmetry of action with individual political groups or vigilante actors. In the context of the carnage inflicted on Iraq that never made it to domestic television, it is also incredible to suggest that the media gave too much coverage to American atrocities.

In fact, the valid objection to the coverage is not that it was partisan and excessive, but that despite the media's self-excoriation, it was only another instance of the extraordinarily skewed and inadequate news coverage that has left American audiences with no sense at all of the suffering inflicted on Iraqis during the ongoing pacification of their country, a suffering measured beside which a single death, however excruciating, does not have equal political significance. Quite correctly and not because it is anti-American, the world press noted the death of Nick Berg as gruesome and tragic for the family, but in the context of so many deaths, of relatively little political importance except in its play in the propaganda war.

"Certainly Nicholas Berg is as innocent a victim of extremist Muslim atrocities as the 3,000 Americans killed on September 11, 2001," writes Ira Simmons in ChronWatch, a conservative website that monitors the liberal *San Francisco Chronicle*, but this is manipulation of language. Berg was not an innocent. He chose to go to Iraq; chose to pursue what some would call war profiteering; chose to work in a highly sensitive field central to the mission of the occupation; and chose against friendly advice to travel alone in dangerous areas openly carrying articles that identified him as Jewish. He had ties to intelligence, spent time in an Iraqi prison, and was in business with an Iraqi expatriate with criminal convictions and influential ties to the occupation. To equate his death with that of civilians killed in their own country is spurious. Estimates indicate that the U.S. has killed four times more civilians than the resistance has. Those are the facts on the ground against which the Nick Berg story has to be set. To suggest an equivalence between a single act, however terrible, and a widespread and institutionalized war crime against a population is moral counterfeiting that betrays the inadequacy and dishonesty of the language of such discussions. Surely civilian does not mean noncombatant, noncombatant does not mean innocent, and innocent under law does not mean lacking in moral or ethical culpability. The proper counterpart of Nick Berg is not an Iraqi or American bystander but a suspected Iraqi spy or someone materially aiding a terrorist group, supposing one can even pick out such a person in a popular resistance.

The claim that the Berg beheading was a random act of aggression was also not an isolated one but a rhetorical tactic repeated systematically to distort understanding of events in Iraq as well as in the wider Middle East. For instance, in April the mutilation of four Americans in the besieged northern town of Fallujah was likewise described relentlessly as a calculated and unprovoked atrocity by terrorists against innocent civilians, when in fact it too was not calculated, unprovoked, or committed by terrorists. And, like Berg, the victims were far from innocent.

Such revisions of history are often attributed to the Pentagon's policy of "embedding" the media in the military, a policy that gives journalists unparalleled access to the battlefield but limits their viewpoint strictly to what the military wishes them to see. Still, professional reporters should have no difficulty in refusing to accept military briefs and press releases uncritically. That most have not is a stunning indictment of American journalism and questions its standing as the epitome of the free press. More disturbingly, external constraints are not the only or even the most important causes for distorted coverage. More than any *a priori* restraints, it is the cognitive framework within which most reporters function that shapes their writing. The subtextual narratives and assumptions of liberal journalism ultimately prove to be drawn from the same ideology that constructs the strategy of the forensic drama.

Just as the legal model presents a seemingly neutral facade that both conceals and amplifies the operation of power, it seems that the rhetoric of journalistic objectivity actually bolsters the preferred narrative of the corporate state. This is clear from the way in which the media covered the first siege of Fallujah, which took place just before the revelations about prison torture and provided the context for those revelations. It was concern about events at Fallujah that led CBS to spike the Abu Ghraib story in mid-April 2004 while the widespread unrest that led to the siege was itself partly incited by popular knowledge of the torture.

Fallujah and Abu Ghraib

Fallujah is one face of the American occupation of Iraq; Abu Ghraib is the other. One presents itself as external policing, the other as internal surveillance and security. Terror and torture masquerade here together as law and order, the violence of the virtuous state.

At Fallujah the killing of around a thousand civilians in April 2004, a ruthless pacification of a crowded city, was recorded in the major media as a raid on rebels. This narrative, in which the bombardment of a population is normalized as a police action against rebels, is the necessary counterpart of that other narrative, in which the terrorizing of the population is normalized as an interrogation of suspects. In both, language that characterizes the state in its internal judicial role, such as police, suspect, law and order, is essential to removing the story from the political realm into the legal. This is done so that questions about the power and legitimacy of the actors that would undermine the state's role are displaced by procedural questions about the acts themselves. The result is that the state's legitimacy in acting is reinforced. Notice that terms like "policing" already concede that the state is the legitimate authority in the area it polices and disguise the reality that under the international legal guarantee of the integrity of states, it is actually Saddam Hussein, unfortunately, who continues to be the legitimate ruler of Iraq. The United States, having altered only political but not legal reality by military force, is compelled to sanctify that force by enlisting the language of law and virtue on its behalf. A discourse of civilization thus inevitably accompanies the state apparatus in its imperial project. The state's violence is always legal and justified—that is the conclusion we draw from the dominant narratives of Fallujah and Abu Ghraib.

Thus the virtue behind state violence is the unstated assumption of the liberal journalism that writes neutrally and from an objective distance about both events and treats them as occurring in two different universes. Take, for instance, an article written by Alissa Rubin, Baghdad bureau chief of the *Los Angeles Times*.[14] While superficially a rather innocuous bit of reporting, liberal in sympathy, its perspective is as distorted as more blatantly one-sided pieces. The first time Rubin attributes any violence to someone, it is to the Iraqis, and describes it is in terms beyond quantification—as "any level"—perhaps because one way to evoke a nebulous horror is to use vague aggregations that loom all the larger the less they are defined:

> A culture of impunity has taken hold in Iraq. There are few limits to who can be taken hostage or how a hostage might be killed. In this environment, virtually any level of violence is acceptable if it is aimed at the occupation. … The loathing many Fallujah residents have for foreigners, an attitude bred of the Sunni Triangle's long-standing insularity and 12 months of deadly face-offs with U.S. forces, has spread.

The "deadly face-offs" are not blamed on anyone so that a spurious appearance of neutrality between the two combatants is created, but the phrase, "long-standing insularity," subtly shifts the blame onto the insularity of the Fallujans.

> "If we force them to choose, they will choose their own," said a senior official in the U.S.-led coalition.

The source—an American military official—is far from objective but his statement, offered with an air of dispassion, implies that Iraqis are driven more by irrational feelings of tribal solidarity. Should one conclude similarly that Australians and British were also tribal for choosing their own when they supported the American invasion?

For Rubin, the situation is disturbing only in terms of the foreign dead. She is able to reference "published reports" and specific details when the dead are foreigners, but where are the reports about the killing of Iraqi civilians that was the initial provocation? For instance, here is the *Guardian* on the subject:

> But as residents ushered reporters into their homes shortly before last week's attack on four American security guards, it was clear that deep communal anger was lurking here, and had reached boiling point. They wanted to show the results of several US incursions over four days and nights the previous week. Rockets from helicopter gun-ships had punctured bedroom walls. Patio floors and front gates were pockmarked by shrapnel. Car doors looked like sieves. In the mayhem 18 lay dead.

Rubin's piece, however, is written entirely from the point of view of an outsider who sees her protected status about to evaporate. American motives are transparent and free of cultural contextualization, but descriptions of religion and ethnicity creep in when Iraqis are analyzed, a tactic that imitates the manner in which television cameras focus on pictures of Shia scourging themselves but draw back from the realities of power polities that actually goad the occupation and resistance. In a neutral, impassive tone the article links the violence of the resistance to the slowing down of reconstruction, economic growth, and democracy. A a reader, lulled by the quasi-syllogistic tone, swallows the contorted logic by which the cause of economic chaos is the resistance and not the invasion and the preceding twelve years of sanctions and bombing. Rubin continues:

> In some measure, the violence against Westerners is viewed as retribution for the violence in Fallujah. Whether that is true or not, belief that Americans behaved as barbarians and that thousands of Iraqi civilians are dead is widespread. According to Arab custom and especially tribal tradition, they should be avenged.

Again we have the gratuitous reference to tribal tradition that demands vengeance. Forgotten are the innumerable editorials in American papers demanding blood for 9/11, the calls to nuke the Middle East in retaliation. Presumably those calls were rational and "just" and not tribal and vengeful. Is it only Arabs who believe that the American army has behaved barbarously? What should we call collective punishment of civilians, falsified evidence about WMD, random shootings at checkpoints, sniping at ambulances, bombings of hospitals and mosques, looting and arson of libraries and museums?

> No one knows for sure what really happened in Fallujah. All the parties involved have an interest in presenting the events in a manner that maximizes their advantage.

Can Alissa Rubin really not know what's happening? But here is Dahr Jamail reporting from Fallujah:

> Iraqi women and children are being shot by American snipers. Over 600 Iraqis have now been killed by American aggression, and the residents have turned two football fields into graveyards. Ambulances are being shot by the Americans. And now they are preparing to launch a full-scale invasion of the city.[15]

His accounts are seconded by Rahul Mahajan and Helen Williams in the alternative press and by Dan Murphy of the *Christian Science Monitor* who agrees with Iraqi and foreign analysts that 700 dead is an accurate number.[16]

In an interview, even CNN's Daryn Kagan, while taking Al Jazeera to task for showing civilian deaths, makes an extraordinary admission in the context of so much self-serving denial:

> Isn't the story, though, bigger than just the simple numbers—with all due respect to the Iraqi civilians who have lost their lives—the story bigger than just the numbers of people who were killed or the fact that they might have been killed by the U.S. military, that the insurgents, the people trying to cause problems within Fallujah, are mixing in among the civilians?[17]

CNN, in other words, wants to spin civilian casualties to help the military, a legitimate position for the Pentagon to take but surely a deeply unethical one for a news organization.

The army, as often happens, seems to be conducting a different war from the real one on the ground. The military announces that 95 percent of dead Iraqis are "military-age males," not women and children. But an analysis in the *Washington Post* confirms the alternative press again.[18] While an Agence France Press report cites slightly larger numbers than others, all the news accounts are actually remarkably consistent about the numbers killed, but none have reached journalists like Rubin, lost in the "fog of war," morally ambivalent, making false equivalences between both sides. At least half of the thousands of dead Iraqis were civilians of *prima facie* the most innocent sort. The dead Americans at Fallujah were mercenaries for an occupying force, guilty of indiscriminate civilian killings. The Fallujah siege was the collective punishment of a densely populated city, indisputably a war crime. But Rubin overlooks such distinctions and invokes Iraq's colonial history and the memory of Ottoman and British humiliation to account for Iraqi resistance, although not because the American invasion reminds her of the older colonial invasions. Quite the contrary. Rubin clearly believes that the American war, a war of liberation, differs from those past wars. The colonial reference is simply intended to display the Iraqis as weighed down by the past and tradition and unable to embrace modernity. Again, religion and race, plausible as exacerbating factors for the Iraqi resistance, are evoked as the primary ones. Again, as with pre-war commentary, history is manipulated without relevance or logic. Again, rhetorical sleights of hand elevate or diminish the status of facts to fit the argument at hand:

> "Now all the people, even the most ignorant, believe the only solution is resistance. The Americans are killing children, destroying homes, killing women," said Sheik Bilal Habeshi.

Even the admission that civilians are being killed is presented as a quotation from a religious leader, reducing its status to a subjective opinion from the "Arab street." Other facts are similarly obscured—shutting down Sadr's newspaper becomes "avoiding confrontation"; a military goal, such as increasing forces to maintain security, is presented as an objective necessity rather than one of several options, another of which could, after all, be complete withdrawal:

> To many Westerners, the ambush and mutilation of four U.S. contractors in Fallujah appeared to be the start of the troubles. But tracing the onset of this downward spi-

> ral, two other events stand out that at the time were viewed by Westerners as relatively ordinary. Six days before the attack on the contractors, newly arrived Marines had entered Fallujah—the first time in months that U.S. forces had done so. In a battle for control near an entrance to the city, Marines killed between eight and eighteen Iraqis, some of them civilians.

Rubin places the "relatively ordinary" killings of Iraqis, including "some" civilians, at between eight and eighteen, but she fails to mention that they concluded a month that had reported a sharp spike in fighting all over Iraq.

Among those killed was yet another journalist, an Arab freelancer for ABC. Earlier, 143 Iraqis had been killed in Baghdad and Karbala.[19] "More than 10,000 Iraqi men, from 11 to 75 years were locked up, kicked in the head, choked, and put in cold, wet rooms for days at a time," with no legal rights or visits, although most were not considered a threat.[20] In one instance U.S. forces fired on a civilian car in Tikrit, killing a three-year old boy and wounding six women and children as well as their male driver.[21] It is in this context that the killings of the mercenaries, gruesome as they were, should be viewed. A context of mass arrests, beatings, Gestapo-like house raids, humiliating searches of women, aggressive shootings of civilians at checkpoints, and deployment of armored vehicles in residential areas in a manner no different from the pacification of Gaza. Rubin continues:

> What appeared as a spontaneous outpouring of anti-American emotions might in fact have reflected a secret compact between Sadr and insurgents in the Sunni Triangle to produce a national uprising around the April 9 anniversary of Baghdad's fall.

The source for the insinuation that the "spontaneous" anti-American emotions might in fact be orchestrated is Adel Abdel Mehdi, deputy leader of the Supreme Council for Islamic Revolution in Iraq and a member of the U.S.-backed Iraq Governing Council. That is to say, besides an American general, the only person Rubin interviews is a member of the regime installed by the United States who would naturally find it expedient to tar a popular resistance as orchestrated in order to sustain the fiction that democratic governments are always on the side of the "people." A popular uprising must always be instigated and planned by insurgents, foreigners, religious militias, or other professional cadres. Blaming people themselves for an insurgence would after all undermine the whole facade of liberation and expose it for a charade imposed on people who palpably don't want it.

Thus, when the U.S. kills civilians, it is always "inevitable," "unintentional," and in spite of the most precocious of smart bombs whereas Iraqis not only always intend the worst but are at fault also for not condemning their own resistance. Rubin's refrain—"the violence of Iraqis"—is an unconscious betrayal of her inability to distinguish legitimate self-defense from aggression and to recognize the illegitimacy of even raising the issue of Iraqi violence, civilian or even military, which in the circumstances is no more than self-defense against theft and murder.

Elsewhere, Rubin argues that reporters have to be cautious about using material from the Iraqi press because

> Iraq is a country saturated by rumors. ... We try to both reflect what the Iraqi street is saying but not to assert its truthfulness or falseness ... we would do so with care.[22]

Considering that Iraq is a war-ravaged country with communications in disrepair, subjected to a propaganda barrage both from the West and other Arab states, the reports from many local groups have been actually remarkably accurate. Iraqi assertions about the absence of WMD, the number of civilian casualties, the nature of the insurgency, and the presence of Israeli intelligence have all turned out to be accurate. Iraqi skepticism about propaganda narratives like the Jessica Lynch rescue, the staged Berg beheading, and perhaps even Margaret Hassan's alleged murder has been justified.[23] Contrast this with America, where despite access to the whole range of sophisticated national and international media outlets, a wealthy and stable society continues to believe that Iraq was behind 9/11, that Iraq had nuclear weapons, and that the UN inspections regime in Iraq had failed. Yet, where are the references to the American "street" and its "saturation with rumors"? What are such one-sided characterizations if they are not deeply Eurocentric?

It would be one sort of failure of journalism and a simpler one if Alissa Rubin were mouthing government propaganda. But she is not. She has questioned, looked for reasons, and drawn inferences in a manner that reflects a liberal search for root causes. But what speaks through her is a set of assumptions whose framework is the inevitability of the state and thus the virtue of its violence. In that framework, democracy, economic prosperity, and secularism are ranged against religion, tribalism, and irrationalism; state terror is law and order and non-state war is terror; and the West is a monolith because of shared values whereas Arabs are always tribal, whether acting individually or in a group. Mouthing the mechanical language of these preconceptions, her own human powers of observation succumb, and, purporting to show her readers what is happening, she only convinces them of her blindness.

An ideology that expresses itself as much through journalists' silences as through their statements, uses a discourse of civilization and barbarism to erase state terror altogether from the picture. We are left with the misperception that the balance of terror goes against us when in fact, overwhelmingly, it is our terror—whether crystallized in physical or psychological violence or incipient in the potential for them that exists in our overwhelming power—which provokes the "terrorism" of the insurgent.

The Silent War

Where in the accounts of liberal journalists like Rubin, so filled with the violence, turbulence, and fanaticism of Iraqis, do we hear the sound that actually overpowers the skies of Iraq—the whine of AC-130 Spectre gunships, Predator drones, the helicopters—Apaches, Cobras, Lynxes, and Pumas—the shriek of F-16 fighter planes "on the go all through the night"? Media analyst Tom Engelhardt finds not a single article of any significance on the air war, either discussing military strategy or even focusing on the dangers to pilots in the Iraqi skies, a remarkable absence. An American helicopter shoots missiles into a crowd in Baghdad outside the armored American enclave, the Green Zone, killing a reporter for Al-Arabiya TV and the clip is splattered across the screens all over the world but not at home.[24] That is the silence in which liberal ideology operates. Engelhardt:

> For eleven years there is a bombing campaign in the no-fly zones and we hear nothing about it, although the destruction of Iraq's air force and air defense systems in advance was the indisputable reason why ground troops could be used almost immediately in the war.

This is the silence in which liberal ideology commits war crimes.

An average of 34,000 sorties per year over three years, the equivalent of fighting Desert Storm every three years, is depicted as "aerial policing" and passed off as a gradualist alternative to the massive strikes on cities, whereas in fact it worked in tandem with them. For instance, during the pyrotechnical bombing of Baghdad, cameras positioned in hotels adroitly focused attention on the theatrics there, although government buildings were the least of the targets. The great majority of air strikes were directed elsewhere against military and civilian targets all over the country. Even in Baghdad, while public outcry may have initially prevented a campaign against the city as ferocious as the one the Pentagon wanted, once the clamor died down the assaults were progressively stepped up while public attention was distracted elsewhere. This is true not only of Baghdad but of cities across the country, such as Fallujah, which has been blitzed on and off unquestioned for a year.

But the ideology of liberalism permits such things to be edited out of reports and out of consciousness. We hear about the cowardliness of mujahideen who fight from behind mosques. We hear nothing of the cowardliness of pilots invulnerable at tens of thousands of feet raining destruction on unprotected cities. Silence is the tacit lie that enables tacit violence.

Air attacks of sustained ferocity are transformed into police operations by a language that converts illegitimate and aggressive external actions into defensive and legitimate internal ones and a war between states into a law-and-order operation, seamlessly eroding the boundaries between one state and another and between states of peace and war. If our peace is militarized, then by what standard are our wars objectionable?

Discourse shifts from that of war and peace to one of government and outlaw, cowboy and Indian, crime and punishment. We enter a Manichaean world of fixed essences in which our violence is not the amoral operation of power but the virtuous enforcement of law, an internal world of imbricated intentions and choices, in which the evil of the designated enemy is always an absolute against which anything we do is justifiable. The justification for our torture is the enemy's terror, we are told, while carefully hidden from view is the truth that torture is only another word for terror and that torture is the necessary adjunct of a war provoked from the beginning with state terror.

6
Context II: Theater of Pain

Erasing a Crime

In a sworn statement, Specialist Sivits describes Specialist Graner punching a naked detainee, an empty sandbag covering his head "with a closed fist so hard in the temple that it knocked the detainee unconscious."[1] But Mr. Womack, lawyer for Specialist Graner, says, "Striking doesn't mean a lot. . . . Breaking a rib or bone—that would be excessive."

Mr. Bergrin, lawyer for Sergeant Davis, who stomped on a prisoner's fingers, says, "He may have stepped on the hands, but there was no stomping, no broken bones."

Secretary of Defense Donald Rumsfeld says, "I'm not a lawyer, but I know it's not torture—probably abuse."

In these statements the distinction between mere ill treatment and torture hinges on the severity of the pain.

Lynndie England says, "Well, I mean, they [the photos] were for psy-op reasons. And the reasons worked. I mean, so to us, we were doing our job, which meant we were doing what we were told, and the outcome was what they wanted."[2]

James Schlesinger, former CIA director, says, "The aberrant behavior on the night shift in Cell Block 1 at Abu Ghraib would have been avoided with proper training, leadership, and oversight."[3]

The distinction here between a mere aberration and psychological torture hinges on the presence or absence of intention. International and domestic law confirm that severity and intention are the criteria in determining if an act is torture. For example, the UN Convention Against Torture and Other Cruel, Inhuman or Degrading Treatment or Punishment (proposed by the UN in 1984 and ratified by the United States in 1994), defines torture as "any act by which *severe* [my emphasis] pain or suffering, whether physical or mental, is intentionally inflicted on a person" in order to extract information or a confession.

In Federal Criminal Law, the torture statute (18 U.S.C. 2340), defines torture as any "act committed by a person acting under the cover of law specifically intended to inflict severe physical or mental pain."

However, at this point, we are presented with two problems. While it's possible to rank certain kinds of physical pain in a hierarchy of severity, what do we do about mental pain? And how do we gauge intention?

On the first point, Article 16 of the UN convention clearly extends protection to victims of mental torture as well, for it prohibits public officials from committing "other acts of cruel, inhuman or degrading treatment or punishment which do not amount to torture as defined in Article 1." Nevertheless, mental pain, or even physical pain that falls short of mutilation or organ failure, has consistently been devalued in recent American legal history. Thus, the United States has balked at Article 16, finding the terms "cruel, inhuman, and degrading" too nebulous. Its reservations are summed up in the March 6, 2003, torture memorandum which turns to domestic law to clarify the meaning of the terms, specifically, to the Eighth Amendment to the US Constitution that deals with "cruel and unusual punishments."[4]

Observing that the framers of the Constitution apparently intended the phrase to apply to "barbarous" punishments, such as pillorying, disemboweling, decapitation, and drawing and quartering, and that the unusual cruelty lay in the method of punishment not the severity, historian Joan Dayan points out that the real background to the Eighth Amendment lies in the slave codes developed by the French in the Caribbean, copied by John Locke and brought to Carolina, from where they spread to the other mainland American colonies. The codes degraded the humanity of the slave through a curtailment of his personhood under law, not through an absence of legal protection but through a "spurious generality, operating under cover of excessive legalism."[5] That is to say, the legal codes that supposedly went into great detail to protect the body of the slave and his security and "minimal needs," actually permitted and, in fact, exacerbated brutal treatment by the use of hypothetical circumstances and omissions or silences that allowed for leeway in interpretation. An injunction against "unnecessary and excessive whipping, beating, cutting or wounding or . . . cruelly and unnecessarily biting or tearing with dogs . . . withholding proper food and sustenance" obviously begs the question. There must, by corollary, be occasions when necessary and proportionate whipping or biting with dogs is permissible.

So we arrive at "intention." If there is no objective external standard, terms like "unnecessary," "excessive," or "cruel" are ultimately interpreted through the eyes of the perpetrator. In fact, after the liberal rulings on prisoner treatment that prevailed in the 1970s as a result of the prison reform movement, American jurisprudence moved sharply away from the objective consideration of the totality of circumstances in prisons and instead strove to penetrate the jailer's frame of mind, his intention, and his perception of the vital necessity of his actions. The mentality and consciousness—the subjectivity—of the torturer came to matter, while the tortured regressed to a mere body, an object on which the state's will, acting though the torturer, could be inscribed.

This view had notable consequences within the U.S. prison system. In *Hudson v. McMillan* (1992), a Louisiana inmate was punched in the face, chest, and stomach by three correctional officers. Justice Clarence Thomas dissented from the Supreme Court's ruling that such maltreatment during handling constituted "cruel and unusual punishment," even without serious injury. Thomas argued that "punishment" had to be restricted to acts intended as a penalty for the crimes committed and could not be applied to random mistreatment:

> A use of force that causes only insignificant harm to a prisoner may be immoral, it may be tortuous [*sic*], it may be criminal, and it may even be remediable under other provisions of the Federal Constitution, but it is not "cruel and unusual punishment."

Again the question is begged. Thomas assumes that an insignificant harm might be torturous yet he is certain that it is not also cruel and unusual.

It will not do to dismiss Thomas immediately as a judicial reactionary. The attempt to separate deliberate and unintended harm has undoubted merit, and he does allow for remedy of the maltreatment under other constitutional provisions. What he (and Justice Antonin Scalia, who joined him in the dissent) does not take into consideration, however, is *context* and it is context, as always, that is crucial.

Consider one well-known form of punishment that does not cause organ failure or injury to the body—prolonged isolation. One might regard it as harsh but non-torturous, but only if one did not know the conditions in modern Super Maximum (Supermax) prisons.[6] This is how Everett Hoffman, executive director of the American Civil Liberties Union of Kentucky describes them:

> Typically, inmates are confined in 8 x 10 foot cells for 23 hours a day in enforced idleness. The cells are windowless and have solid doors, so that the inmate cannot see or hear anything going on outside the cell. Inmates are "cell fed"—their meals are delivered through slots in the cell doors, with no verbal or visual contact with the guards delivering the meals. No furniture or other amenities are allowed beyond the concrete and steel furniture in the cell—no television, no radio, no tobacco. Inmates in Super Max units are allowed one hour a day of solitary "recreation" in a concrete enclosure, their movements monitored by video cameras. Inmates are within close proximity of staff only when they are being visually searched as they stand naked before a control booth window before their one hour of "recreation." Typically, they remain shackled in front of their families during non-contact visits conducted behind clear partitions. There is always a physical barrier between the inmate and other human beings. They are deprived of human contact or touch for years on end.[7]

However, even before the advent of these concrete-and-steel remote-controlled catacombs, punitive isolation was morally problematic. In the 1840s, while touring the Eastern State Penitentiary in Pennsylvania where isolation was first introduced into the penal system in America, Charles Dickens remarked, "I hold this slow and daily tampering with the mysteries of the brain to be immeasurably worse than any physical torture of the body."[8] Some of the effects of even short-term isolation are described in a 1973 *Harper's* article on the treatment of American prisoners:

> The exciting potential of sensory deprivation as a behavior modifier was revealed through an experiment in which students were paid $20 a day to live in tiny, solitary cubicles with nothing to do. The experiment was supposed to last at least six weeks, but none of the students could take it for more than a few days: Many experienced vivid hallucinations—one student in particular insisted that a tiny spaceship had got into the chamber and was buzzing around shooting pellets at him. While they were in this condition, the experimenter fed the students propaganda messages: No matter how poorly it was presented or how illogical it sounded, the propaganda had a marked effect on the students' attitudes—an effect that lasted for at least a year after they came out of the deprivation chambers.[9]

Yet under the Prisoner's Litigation Reform Act, signed into law by Bill Clinton on April 26, 1996, and intended to reduce frivolous litigation, a prisoner must suffer actual physical injury in order to be considered for injunctive relief. If it did not produce visible physical damage, even the most prolonged isolation would be disqualified under this standard.

Mental torture or degradation thus continues in U.S. prisons unnoticed, in the gaps in an ornate structure of meticulous but arid jurisprudence prohibiting torture. The arid legalism is the precise rhetorical counterpart of the sterile environment of the Supermax itself, both in hiding its inherent violence and in displacing it back onto the victim through self-mutilation or insanity. By admitting "intention" into the argument, the law depicts the victim as deserving the circumstances in which he finds himself, however harmful they might be, so long as he can be defined as guilty and so long as the harm can be defined as accidental or unintended.

Accordingly, in pro-war circles, the torture at Abu Ghraib was absolved by erasing the notion of intention and replacing it in public discourse with an urgent rationale, national security. Conversely, the killing of Berg was magnified by ascribing an *excess* of intention to the killers while depriving them of *any* rationale whatsoever. That is to say, whereas Abu Ghraib was whitewashed by arid quibbling over forensic and procedural detail in the Senate hearings and by media obsession with a convoluted and arcane trail of "torture memos," the Berg killing was magnified by the strategic deployment of heated and value-laden language in opinion journals and Internet commentary that played directly on public sentiment.

This two-pronged strategy illustrates how the abstract, seemingly value-neutral language that turns the unacceptable into the acceptable, the false into the true, and myth into history is always accompanied by the sensation-driven and emotionally charged language that does precisely the opposite and makes the normal aberrant, the rational irrational, and the human monstrous or heroic.

These two languages fit the parameters of the forensic and the pulp drama as I have described them, but they are also more complex and broadly relevant than either term suggests. The personal details that color the stories of the Abu Ghraib reservists, for instance, also color the stories of the Fallujah siege, the rescue of Jessica Lynch, the martyrdom of Nicholas Berg, and even the hunting of Saddam Hussein. But while the first two stories are not given a mythic dimension, the others are. They come to dramatize deeply rooted cultural archetypes that evoke our collective emotion. We can see in them, successively, bound Andromeda rescued by winged Perseus, the self-immolating demigod who appears and reappears from Attis to Christ, and the dragon of pagan and Christian imagination cornered in his labyrinth. They are soteriological myths, myths of salvation, and they feed a national myth of a country that takes on itself the burden of liberating others.

Such myths amplify instances of heroism, martyrdom, or villainy, but only as long as it is *our* heroism and martyrdom and our enemy's villainy. However, when it is our villainy, as at Abu Ghraib, or their martyrdom, as at Fallujah, the descriptions, though still personal, are no longer cast in the poetry of the heroic but in the bureaucratic jargon of error (collateral damage), the cultural critique of regression (tribalism at Fallujah, fundamentalism with Graner/ England/Al Sadr) or the medical diagnostis of illness or perversion (as with Graner/England) so that the underlying events appear exceptional and not emblematic, trivial and not crucial. When the villainy is ours but the fault lies at higher levels of the state, the language ceases to form a personal narrative and disaggregates into the shapeless jargon of bureaucracy, shifting attention away from the actors to the process, diffusing their responsibility like pixels on a screen.

The alternate and interpenetrating use of these two languages characterizes the coverage of Abu Ghraib as it does the rest of the Iraq war. It suggests whether intention or motivation will or will not be ascribed to the actors and explains why certain acts of violence are christened terror and others are not, why certain experiences of pain are considered suffering and others are not.

Constructing a Crime

The Berg killing, although demonstrably less important than Abu Ghraib, was made to trump it by a mixture of the two strategies. The pulp drama turned the killing into a monstrosity while at the same time it removed it from politics and constructed it as a criminal act. The perpetrators were deemed unjustified, the victim completely innocent, and the act especially heinous.

"It's very troubling there's not outrage about the cold-blooded murder of this American," said Senator Susan Collins (R-Maine).[10]

A killing that is a murder is removed from the realm of politics, where groups contend for power, to the realm of law where rights and claims are adjudicated under a dispensation already agreed on through politics. That is, we no longer debate the killing in terms of moral questions arising out of differences in power but debate it instead in terms of moral questions arising in an apolitical or post-political legal context. Treating the killing as a crime assumes that the political dispensation has been accepted by the opposing parties whose claims are being adjudicated, a rhetorical tactic that efficiently removes from the debate the question of whether that dispensation is legitimate or illegitimate

The first tactic in constructing the beheading as a crime was to depict the killers as acting without motivation. Thus they would be seen not as political assassins who demanded negotiation but as criminals deserving only punishment. Right-wing commentators uniformly refused to admit any connection between American actions and the beheading, just as they had previously denied any connection between 9/11 and American foreign policy. Yet, both the hijackers and Berg's executioners explicitly described what led them to act violently and laid out their political objectives. For the former, the deaths of Iraqi children under sanctions were the grievance, the immediate withdrawal of American troops from Saudi Arabia the demand. For the latter, the sexualized torture of Iraqi prisoners, especially by women, was the provocation; an exchange of hostages the immediate demand.

But a fiction is needed to sustain the national self-perception of an unspotted nation defending itself righteously from total evil, and, as usual, it was concocted almost immediately by the avatar of the American street, Rush Limbaugh, "If anybody—and I don't care who they are—if anybody tries to tell you that these pictures from this prison are responsible for the death of Nick Berg, I want you to stand up, and I want you to tell them to stuff it. This is just Al Qaeda being who they are. Al Qaeda beheaded Daniel Pearl before there was any knowledge of whatever went on in this prison in Baghdad."[11]

Senator Joseph Lieberman editorialized in the same vein: "Prison abuse must not blur the enormous moral differences between us and those we fight in Iraq, and in the worldwide war on terrorism."[12]Dr. Walid Phares, a Lebanese expert in political Islam employed by the public relations group Benador Associates, blamed anti-Americans for the "horrid logic" by which the abuse "morally legitimized" the "slaughter of Berg" and asserted that there can be "no moral equality between the two."[13] Phares, a professor at Florida Atlantic University, was during the Lebanese civil war in charge of foreign affairs for the World Lebanese Organization, an umbrella coalition of several right-wing militias, including the Guardians of the Cedar, which has been deemed a terrorist group by the US Congress, and the Phalange, which was complicit in the massacre of between 700 and 1,500 civilians at the Palestinian refugee camps at Sabra and Shatilla in 1982.[14]

The second element in establishing the killing as a crime was to portray Berg as an innocent. Internet commentator David Thibault, for instance, called Berg a "defenseless civilian," although even right-wing bloggers willing to use Berg to score points were uneasy about his bona fides as an innocent.[15]

Finally, commentators were quick to assert the uniquely horrific nature of the beheading. An article in the *New York Post* employed nine different epithets in its description—horrifying, gruesome, sickening, mercilessly, savage, brutal, grisly, stomach- churning, monsters.[16] Captioned "Nick Berg: Jewish like Daniel Pearl," the article suggested a singular crime of anti-Semitism. In fact, beheadings have been horrifyingly common in postwar Iraq and have victimized primarily Iraqis, not foreigners, although it is the handful of foreign victims who have garnered all the press. Neither Berg nor his captors mentioned his religion, so the reference to Pearl seems intended to draw a connection where none seems to exist. Nor is there anything intrinsically more horrible in being beheaded than in being blown apart or mutilated by a cluster bomb, or burned to death by napalm, as over a hundred thousand Iraqis have, without much comment on them individually.

Of course, it is precisely because the methods that the state employs are no less—and in quantitative terms often very much more—horrific than the methods of the non-state actor, that the latter has to be cast as absolutely evil in order to undermine any perception of moral parity between the two which might result from comparing their actions. So while the Abu Ghraib photos were deemed unrepresentative, the Berg beheading was said to represent the essence of the enemy. The *Dallas Morning News* editorial page of May 13 ran an edited photo of one of the assailants holding Berg's severed head aloft, with the headline, "This Is the enemy: Vile Image Shows the World Why We Should Fight." Sean Hannity aired a 30-second audio clip because "it is horrible and it is evil in your midst."[17] *CBS Evening News* producer Jim Murphy explained, "By showing even that little bit, you get a better sense of what some very bad people are willing to do to Americans."[18]

Reframing the Context

Again the legal model suggests the strategy that is at work here. Since the American justice system, unlike the French, is adverserial, cases are established in court not by an independent fact-finder but by the two opposing counsels.

The result is that the facts underlying a case are as much a matter of dispute as its legal interpretation and lawyers fight to prove or disprove them like hired guns, constrained only by their client's interests. This was famously expressed by Oliver Wendell Holmes when he noted that his job was not to achieve justice but to apply the law. Likewise, one could say of the American media, its job is not to tell the truth but to convey the message. A well-funded and insistent message, however false, is often reported without any evaluation whatsoever. When journalists do evaluate politicians, it is often not in substantive terms—are they being truthful?—but in terms of their performance—did they do well or did they stay on message? Debates over style and technique overwhelm analysis of substance.

Of course, this is only possible in the historical vacuum in which American politics is often debated. What right-wing commentators see as "context" turns out unsurprisingly to be not history but law or process. Here is Jonah Goldberg explaining why the photos of Abu Ghraib need to be suppressed:

> These pictures are ... so offensive to Muslim and American sensibilities, whatever news value they have is far, far outweighed by the damage they are doing. "Context"—the supposed holy grail of responsible journalism—is lost in the hysteria and political grandstanding. ... Lost is the fact that in America torturers get punished, while in the Arab world they get promotions.[19]

Two contrasted world of essences—Arab and American—rather than history or politics is the context where we must look for an explanation of Muslim and American sensibilities. But is Goldberg right even on his own terms? It seems not. Has John Kerry who has publicly admitted in the past to committing war crimes in Vietnam, including shooting an unarmed civilian in the back, or Bob Kerrey, who slit the throats of some dozen women and children in Thanh Phong village in February 1969, been in any way punished?[20] Apparently not. In the case of John Kerry, his Vietnam record was used to "promote" him precisely in the manner that Goldberg claims is the distinguishing mark of Arab societies alone.[21] As for the seven reservists, making an example of them merely obscures the lack of accountability of senior officials. In America, as in the Arab world, crimes in the name of the state have rarely hampered a politician's rise to power.

So, the contexts commentators present are self-serving and very often partisan, but a more significant distortion is actually common to both parties—in

America, history and international politics are to an extraordinary degree refracted through domestic culture and politics. Iraq recedes to mere background in a culture war between the Left, by which is usually meant the liberal center, and the Right, where the mainstream has increasingly shifted. The culture war recapitulates Vietnam-era divisions in which the right is associated with patriotism, national purpose, and anti-communism and the "left-liberal" with treachery, self-doubt, and fellow-traveling. Vietnam is less about Vietnam than it is about the American reaction to the war, the humiliating defeat, the loss of prestige, and the rancorous divide between traditionalists and the sex, drugs, and rock-and-roll generation. To a degree quite baffling to foreigners, American politics is driven by this psychological wound. Any criticism of the Iraq war is automatically construed as a resurgence of hippie excess, self-indulgence, disloyalty, and failure of the national will.

For one conservative, for instance, Abu Ghraib is a "pornographic orgy of obsessive national self-flagellation."[22] This only echoes Jonah Goldberg, who writes, "When shocking images might stir Americans to favor war, the Serious Journalists show great restraint. When those images have the opposite effect, the Ted Koppels let it fly."[23] The jibes at the "liberal media" are simply variants on Limbaugh's popular anti-intellectualism. Goldberg forgets the equally shocking pictures that might have dissuaded Americans from war had they made it to CBS—of Iraqi children blown to bits by air strikes, or mutilated by cluster bombs, or shredded by sniper bullets.

Other conservatives attacked the media not only for partisan bias but for inciting violence, "Where is the rage, Mr. Kerry? Where is the rage, Mr. Kennedy? The perpetrators of this horrible crime have stated that it is in retaliation for the alleged abuses perpetrated on Iraqi detainees. This is a clear sign that those who have made much hay about what happened in that compound are to be blamed."[24]

After having denounced as fellow travelers anyone who suggests that terrorists might have defensible political grievances, conservatives see nothing illogical in arguing that the Berg killing might have resulted from the assiduous stoking of outrage over Abu Ghraib by liberals. Lost in the cacophony about the so-called liberal media is the inescapable fact that the liberal media in fact shares many of the Right's most questionable assumptions. For instance, in rebutting Goldberg's criticism, Howard Katz of the *Washington Post* uses the Right's own argument about terrorists—they don't need a reason.[25]

A legalistic discourse enables us to reframe our violent acts as rational, limited, and defensive, while emotionally charged language reframes our enemy's response as irrational, unlimited, and unprovoked. The bureaucratic language of law erases the violence of our acts while the language of mythology amplifies theirs into monstrosities threatening us from a pale of unreason and regression.

The Language of Normalization

The contextual vacuum is of course created by more than language. Contributing to it is the practical temper of American culture, suggested by Henry Ford's famous comment that history is bunk. The business of America is business and the model of the thinker in American history is either the recluse at Walden or Emerson's scholar-activist who "grudges every opportunity of action past by, as a loss of power."[26]

In a famous book of the 1960s Richard Hofstader traced the roots of this anti-intellectualism to geographical isolation, democratic populism, and a culture of social mobility that rewards self-reliance.[27] But it is significant that while popular anti-intellectualism is hostile to the disinterested erudition of the Ivory Tower, it also naively idolizes experts. From having spent a large part of their history struggling with natural hazards as they expanded their frontiers, Americans tend to see reality as a series of physical challenges or technical problems to be overcome or solved and are inordinately willing to trust those they think have the skills to do so.[28] These experts, lacking both the broad erudition and interpretative skills of humanistic scholars, as well as the methodological and conceptual rigor of the physical scientists, are properly called technicians, since they use a rather narrow body of specialized knowledge to solve technical problems. But popularly, they are regarded as scientists and are presumed disinterested. Since what constitutes a problem and what makes for a solution are not self-evident but rely on the terms in which they are defined, the disinterest is questionable and is at the command of whoever sets those terms. Experts in public life are employed largely by the government, the military, big business, and the think tanks, research facilities, and regulatory bodies that go along with them, so the problems public experts solve are what their employer—the corporate state—defines as such, and the recommendations they propose are also what their employer must implement. The incentive to oppose the state's preferred position on something is thus usually nil.

Even if experts manage to think independently, their training does not help them make independent judgments of value, for the new technocrats are largely drawn from either the law or the so-called soft sciences, especially the management and policy sciences.

Furthermore, while in England politics may fall under the discipline of modern history, in America it is conceived as a social science, overlapping political economy and behavioral psychology, and is studied in a historical vacuum, as though nations were bodies moving with quantifiable direction and force in a Newtonian world. Behaviorism, the view that man is infinitely malleable, was in fact the pervasive philosophy in academia when the uniquely American discipline of political science was created in the early Cold War years in the shadow of the atom bomb.[29] Concerned with minimizing human error and controlling human behavior in a broader sense as well, the government massively funded research in the sciences dedicated to the management of men, from behavioral psychology to political science and areas studies. In 1951, a Social Science Research Council report even argued that the best thing for U.S. domination of the world was "the launching of scores of area programs."[30]

More relevant to the story of Abu Ghraib, in 1962 a professor at the Massachusetts Institute of Technology (MIT), Edgar Schein, suggested that prisoners offered a ready-made population on which experiments in physical, psychological, and chemical techniques of behavioral modification could be performed that could then be used in other circumstances. Schein, who founded "organizational psychology" and invented the term "corporate culture" has had enormous influence on the management sciences and human resources studies, but it was from totalitarian regimes that he learned his methods. Studying the torture and brainwashing techniques used on American prisoners of war by North Koreans and Chinese, he proposed isolation and sensory deprivation as methods to cut prisoners off from others and make them easy to manipulate. The "Psychology of Invisibility," as he called it, relied on destroying the external validation needed by the psyche.[31] He treated it with scientific detachment as something entirely divorced from ethical scruples:

> I would like to have you think of brainwashing not in terms of politics, ethics, and morals, but in terms of the deliberate changing of human behavior and attitudes by a group of men who have relatively complete control over the environment in which the captive population lives.[3]

Sensory feedback reduction, Schein felt, would crack inmates' mental defense systems, which could then be filled by state propaganda.

These are the sinister roots of statecraft which are concealed by the bureaucratic jargon policy scientists like to employ.[32] Statistics and charts are used misleadingly to confer scientific precision on analysis that is actually political. Abstractions turn the figments of grammatical structure into reality. What does the vapid notion of *rapid dominance* really mean, for instance? The use of the passive voice eliminates the subjects of sentences and devolves responsibility to the machinery of actions and processes, and not the human beings who operate the machinery. Models from science and technology are misapplied in dangerously different contexts and are then accepted uncritically. These developments can be blamed partly on the public's excessive veneration of technical expertise, its *technolatry*, but they can be blamed even more on aggressive marketing techniques borrowed from business. It is not coincidental that public relations—the craft of managing public perception—was born at the same time as political science and that the two together supply the art and science of government language today. It is not coincidental that the scientists of prison control were also the scientists of workplace management. From the work gang and the labor camp to the gulag is only a step.

To hide this seamless reality is the task of official jargon, which is as ugly aesthetically as what lies behind it is morally repulsive. Information specialists spread disinformation; a biblical sounding acronym, MOAB, places a righteous halo on a 21,000-ton bomb; under the linguistic cover of collateral damage, we are free to bomb children, the elderly, and the sick; it seems that if we only christen it a Daisy Cutter, a thermonuclear device boring through molten rock into the bowels of earth will leave in its wake a confetti of petals and leaves. While in ordinary language pacification means making peace, used by government, it is the annihilation of cities and the massacre of populations. Precision weapons and surgical strikes conceal the lethal penumbra of destruction inflicted by even the most accurately targeted strikes. GPS-guided bombs, for instance, may hit within 10 meters of the target 80 to 85 percent of the time, but even the smallest, the 500-pound bomb, with a blast radius of 400 meters, shakes a whole neighborhood, smashing windows and doors. In Gulf War I, 10 percent of the weapons were precision-guided while in this war 80 percent were, but the perverse result of the increase in precision weapons has only been an increase in their use.[33] The coalition sent out over 1,700 air sorties on one day alone, dropping 504 TLAM and CALCM cruise missiles on Baghdad, more than were used in the whole of the first war.[34]

Or consider a term like "nonlethal," which tenderly relieves us of our anxieties over civilian casualties. Of course, plastic bullets are lethal, only less so than conventional ones. Plastic bullets penetrate the eyeball and explode in the brain and their deceptive innocuousness only encourages indiscriminate use. Plastic handcuffs, if tied hard, cut circulation and nerves and damage limbs permanently. Psychological torture that drives adults insane in a matter of months is called "abuse" and reduced to mere indiscretion or overzealousness. Hoods, like those at Abu Ghraib, suggest gentle restraint until we learn that they are made of sackcloth, soaked in feces and urine, strapped at the neck, and kept on so long they suffocate the victim. Even government directives blandly admit that the real purpose of nonlethal weaponry is to increase acceptance of violence and not to reduce violence.[35]

Even those who recognize the Orwellism of modern political language do not always escape its effects. Lacking the precision of science or the complexity of the humanities, the aridity of jargon passes for scientific rationality, the very colorlessness of its descriptions of death and destruction becomes a measure of their necessity and legality. Associated daily with the ordinary and legitimate actions of government, it finally becomes acceptable when used by government to justify extraordinary and illegitimate actions. It becomes persuasive by default. With public relations experts increasingly indispensable to all areas of public life, from the running of political campaigns to the conduct of military affairs, bureaucratic language becomes an irresistible instrument of coercion.

Inevitably, we end up with orchestrated press releases masquerading as news on the media conglomerates.[36] The conglomerates themselves are driven on one end by the advertising needs of the same businesses that lobby and control government, while on the other they service a public molded and managed by advertising. The result is plastic perceptions, virtual reality. This, rather than naive insularity, is what permits propaganda to succeed. Forty percent of the American population does not own a passport and most—if we are to believe the polls—cannot place France, let alone Iraq, on a map. But it is not ignorance itself that is at fault in American failures in diplomacy or strategy but the void it creates into which elites can project the fabrications of the public relations industry.

The bureaucratic language of law and the management sciences erodes the sharp outlines of reality into a haze onto which propaganda imposes its own powerful images. In the vacuum of an insular public consciousness, the past and the distant are fragmented without history or logic, then reunified by a monochrome of emotion into those hypnotic images of the mythic and monstrous that emerge from the subconscious. While the discourse of legalism and scientism makes the government's case in rational terms, myth makes it in irrational terms.

The Language of Monstrosity

The sensationalized language of the pulp drama draws naturally from the realm of the myth, which is visceral, not fully conscious, and therefore easily manipulated.

Having constructed the Berg killing as a crime and eliminated or neutralized its context through the rhetorical tactics of bureaucratic language, propaganda works to make the perpetrators as monstrous as possible. Religion is the perfect locus for this for several reasons. Exaggerating the role of religious fanaticism in terrorism fulfills the need to have the enemy defined as evil by his very nature. It fulfills the need to provide an impetus that cannot also function as a reason. It provides the enemy with intention but robs him of rational motive. It defines him as irrational, atavistic, and tribal, so that his motiveless malignancy can foreclose even the possibility of negotiation with him. The individual motives of the actors are erased or made fungible and a generic terrorism is created, unyielding and eternal, uncaused and ahistoric. Ultimately, defining the terrorist's irrationality in terms of religion prevents him from evading responsibility. To consider someone truly mad would, after all, absolve him of motivation and thus accountability. So, paradoxically, the terrorist is constructed as both culpable and irrational, both coldly calculating and psychopathically savage. This is to understand the enemy not as human like us, but monstrous. And those precisely are the images we encounter in the media.

Daniel Pearl's killing is linked with Berg's to emphasize their common Jewish identity and gloss over the non-Jews, including Iraqis, who have also been beheaded. Berg's passion for his religion is not described in terms of fanaticism, yet Iraqi males of the same bent are inexorably fanatical. Thus, the ritualistic Berg killing typifies Islam but the anti-Muslim sadism at Abu Ghraib does not typify Christianity.

Iraqi human rights minister Bakhtiar Amin refers to the assassins as "psychopaths."[37] An Internet commentator calls them "barbaric animals" who "bark" their religious slogans while committing "satanic actions." He applauds the Bush

White House for trying to "exterminate these insects."[38] Terrorists regress from barely human to animal to insect and finally to "slime" in a steady progression through the chain of being to nonexistence.

Even a Democratic Party operative, Steven Zak, complains about the "self-flagellation" of the Left's anti-Americanism.[39] For him, Abu Ghraib is merely "nonlethal humiliation," born of "frustration" whereas the mutilation of the contractors and the killing of Berg, like "the cold-blooded murders of a pregnant 34-year-old Israeli mother and her four daughters ... by the Islamic allies of our enemies in Iraq," display evil "not seen since the Third Reich." American guards are not "thugs"—that word must be reserved for Hussein, Yassin, and Rantisi.

A neoconservative commentator could not have been shriller than Zak:

> We're there because Iraqis, collectively, have created a hellhole that threatens the world, not to mention a nightmare for themselves. Nearly one thousand Americans have died trying to clean up their mess and for that we don't owe any apologies—not for damaged mosques that house terrorists, not for occupied "holy" cities, not for anything we're trying to accomplish. Yet our repentant posture never seems to end.

The single act of an unnamed and indefinite group is identified here with all Islam, not merely some militant version of it, the religion itself is questioned in derogatory quotation marks, and finally Iraqis are elided with Palestinians and judged "collectively" as complicit in their fate, thus legitimizing their collective punishment and indeed "anything we're trying to accomplish." Open season indeed.

As in the coverage of Abu Ghraib, several different political situations are lumped together to provide a broad target, Islam, so that the discourse of civilization and barbarism can be revived. "It is very difficult not to think that, after all, there may be a hopeless clash of civilizations taking place between the Middle East and the West. It is impossible not to ask whether there is inherent violence and lack of civility in Arab society," writes Meyrav Wurmser of the Middle Eastern Media Research Institute, apparently without irony or recollection of two world wars and a multitude of bloody colonial and proxy wars fought by Europeans or Americans.[40]

Wurmser continues, "It now has become clear that we are confronted with a deep malady. So many years of corruption, despotism, and tyranny—not just a century of Arab ideologies, but also centuries of Ottoman imperial rule and centuries of Arab tyrannies before that—have distorted, even sickened, Arab societies."[41]

Again, as with the formulation of terrorist madness, the formulation of Muslim sickness is paradoxical—Arabs are sick but too sick for healing. Their malady needs a more brutal purging. In Vietnam, we destroyed villages to save them from Communism; in Iraq, we destroy cities to cure them of Islam.

Religion allows us to see Muslims as diminished human beings, for if modernity makes us full individuals, then a religion defined as premodern and tribal must make its followers an undifferentiated animal-like mass, and customs that are strange must make their practitioners barbarous. Religious clothing and customs occupy our attention inordinately. Consider the attention paid to the return of the veil in the aftermath of war, the scourging practiced by the Shia, the chanting of Allahu Akbar during the beheading. What does this suggest if not fascination, even if it is one mixed with revulsion? The chant is surely to have been expected from Islamic killers—if that is what they were—and is not different from the Christian prayer that is said before war, or before the proceedings of Congress, or at the prayer breakfasts that are almost compulsory in the White House, or before football matches, or at any of a number of perfectly secular events. Yet, the chant and the ritual that endow the beheading with meaning and solemnity for its perpetrators, is for the same reason fraught with horror for its American viewers. The numinous quality both repels and excites by compelling us subliminally to pay attention to a dimension we have banished from explicit expression in politics. Religious rituals mark a cyclical and eternal time outside the linear time of the rational state. While our own rites, having long been domesticated, participate seamlessly in the temporal realm, theirs, erupting from some dimension beyond, appear to us as monstrous and compel us to ascribe greater power to them than even their creators seek. In a bizarre paradox, the very meaning with which the terrorist endows his killings thus becomes proof of his irrationality, while the sheer meaninglessness of ours—the accidents, the collateral damage—validates our rationality.

Terror as Communication

Indeed, it is the terrorist whose acts are rational. The terrorists' rationality is this: he can claim our attention on no other grounds. He cannot compel us in any other way—physical, financial, or legal. We annihilate his person, his family, his home, his factories, and his state with relentless bombing. We refuse his pragmatic barter of land for peace, persons for money, or prisoner for prisoner. The beheading of Berg, as of all the hostages, Italian, English, Japanese, Korean, Polish, who followed him in their video incarnations, were preceded by pleas to release the prisoners of Abu Ghraib, especially the ones we do not hear about, the women. It is surely neither irrational nor unreasonable that a country should want women released from degradation and assault at the hands of alien men. And it is surely both reasonable and rational that when law fails—as the United Nations failed, as the rights of statehood, and the protection of international law all failed—a country may turn to what is left to it to resist. What is left is pain; pain conceived as communication; terror as theater; the power of violence not over the body but over the imagination, as imagery that forces us to look again at a history we daily efface and rewrite with our weapons.

Before it is a crime, then, a beheading is perfectly an act of communication, or it would not have been recorded. Recorded, it creates a new relationship between the weak and the powerful. Within its artificially created time and space it creates a representation of power in which the terrorist reclaims his existence as our equal, able to inspire us with the same fear that we inspire in him. Through imagery, he differentiates himself from "insects," "the slime," and becomes al-Zarqawi, a man who at last has a name and whose face we are compelled to recognize.

Again, we find a paradox. The more we scorn dialogue with the terrorist, the more we endow him with the numinosity of the abyss. The more we shudder at the horror, the greater becomes its power to move us to irrational action. Contrary to the popular cry, we *must* negotiate with terrorists. It is through negotiation alone that we permit reason to cut into the dance of death and reclaim our own humanity that stands by hypnotized. Otherwise, we condemn not him but us to the abyss. But it seems that is precisely what we want. We covet the abyss. It is we who are monstrous in our unreason.

Consider how the state takes hostages with impunity. Not merely one or a dozen but entire populations. Under the sanctions, a half-million children were held hostage, ransoming their country's future, its health, its future generations. And wasn't it also hostage-taking when American planes conducted the longest continuous bombing campaign in history and demanded of a leader who had been disarmed for ten years that he disarm yet again and again under the threat of annihilation?

And when his nuclear nakedness was held up to the world by the IAEA, by UN inspectors, even finally by American inspectors, with an insatiable lust for violence we promised the people of Iraq, of whom half are children, that we would rain bombs on them of a might they had never seen. Glorying in our unfettered power, we unleashed what we called "shock and awe," launching between 1,400 and -2,000 sorties every 24 hours, that is, almost 30,000 in just over two weeks, dropping in three weeks between March 20 and April 9, 2003 more cluster bombs than were dropped in six months in Afghanistan, firing in just one day 400 cruise missiles, as many as were fired in forty days in Gulf War I.[42]

Do we forget that such carpet bombing was precisely the charge laid against the Nazi minister Hermann Goering at the Nuremburg Tribunal and that it is a violation of the civilian protection clause of the 4th Geneva Convention, its Protocol I of 1977, as well as of "customary international law," which counts it as "indiscriminate attack"?[43]

Do we forget or is it what we really intend? In their 1996 National Defense University opus, which lent its title to the shock and awe campaign, Harlan Ullman and James Wade admiringly pointed out photo and film images of "the comatose and glazed expressions of survivors of the great bombardments of World War I" and advocated "instant, nearly incomprehensible levels of massive destruction directed at influencing society writ large, meaning its leadership and public, rather than targeting directly against military or strategic objectives. The employment of this capability against society and its values, called "countervalue" in the nuclear deterrent jargon, is massively destructive strikes directly at the public will."[44]

But all this is not accounted as terror or sadism or barbarism. But when one young man, unfortunate to be where he was but apparently not guiltless, was dressed, named, and then killed—albeit with brutality—then and only then was terrorism born.

Terror as Pornography

If we examine why it is we refuse rationality to terrorists who offer us nothing but reasons, it becomes evident that it is because we refuse to admit our own irrationality. It is because we do not need or want reasons. The reasons we offer grow, metamorphose, vanish, but our will to violence remains. The provocation does not arise from our victim, for when he meets our demand, we remain insatiable. Our victim is irrelevant to a violence that merely finds an object in him.

Before the 2003 invasion Senator Mel Martinez in a debate with Betty Castor said that American and British pilots in the no-fly zone "were risking lives" to protect the Iraqi population.[45] From the end of the Gulf War in 1991, thousands of sorties were run, ostensibly to protect rebel groups from Iraqi bombing. They were unable to show one instance of doing so, but they did routinely hit Iraq's air defense systems and kill hundreds of civilians, including children, yet Centcom denied targeting civilians. Protecting a population from 33,000 feet is no more than a fantasy, and by late 2002 leaflets picturing cowering Iraqi families and Arabic warnings showed that the fantasy was not of protecting but of terrorizing.[46]

At Fallujah in March, the Americans shut down the main bridge, cut off the hospital from the town, and dropped 500-, 1,000-, and 2,000-pound bombs; AC-130 Spectre gunships that can destroy a block in under a minute raked the town; roughly 900–1,000 people were blown up, burned, or shot, two-thirds of them noncombatants. Was this terror?

"U.S. Urges Civilians to Flee Targeted Falluja," reads a Reuters headline on November 5, 2004, but the article beneath describes the targeting of all males between 18 and 45 in a population of 100,000, although the actual militants numbered only a few thousand. Was this terror?

Marine Staff Sergeant Jimmy Massey described how men under his command in the Seventh Marines, killed "30 plus" civilians within 48 hours while on checkpoint duty in Baghdad in March 2003.[47] In some incidents, Iraqi civilians were killed by between 200 and 500 rounds pumped into four separate cars, which each failed to respond to a single warning shot or to hand signals at a Baghdad checkpoint.

Acting insistently in the full knowledge of "unintended" side effects makes us as guilty as those acting intentionally. Consider that in January a UN study warned that 500,000 Iraqis could be injured in the early stages of a new U.S. invasion, and because U.S. air attacks would probably destroy Iraq's infrastructure, up to three million more could face dire malnutrition in the fallout.[48] On January 25, 2003, the *Los Angles Times* reported that it had uncovered Pentagon plans to unleash nuclear weapons upon Iraq, even though, as we now know, there was no credible military threat.[49] Can we pretend that we did not intend those consequences we knew of well in advance?

Consider that the water supply to Fallujah was cut off, as also to Tall Afar and Samarra. This affected up to 750,000 civilians and was apparently part of a deliberate American policy against cities under attack.[50] Yet though Fallujah has been under almost constant bombardment from the original siege in March up to the latest offensive in November, it is still only "occupied but not subdued" and Zarqawi has yet again escaped, as he surely must if we are to have a war on terror.[51] How different is this from the British "saturation bombing" of Dresden that was fully intended to terrorize through the incineration of civilians? Let us desist altogether in perpetuating the patent absurdity that the United States does not "intend" casualties.

It is because we turn the issue into a certain kind of morality play, a legal drama of wicked and virtuous "intent" that we are unable to see that terror and also torture cannot be understood only in those acts committed purely in order to inflict pain.

We are mesmerized by a pious theater in which the pain we inflict, however genocidal, is insignificant because it was unintended and we had reasons, whereas the pain they inflict, however limited, is monstrous because it was intended and they had no reasons.

Justice Thomas's ruling plays to the crowd that patronizes that theater and identifies only with the subjectivity of the perpetrator who plays the lead role in it. Thomas, attempting to situate torture in the mind, that is, the intent and good faith of the perpetrator rather than in the body, that is, the deprivation and injury of the prisoner, privileges the former and diminishes the latter.[52] Defining torture from its causes rather than its effects not only disparages the victim but the reality of the body in which the victim suffers and to which the victim is reduced. In that denigration of the physical world we can a read a whole history of cruelty to human flesh sanctioned by ideology. In eroding the Eighth Amendment prohibiting cruel and unusual punishment, Thomas looks back to colonial ideology from which the slave codes were imported and which enabled the degradation of the native into an object of manipulation. Denying the concrete reality of a body, a person, and a population is thus an incremental series that is *enabled,* not checked, by the structure of law and legal reasoning, which substitutes in its place a series of abstractions—the mind, theory, and system. The privileging of a system of ideas over flesh and blood reality is precisely ideology.

Nor can we evade this conclusion by insisting that there is some "virtuous" pursuit of information that justifies the substitution of ideology for flesh and blood. At Abu Ghraib and Guantanamo, we are not really searching for vital clues to avoid a concrete "ticking bomb" contingency, because, as Ullman explains, the "rapid dominance" of the state is not content with the bits and scraps of information that such an interrogation might yield but needs the magisterial collection of "sufficient and timely environmental information" in "logistics, demographics, and infrastructure," encompassing the entire population and all it requires to live—"geography, road/sail/ship lanes, utility sites and corridors, manufacturing, government sites, military and paramilitary facilities, population demographics, economic and financial pressure points (such as oil wells or gold mines), and major dams and bridges." Which is to say that what the state demands is omniscience, an infinite movement into internal space. A movement that entails the physical and mental torture of the individual as much as the thrust into geographical space entails the subjugation of populations. Terror and rationality slip hand in hand through the hidden cells of detention centers, the gray zones of secret special operations, and the silent bombing at the no-fly fringes of our consciousness.

The torture at Abu Ghraib, like the bombing of Iraq, moves toward such limitless rationality that it becomes completely irrational, gratuitous, and without any purpose beside the display of power and the desire to make an example of. Since we cannot win hearts, let us win minds through the persuasion not of reason but fear. This diminishment of the victim to an object rather than the acts themselves is what makes the torture and terror of the warfare state ultimately pornographic, for while the theater of the terrorist-insurgent seeks to communicate and is to that extent rational, our theater appears to be only a perverse enjoyment, a tasting of our freedom from all constraint, the self-pleasuring of power delighting in its own performance.

More than forty pictures posted on a commercial website by a Navy SEAL's wife testify to this.[53] Dating as far back as May 2003, they show jubilant SEALs sitting on hooded, handcuffed, and bloodied prisoners in the back of a pickup; in the aftermath of a house raid, one prisoner lies on his back, a boot on his chest; another has an automatic weapon held to his head, a gloved thumb poked into his throat; blood drips from heads; a family huddles on the floor here; there, rubble and overturned furniture. The photos surfaced during an investigation of another case in which SEALs posed in the back of a Humvee for trophy pictures with a prisoner who died hours later at Abu Ghraib. There are eyewitness reports from refugees that some soldiers in Fallujah were tying the dead bodies of resistance fighters to tanks and driving around with their "trophies."

In October 2004, cockpit video footage surfaced showing a pilot targeting unarmed Iraqis on the street in Fallujah and asking his mission controllers whether he should "take them out." They assent and there is a huge explosion in the crowd. A second voice on the clip exclaims with audible satisfaction, "Oh, dude!"[54]

The conclusion is inescapable. The terror that is held up to us like a red rag is actually of our own making and allows each objective when reached to immediately recede, leaving an insatiable void into which we thrust with greater and greater violence, inflamed by weakness in a theater almost of sadism. As with terror, so with torture. That 90 percent of prisoners have nothing to tell us can hardly stand in the way of our inflicting pain on them if information is not the objective as much as it is the exercise of power on the helpless will. In any case, extraction of the most vital information—and information is always the most vital when the pain inflicted is the worst—does not absolve us. Rather than use some elusive and easily camouflaged notion of intention that is only operative when the moral and legal conventions in which it is couched are accepted and obeyed by both sides, we ought to examine the actual contest of force before us.

Analogies reveal what the language of law conceals. We do not permit a man, however restrained, to fight a child, however pugnacious. The great inequality of power presupposes an unfair contest.[55] We do not allow a man to blow up a building containing hundreds to avenge the death of a friend. The disproportion in response overwhelms the justice of the intent. We do not exonerate a man who punishes his neighbor's dishonesty by burglarizing his house. He was not the legitimate authority to mete out punishment. In these contests of force, the intent and motive of the actor are secondary to the effects of power on the victim. As in wars between states, considerations of the motive and intents of the states are secondary to the effects on the object of intervention, whether it is the body on which torture is inscribed or the population on which terror is rained. If we accept the validity of these analogies we must concede that in them the notion of intent in these matters is irrelevant and self-exculpatory. It is inequality in power, illegitimacy in its use, and disproportion in its application that constitute the essence of terrorism as it does torture. It is the humiliation and subjugation of whole populations through normalized physical and psychological violence and detention that constitutes terror or torture, especially in its most insidious form, the rational violence of the modern state to which we are blinded by language and ideology.

7
Ideology I: Prometheus

Ideology prevents the citizens of the state from recognizing its violence and allows the state to rewrite the general terrorizing of a population through detentions and torture as the inevitable and just operation of law. Since overt coercion would be unacceptable and since only a handful of elites can be bribed into complicity by tangible rewards, the state must convince the mass of its citizens of its inevitability and virtue through ideology. The tale of Nicholas Berg is a powerful key to that ideology.

Like the tale of Abu Ghraib, in its telling it foregrounds the personal and sensational. Unlike Abu Ghraib, it is not repellent but heroic and even messianic. The story of a young Jewish boy who sacrifices the comforts of American life to help the downtrodden of Africa, in Ghana, who finally sacrifices life itself for the suffering people of Iraq resonates deeply with archetypes that are not only religious but national.

Pagan Inflections

Berg's telecommunications tower company, Prometheus Methods, invokes a myth—the myth of the Greek titan who stole the secret of fire from the gods and was then punished eternally for bringing to birth a new world. Individualism, maverick defiance, talent for innovation, belief in the future, and a sense of responsibility in bringing it to fruition, those traits that Americans most passionately believe about themselves find expression in the myth of Prometheus. It is worthwhile to explore why that myth has acquired deeper significance in American political culture today.

American exceptionalism, its traditional sense of being different from other nations, is bred from the biblical injunction to be a city on a shining hill and a light unto the heathen, but these days it carries a distinctively pagan inflection.

Prominent members of the State and Defense Departments call themselves Vulcans from their conviction that the use of American force is overwhelmingly good and unavoidable.[1] The most influential intellectual current in American politics today—neoconservatism—rejects Catholic "just war" theories[2] and draws inspiration from Leo Strauss's cryptic interpretations of pre-Christian philosophers.[3]

Likewise, the story of Prometheus draws on pre-Christian themes to reinvent the dying savior as one who does battle not with evil incarnate—Satan—but with the traditional gods, the Olympians, keepers of law and tradition. Still godlike in capacity, he is no longer the ethical Jewish savior but the heroic Greek, and his mortal enemy is not the law-breaking Lucifer but the establishment on Mount Olympus. Like the trickster god who wrested the secret of fire from Zeus on behalf of humankind, the intellectuals of the New World Order, the new Prometheans, see themselves as using stratagems to wrest the leadership of the world from the old order of international bodies, international law, diplomacy, negotiation, and compromise.

We can identify certain concrete themes in the program of the Prometheans: a fascination with advanced technology not only of weaponry but especially of communication and information, including everything from the exploitation of information networks to psy-ops and mind-control techniques; a tendency to secrecy, covert actions, and the creation of extralegal channels; an emphasis on maneuverability, flexibility, lightness, and speed in the deployment of forces; a radical reordering of the military that blurs the line between military and civilian functions and penetrates the civilian population through the use of guard and reserve forces, the training of police SWAT teams, and the deployment of covert paramilitary forces; the embrace of privatization and of operational models drawn from business; an unconstrained and unapologetic symbiosis between business, government, and military; a nationalist and patriotic rhetoric that is almost religious in tone.

Totality and Secrecy

Tower and Cave: Analyzed, these disparate elements reveal a pattern—they tend toward unity and secrecy. Between private and public, civil and military, domestic and foreign, the mental and the physical, even the simulated and the real, boundaries are erased and made seamless through physical restructuring, the financial mechanism of the market, and networks of propaganda. Likewise, every part of the Promethean program tends toward invisibility—from covert operations to the exploitation of far-flung bases, from stealth air strikes to satellite spying in outer space, from nonlethal weaponry and psychological operations to backroom deals, each element attempts to mask itself. Indivisible and invisible, the state, totally hidden, presents itself as an inevitability and the end of history.

This is the essence of the current Revolution in Military Affairs theorized by such futurists as Andrew Marshall. In today's RMA, belief in the centrality of surveillance and the information war is combined with the conviction that the "whole theater should be held at risk" leaving the enemy "no sanctuary." When the theater is anywhere in the world, it follows that no population is without risk.

Both indivisible and invisible, information networks lie at the center of this total state, in their broadest sense encompassing everything from academic treatises and public information to "black" espionage. Ideology moves to the center as the advance of the total state accelerates and with it moves the staging ground of ideology—electronic communications, computer and information networks, and information technology, the fire of the modern Prometheans. It is through these networks that they do battle as defiant revolutionaries on behalf of a higher imperative, a greater good. That this might be self-deluding rhetoric is a different question. The Prometheans in their own minds, at least, lead the state in its most rational and virtuous incarnation.

***Synchronicities*:** The story of Nick Berg feeds very deeply on these hidden wells of cultural mythmaking. The technological prowess of a young man like Berg embodies the youthful and pragmatic optimism of the American ethos, where every problem must have a solution and where technology is always part of that solution. The dot-com bubble of the Clinton years may have burst, but the endless optimism about the Internet and chip technology remains strong and expresses itself in a popular fascination with technological wizards and wizardry, whose chief failing is to be unable to see through misleading transpositions of technological paradigms into other fields or to distinguish between true technological genius and marketing skill.

What are we to make of the singular events in Berg's story that resonate with Promethean themes? He was a civilian contractor, a tower repairman, a telecom wizard. Yet it is hard to credit that a young man not registered with the Coalition Provisional Authority could have been wandering through Iraq with telecommunications equipment, working at some of the most sensitive sites in the country. While most contractors travel directly to Baghdad, Berg landed in Jordan and found his way by land into Iraq. If he was a one-man radio-tower operation, would he have been able to work in Iraq without first being contracted in the United States by a larger company? Would he insist on traveling alone? Familiar with Middle Eastern languages, well traveled in the region, politically active, could it be that he was connected to intelligence in some way? In late November 2003, as the occupation grew increasingly covert, swarms of special forces operatives were trying to infiltrate the insurgency and police the population itself. Berg's apparent involvement in Oklahoma with the 9/11 terrorists and his ties to Republican operatives are too curious to dismiss and suggest that he may have been a part of that covert war playing out in northern Iraq, where we know he spent time working on towers.[4]

He was also part of the web of influence spun by unsavory expatriates over the formulation and execution of the invasion. His partner, al-Taee, who had ties to the Russian mafia, was a vocal proponent of the war and a supporter of Ahmad Chalabi, the convicted embezzler whose questionable intelligence fueled the case for the war. Taee was also an associate of Paul Wolfowitz, who actively promoted Chalabi.[5] On August 9, 2002, as president of the Iraqi American Council, Taee coordinated meetings of Iraqi-American groups and Iraqi opposition leaders, including Chalabi (Iraqi National Congress), Massoud Barzani (Kurdistan Democratic Party), Jalal Talabani (Patriotic Union of Kurdistan), Iyad Allawi (Iraqi National Accord), and Ayatollah Baqr Al-Hakim (Supreme Council for the Islamic Revolution in Iraq) with Secretary of State Powell, Undersecretary of State Marc Grossman, and Undersecretary of Defense Feith.[6] How did Berg, then working as a janitor at Oklahoma University, end up with a man so well connected politically and why does he refer to him misleadingly in his e-mails home as his office manager? How did Berg meet filmmaker Michael Moore who filmed an interview with him before he left for Iraq in the course of producing the documentary *Fahrenheit 9/11* which does not, however, include that 20-minute interview?[7]

According to a friend of his, in the last eighteen months before his trip, Berg had become more religious, traveling to Israel to study Arabic and Hebrew just before leaving and studying the Torah at an Orthodox Kesher Israel Congregation.[8] The congregation is affiliated with the United Synogogues of Conservative Judaism which supports Zionist goals such as the return of diasporic Jews to Israel and the expansion of Israeli territory.

Like a Rorschach, the Berg story assumes the shape its viewer brings to it. Right-wing bloggers note Michael Berg's left-wing credentials as a member of the antiwar A.N.S.W.E.R. and imply that his son was actually traveling to Iraq to help the insurgency.[9] Coincidentally, Prometheus is the name of a collective of progressive radio activists located in Berg's hometown that encourages community broadcasting and fights for independent media at home and abroad. One of its board members is an aggressive sponsor of international democratic revolution—the Open Society Institute of billionaire international financier George Soros.[10] Did the idealistic Berg turn into a jihadist like the American Taliban, John Walker Lindh? Did he infiltrate U.S. telecommunications and pass on information to the insurgency? And was Taee, with his Russian mafia links, somehow involved in his death, or at least in the staging of the video that supposedly depicted his death? Leftist antiwar blogs suggest the opposite. They point to Berg's rediscovery of his Jewish beliefs and his travels to Israel and ask if he had been recruited by Israeli intelligence, if not directly at least as a *sayanim*, a civilian helper, whom the Iraqi insurgency unmasked.[11] They ask if Michael Berg's antiwar identity was a cover for his son's CIA or Mossad affiliation, whether Nick was playing a dangerous double game with Iraqis, and whether ultimately he became dispensable to either the Iraqis or the Americans, or to both.

Berg's e-mail correspondence shows that he worked on transmission towers at Abu Ghraib and intended to work for the Iraq Media Network, the public radio and broadcast system designed by the CPA to function independently, but which from the start was so subservient to the coalition that Iraqis had come to regard it as an American propaganda outfit.[12] Abu Ghraib, according to General Janis Karpinski, had been set up as a convenient pen to hold detainees outside close supervision and was the focus of intense efforts to gather human intelligence.[13] Was it simply coincidental that the tower expert worked at the towers of Abu Ghraib, where presumably some of the most vital information about the insurgency might be housed?

How shall we think of Berg's reclusive and intensely physical life, his obsessive climbing of immense towers even in dangerous weather, his disinterest in women, his absorption in religion, the restless wanderlust that took him across Africa and the Middle East, his bouts of vagrancy?[14] If not homoerotic, they at least suggest the temperament of an outsider driven by a spiritual angst, a desire to transcend himself in ceaseless activity. We might say the same, strangely enough, of the Promethean tendency in American politics.

Like an archetype, Berg's towers reappear in the politics and imagining of this war in the demolished twin towers of the World Trade Center and the spy towers of Abu Ghraib. They forge a link between the embattled frontiers of empire and its heart, between caves in Afghanistan and towers in New York, between the veiled lives of Afghan women and the penetration of markets.

At Abu Ghraib, in one way of speaking, the cave meets the tower. The sexual torture that was enacted secretly in cell blocks at night, in *Animal-House*-like hazings, comes to light through the network of the tower, the digitalized all-seeing eye that records and transmits it reduplicated a thousand times in the pornography of war. Networks of images are superimposed on networks of money; propaganda and power circulating in the neoliberal market thrust out into the farthest reach of space, penetrating and laying bare the innermost mind.

In Arabic, *Abu Ghraib* means the "father of the raven" and so cave and tower meet under the wing of the prophetic bird, the omen of war, the messenger from the world of the dead. These meanings from pagan Europe are transformed in the Middle Ages when the raven becomes a symbol of confession and penance,[15] replicating in its metamorphosis the shift in the source of authority from the outer world of power and its effects to the inner world of morality and causes, from the material to the spiritual.[16] So, again, at the heart of rationality we find the irreducible seed of irrationality. On the sinews of state and power, we find tattooed the insignia of religion. We move from the confessional to the interrogation cell and from penance to torture under an eye indivisible and invisible.

Invisibility

The centrality of information networks in both their afferent (intelligence-gathering) and efferent (intelligence-disseminating) aspects underscores the Promethean belief in the importance of the spiritual—the mental, moral, and psychological elements—in the polity they imagine. For this reason espionage and propaganda have become central for the Prometheans, and both operate in a manner essentially invisible to the public.

The expansion of afferent functions has been stupendous. Ultimately, it is not from the framework of the so-called war on terror but from this expansion that we have to understand Abu Ghraib. It demonstrates that what drives espionage and interrogation in Iraq is not some extreme "ticking-bomb" contingency but the state's own inexorable drive to totality. Otherwise, why is it that interrogations and torture continue in Iraq when it was already well-known by early 2004 that the prisons there were peopled by either petty criminals or bystanders? [17]

Step by step the logic of the spy state unfolds: Admiral Poindexter's controversial Total Information Awareness program was the most comprehensive surveillance project ever conceived until, in reaction to public outrage, Congress canceled funding in 2003.[18] This was followed by the floating of the crime-fighting computer database known as MATRIX in some states.[19] The most crucial point of these spy programs is that access to some of this data may be given to the CIA, which normally is not supposed to spy on citizens. Some officials even suspect that terrorists will not be the only subjects. That suspicion became concrete on December 10, 2004, when Congress approved an intelligence reform package with little-noticed changes, such as provisions to loosen standards for FBI surveillance warrants and to allow the detention of suspects without bail. These were originally part of an extension of the controversial Patriot Act, which leaked to the media and dubbed "Patriot II" was never introduced as a bill.[20]

Now reintroduced as stand-alone legislation, the new provisions speed the journey to secret arrests, warrantless surveillance, and indefinite detentions, the first harbingers of a police state. The National Intelligence Reform Act of 2004 lays the foundation for a de facto national ID card and links hundreds of federal, state, and local as well as commercial databases, including critical infrastructure like telecommunications and computers, thus enabling simultaneous surveillance of everything from credit reports to insurance claims.[21] According to the Intelligence Resource Program, in 2004 the United States was spending more than $40 billion on intelligence, a 50 percent increase over 1998, more than the GDP of several nations, about double in real terms what was spent on intelligence at the height of the Cold War, and more than what is spent today on NASA ($16 billion) and Homeland Security ($31 billion).[22]

"Ironically, at the same time that the administration has been making it harder and harder for the public to learn what government agencies are up to, the government and its private sector partners have been quietly building more and more databases to learn and store more information about the American people," says Senator Patrick Leahy (D-Vermont).[23]There is a real and grim parallel between the gray future of perpetually monitored American citizens and the luckless present of the inhabitants of Fallujah, subjected to the retinal scans, ID badges, and militarized work gangs of the imperial state.[24]

The afferent network extends to the new American frontier in outer space. In 2001, a panel that included Donald Rumsfeld, before he was secretary of defense, described America as frighteningly vulnerable to space attacks and concluded that the United States was "an attractive candidate for a space Pearl Harbor."[25]

Today, satellites are already involved in "force enhancement," while in the Iraq, Afghanistan, and Kosovo wars, dozens were spying, mapping, providing coordinates of targets, warning of attacks, disseminating intelligence and intercepting messages at all times of day and in all weather over the entire globe in keeping with the motto of the National Reconnaissance Office that "we own the night."[26] When such sleepless watch is being kept, national defense recedes as a plausible motive and surveillance becomes an end in itself through which the corporate state seeks almost jealously to provoke rather than deter enemies.

With Iraq shrouded from one end to the other in American radio towers and satellite disks, gathering information becomes only a pretext for disseminating disinformation.[27] A wandering tower-repairman like Berg might not only learn a number of things, he might be useful for planting a few of them.

So unsurprisingly, wherever information-gathering and espionage operate, they are accompanied by massive propaganda. In this too, the Iraq war was a watershed with its unparalleled control over reporting through a policy of military scripting and vetting and the "embedding" of reporters in the military to provide them with a frontline but controlled glimpse of the war.

Central to the propaganda war was the public relations packaging of various expatriates to present an Iraqi face to a Washington endeavor. "Iraqization" is a cynical strategy to reduce American casualties, neutralize Arab opposition in other Arab countries, and legitimize a puppet regime. In December 2002, a key member of the Iraqi American Council—Bassam Ridha al-Husaini—was reportedly one of fifteen Iraqis flown to Washington by the State Department for two days of "media training" under the Future of Iraq project. Two months later, al-Hulsaini told a war rally in San Francisco that the "Iraqi people are waiting for this liberation." Whether Taee was also trained in public relations or not, he addressed similar rallies sponsored by Clear Channel, the media conglomerate, at which he made the case for war, claiming that Hussein had killed his relatives.[28] Iraqization is defended as necessary to win hearts and minds, in the tired phrase, but increasingly its PR aspect substitutes for, rather than complements, its diplomatic aspect. In this it reflects the more general failure of both the White House's Office of Global Communication as well as the State Department's Public

Diplomacy and Public Affairs Office, headed by a former PR expert for IBM, to successfully graft product "branding" strategies from the business world to the complex world of intercultural communication.[29] Furthermore, for the Prometheans, PR has become less and less about manipulating public opinion than about deceiving it through what are no more than psy-ops.

Jumana Hanna was one of those Iraqi faces that sold the war to America. A wealthy Assyrian Christian, she won sympathy for the lurid torture and rape she claimed to have suffered in jail and at Uday Hussein's hands. Central to her story—all of which proved later to be fictitious—was an account of her marriage to an Indian immigrant, supposedly forbidden under Saddam. No one bothered to check this detail because it fit in so perfectly with the Promethean liberation theology that proclaims both racial and sexual equality. In fact, such marriages were perfectly legal under Saddam.[30] Was there some calculation involved in the appearance of this story in the *Washington Post* in July 2003 just at the time when stories of the real torture of Iraqi women at Abu Ghraib and elsewhere were threatening to be publicized?[31]

Consider also why the stories of those women remain submerged while those of men tortured and humiliated was allowed to flood our consciousness. In this way, actions that should serve as an indictment of the state turn into an advertisement for it. The images of torture serve as propaganda weapons both against the victims, redefining them to themselves, but also against the domestic population, allowing torture to be masked as humiliation while subtly inflaming the lust for violence.

The convergence of psychological warfare against foreign and domestic populations is helped immeasurably when information is centralized. Though the Pentagon was forced to shut down the controversial Office of Strategic Influence when it was reported that it intended to plant false stories in the international media, much of the work of OSI, formed in the aftermath of 9/11, appears to have continued in other government offices, like the Office of Special Plans headed by a fervent partisan of the war, Douglas Feith, which we now know "stovepiped" intelligence tailored to the hard-line neoconservative agenda into the White House, bypassing normal vetting.[32] Whatever merits such departments might have had in filling the vacuum left when budgets for the State Department's diplomacy programs were ravaged and the U.S. Information Agency—the centerpiece of anti-Communist efforts during the Cold War—was cut back in the 1990s, they have ultimately paved the way for an unparalleled extension of the information war.[33]

Item: In late 2003, a still secret 74-page directive signed by Rumsfeld called "Information Operations Road Map," floated "a plan to advance the goal of information operations as a core military competency," and elicited proposals for a "director of central information," responsible for "authoritative control of messages"—public or covert—across all national security and foreign policy operations. It was presented in October 2004 to a senior Pentagon panel including none other than Douglas Feith.[34]

Item: Four-star military officers now represent the United States abroad in a manner unparalleled since World War II, and much of the Pentagon's work in this area, a relatively unknown field called Defense Support for Public Diplomacy, is managed by Ryan Henry. Henry, it turns out, was principal deputy to the under secretary of defense for policy, that is, deputy to the ubiquitous Feith.[35]

Item: Proposed amendments to a classified Defense Department directive on Pentagon policy in coming years, titled, "3600.1: Information Operations," would widen the target of aggressive information campaigns from enemy leaders to leaders of allies or even neutral states.

Item: In mid-September 2004, commanders in Iraq decided to combine public affairs, psychological operations, and information operations into a "strategic communications" office run by Erv Lessel though it ultimately came under the office of the under secretary of defense, that is, again under Feith.[36] Thus, until his departure from the DOD in January 2005 for "personal reasons," one individual, Feith, coordinated almost all propaganda work, making it even more astonishing that there has been no public scrutiny of his role, not just in Abu Ghraib but in the war in general.

This blending of military public affairs and psy-ops, which even General Richard Myers has strongly criticized, turns the state's propaganda operations directly against its own citizens to an unprecedented degree. For instance, three weeks before the second assault on Fallujah, CNN was targeted to relay the false information that the assault had begun. The hope was that this would provoke the insurgency to make a move that could be countered in advance, but it also had the effect of side-stepping domestic media scrutiny.[37]

Admit that propaganda is a bludgeon aimed mainly at the domestic population and it becomes evident that the corporate media "exposé" of Abu Ghraib could not have been anything but manipulative. But Abu Ghraib is part of the propaganda war in another way—it is a bludgeon against the enemy population.

We have to ask why, in spite of all the self-professed solicitousness about Muslim sensibilities, these particular pictures of male sexual humiliation were brandished so vigorously. Why these, and not the beatings or shootings? Were they calculated to multiply the pain of the victims into a collective trauma in the Muslim world?

That suspicion fits well with other developments in the Promethean state. In September 2003, Vice Admiral (Rtd) Arthur Cebrowski, director of the Pentagon's Office of Force Transformation, told members of the Armed Forces Communications and Electronics Association (AFCEA) that "Net-centric"operations could in low-intensity conflict help the U.S move beyond "asset-based war to "elite" war focused on "ideas and their proponents"—what some call Fourth-Generation War.[38] Threats to national security, he argued, are no longer to be found only at "the fault lines that run through societies." U.S. forces are to be prepared to operate "deeply within societies and in urban areas" against the elites and against the "ideas and plans" and "the processes and technologies" that support them. This entails a massive emphasis on intelligence and surveillance not only through the Internet, but also through what Cebrowski calls "all three domains of warfare"—"the physical, the cognitive, and the informational."

The "white" side of this cognitive war extends to the political control of the knowledge base and threatens to encroach on academia. For instance, a recent federal bill seeks the creation of an advisory board, in itself unexceptionable, to "monitor and evaluate" foreign language and area studies programs funded by Title VI, a program that was a product of the Cold War conviction that area studies were vital to the national interest. The new board, disquietingly stacked with representatives from Congress, Defense, Homeland Security, and the NSA, attempts to take back these programs from scholarship that is critical of the effects of U.S. policy in the third world.[39]

Another program puts the CIA right on campus. Section 318 of the 2004 Intelligence Authorization Act, recently approved by Congress, appropriates four million dollars to fund a pilot program named after the Republican chair of the Senate Select Committee on Intelligence. The Pat Roberts Intelligence Scholars Program (PRISP) trains CIA operatives and analysts in American university classrooms for careers in the CIA and other agencies. PRISP is the brainchild of University of Kansas anthropologist Felix Moos, who in the months after 9/11 got his friend, former CIA director Stansfield Turner, to lobby the Senate and CIA to fund a merger among anthropology, academia, intelligence analysis, and espionage training. Most experts also estimate that the presence of CIA-affiliated professors on campus, already large, has grown since 2001.[40]

That is the domestic front. On the foreign front, there are programs to plant stories in the international media or infiltrate their sources.[41] In Iraq, de-Ba'athification involves changing school curricula and textbooks.[42] The ideological battle plan is to paint U.S. policy as constantly extending the domain of universal law and reason, of civilization.

The "black" or covert side makes use of surveillance, disinformation, and psy-ops, as well as of highly classified techniques of nonlethal, or more accurately, sublethal crowd-control weaponry, ranging from foam nets to electromagnetic manipulation of cognition, that is, to mind control. Many of these techniques were already well under way in the Clinton years.[43] Viewed in this light, the interrogation techniques of the prison camps—stress positions, strobe lights, incessant rock or rap music, extreme isolation or sensory deprivation, the photographing of humiliation—no longer seem aberrant or exceptional but completely in line with practices that were being used or planned in classified research. The prisons merely provided the experimental lab, with prisoners the guinea pigs, for a practical experiment in the forms of mental subjugation.

CIA psy-ops have been a long time in the making and rely on everything from KGB-inspired psychic research to the more bizarre reaches of the counterculture.[44] Esalen, Reichian rebirthing, primal arm wrestling, and different forms of group sex have all played a role. In *The Men Who Stare at Goats*, British journalist Jon Ronson traces the use of some of these techniques to a disillusioned officer, Jim Channon, who returned from Vietnam convinced that the American army needed to toughen itself mentally and employ cunning as well as firepower. A few of Channon's efforts yielded the purely bizarre. There were, for instance, experiments at Fort Bragg in which soldiers tried to develop the psychic ability to slay the enemy at sight by staring into the eyes of goats. Other programs are the obvious ancestors of the kind of torture practiced on prisoners in Iraq and Guantanamo. At Al Qaim in Iraq, some prisoners were blasted with the "I Love You" song from the children's show *Barney, the Dinosaur*. When the incident became public, most British journalists, even veterans, insisted on treating it lightly. Ronson, a humorist, was ironically one of the few to recognize that there was nothing either funny or painless about blasting a song tens of thousands of times at someone shut in a metal container in desert temperatures of over 50 degrees Celsius (122 F). He points out the ingenuity of using a popular children's song, which if discovered could always be passed off as a joke and used to inoculate the public against further revelations of abuse. Few would recognize it for severe psychological torture.

On the other hand, some of the music played to detainees was not intended to cause pain at all, although the objective in playing it was not any less sinister and can be linked to the work of the Nonlethal Program at the Los Alamos National Laboratories, headed by Colonel John Alexander.[45] Alexander, the inventor of the nonlethal field in America and a pioneer in the use of acoustic weapons, is known to have collaborated with researchers at the Moscow Institute of Psycho-Corrections who had developed a technique to analyze the human mind electronically in order to manipulate it.[46] In the Russian psychotronic research, subliminal commands are coded in key words that are masked and transmitted in "white noise" or music. Alexander is also a former Green Beret who participated in the Phoenix Program, the CIA's deadly targeting of the Vietnamese people through assassinations, free-fire zones, and other so-called counterterrorist methods.

A DOD directive remarks that nonlethal weapons are not to be limited to the "lower spectrum of conflict," that is, peacekeeping and humanitarian missions, but can be used in every kind of military operation to enhance their "effectiveness and efficiency."[47] And here the cat is out of the bag. Nonlethal weaponry is not meant to replace but to *enhance* conventional weapons.[48] It seems very likely that psychotronic weapons were conceived not merely to supplement but also to act as a convenient *cover* for conventional torture or war. And even if that were not the original intention, that is exactly how they have been employed so far, both in domestic and foreign settings. While the desire to reduce civilian casualties and minimize pain may be admirable in theory, any hypothetical advantages of sublethal techniques are outweighed by their real disadvantages—their invisibility and greater acceptability to the public. Precisely because of their supposed harmlessness, they are almost certain to be used with greater and greater frequency against ordinary citizens engaged in any kind of resistance to the government, even the most nonviolent.

Just as the spy network uses terrorism as the pretext to surveille the general population, law and order—which may eventually mean no more than enthusiasm for the neoliberal order—becomes the excuse to turn mind-control techniques against the population. In the gray zones of borders, occupations, prisons, workcamps, and protests, the corporate state maintains a low-grade and perpetual quasi-war at all times and in all places under its dominion. In this quasi-war, corporate merchandise and advertising act like psychotronic weapons by commodifying and inserting the imagery of war into the public imagination. This is attested to by a burgeoning industry of action films, video games, and violent pornography that blurs the line between entertainment and news, simulation and reality. The videogame series, *Kuma War*, for instance, models its action on real military operations in Iraq—the fight with the Mehdi army in the south, and the hunt for Uday and Qusay Hussein.[49] Such simulations, like violent porn, desensitize young males by promoting a model of aggressive masculinity that feeds recruitment in the warfare state while also preparing a larger public to accept state violence as virtuous, necessary, and inevitable.

Indivisibility

The second prong of the Promethean strategy, the unification of defense and of its civilian and military elements, also prepares the ground for the policies of Abu Ghraib. Unification relies on the adoption of high-technology and maneuver modeled on the German Blitzkrieg, as well as on cost-cutting strategies borrowed from businesses. Rumsfeld's new model army relies less on regulars and more on guards and reservists and also, as Abu Ghraib demonstrates, on private contractors and special forces. The object is to cut back on costs, much as businesses have taken to relying on temporary workers and outsourcing for the same reason. The cost-cutting also includes cutbacks in training, supplies, shelter, military equipment, and medical help for these units, a decision which we have seen contributed significantly to the abuse of prisoners.[50] In weaponry, the revolutionaries look to high-technology to raise efficiency, dispense with bodies, and integrate functions. There is a political rationale behind this as well as an economic. Fewer American casualties means less pressure from the public. Rumsfeld's "transformation," derived from his experience as a CEO, involves deployment in phases in simultaneous air and land strikes, rapid movement on the model of the Blitzkrieg, and extensive use of special operations units.

The new restructuring is not so much the militarization of civil society, as some argue, but part of a corporatization of both civil society and military, undertaken for the sake of the private sphere (that is, private as to ownership) which is relentlessly enlarged at the expense of the public. However, this private sphere is not the old libertarian ideal but a coercive model that combines aspects of corporations and government and is no longer available to all. The new "private" sphere of corporatism is ultimately available only to small, hidden groups of elites. For this reason the mechanism of public law is useless as a tool to analyze or correct government abuses. Much of what takes place is private, that is, secret. Government has been usurped by private interests pursued privately.

To legitimize this arrangement, Prometheans look neither to the law, with which they have a troubled relationship, nor to the will of the people, toward which they show suspicion, but to a reading of history and philosophy that privileges them as the inheritors of the liberal, democratic, and capitalist state, the expression of enlightenment rationality, and the best hope of mankind.[51] Because they define the state as embodying the most progressive values of society, they obscure its coerciveness. It is the Prometheans' affiliation with the socially progressive that blinds them from seeing that torture-lite proves eventually to be not only not "lite" in many instances but actually more deeply traumatizing and antihuman in its premises than many forms of torture that are physically more brutal. For neoconservatives and liberals alike, there is indeed "good torture" and "good war," such as, Kosovo or even Iraq, before it proved to be bloodier than they anticipated.[52]

The similarity of the social agenda and *weltanschauung* of the neoconservatives to liberalism should not be surprising, because although they strongly support American military strength and corporate interests, they originate on the left as social democrats and, in a few cases, even Trotskyites who only moved to the right on foreign policy in response to the Vietnam War.[53] When they did, they carried over their "revolutionary" roots in the cadres and networks through which they operated. The neoconservatives see themselves as a revolutionary vanguard, only in the services of capital rather than labor, and their "private" and transnational networks of business, family, and ideology have come to dominate institutions supposedly serving the national interest.

Project for the New American Century (PNAC), the think-tank which in a notorious paper in 2000 proposed American world domination, is run by the editor of the neoconservative *Weekly Standard*, Bill Kristol. Bill Kristol is the son of Irving Kristol, the godfather of neoconservatism, and his wife, Gertrude Himmelfarb, a neoconservative historian at Chicago University. The *Weekly Standard*, like Fox News and the *New York Post*, is owned by the stridently pro-war newspaper magnate, Rupert Murdoch. Norman Podhoretz, former editor of the neoconservative *Commentary*, is the father-in-law of Elliott Abrams, who was convicted in the Iran-Contra affair. Podhoretz is also the director of Near Eastern affairs at the National Security Council and his wife, Midge Decter, is a veteran of the old anti-Communist group, Committee on the Present Danger. So are Wolfowitz and Feith, who were also part of Team B, the intelligence advisory group responsible for grossly exaggerating the Soviet threat in the 1970s and '80s in order to enable massive budget appropriations for defense. Richard Perle, a prominent hawk, is a fellow at the American Enterprise Institute and on the board of Hollinger International, a right-wing media conglomerate that includes the *Jerusalem Post*, for which Decter writes, and the London *Daily Telegraph*. Hollinger's board also includes the columnist George Will. Hollinger itself is run by Conrad Black, the chairman of the editorial board of Podhoretz's *National Interest*, which Black partly subsidizes through the Nixon Center. Also at PNAC is Francis Fukuyama, author of the most influential book of democratic triumphalism, *The End of History*. Charles Krauthammer, a *Washington Post* columnist, is a friend of Wolfowitz. These neoconservatives, whether in the press or in policy, frequently team up to write their vehement tracts, sacrificing their professional integrity to support their ideological bias.[54]

Members of PNAC now control the commanding heights of policy making. In Bush's first term, Wolfowitz was Deputy Defense Secretary, second at the Pentagon; John Bolton was Under Secretary of State for Arms Control and International Security; Eliot Cohen was a member of Rumsfeld's Defense Policy Board and the NSC; Stewart Libby was Cheney's chief of staff; Dov Zakheim, Undersecretary of Defense under Reagan, was Defense Comptroller until his resignation; Stephen Cambone was Undersecretary for Intelligence and also influential in pro-nuclear circles. Especially powerful are two organizations, JINSA (Jewish Institute for National Security Affairs) and CSP (Center for Strategic Policy), whose members have come to occupy innumerable influential government posts from where they press the same agenda as their ideological fellow travelers in the think tanks and media outlets. The hard-line position they advocate rests on national missile defense, abrogation of arms-control treaties, and preemption—and goes hand in hand with unquestioning support for the Israeli right. Government has been effectively captured by such private lobbyists as JINSA and AIPAC and such think tanks as the American Enterprise Institute (AEI) and Middle East Media Research Institute (MEMRI), which are driven by transnational business and foreign rather than strictly national interests.[55]

Typical of the "revolutionary" style of functioning, many of these pro-Israeli lobbies work in a top-down manner in the manner of business lobbies rather than in the grassroots fashion of other ethnic constituencies. For instance, AIPAC (American Israel Public Affairs Committee) makes use of a kind of "astro-turf" lobbying in which front groups send in mass mailings in imitation of genuine citizen groups.[56] The interlocking system orchestrates media reports and opinions to frame issues in particular ways so that certain themes appear, are reiterated until they have the required effect, and then vanish simultaneously. Consider the manner in which the prison abuse story broke, not in December 2002, when the *Post* first published a revelatory piece on torture in Afghanistan,[57] not in October 2003, when AP ran a story about torture at Abu Ghraib itself.[58] But only in May after the corporate media—CBS—took it up on the heels of Hersh's exposé. Even then, in spite of a flood of reports, certain stories, such as the one on child abuse, remain stubbornly hidden while others, such as the formulation of the torture memos, receive sustained coverage. The tone is set and the issues are framed, the bias lying as much in what is omitted as what is stated.

With the clout of the lobbying, media, and policy networks behind them, neoconservatives have replaced career civil servants with political appointees and nullifed the traditional checks and balances between branches of government. They have unified all intelligence-gathering and propaganda functions under defense and then usurped those functions through personal networks, effectively overturning any constraints placed by law against consolidation of power in the executive.[59] Congressional oversight of intelligence, mandated since Nixon, is often bypassed, though an independent intelligence agency is nonetheless supposed to be part of the checks and balances against an imperial and secretive executive.[60] Now those checks have vanished entirely, leaving the executive unrestrained. Whoever has the ear of the president has nearly limitless power to overthrow law, precedent, and the expertise of career civil servants. That was precisely what happened when lawyers from the Judge Advocate General's office were marginalized in 2003 by Pentagon appointees hell-bent on implementing policies that involved military dogs, extreme sensory deprivation, and psychological torture, policies that shredded the Geneva Conventions and the Uniform Code of Justice.[61]

Intelligence too is now centralized.[62] In the Bush second term, White House loyalist Porter Goss has been appointed director in an effort to bring the CIA to heel, ignoring the recommendation of the 9/11 Commission, which was to create an independent intelligence czar.[63] Counterterrorism experts, like Michael Scheuer of the CIA and the White House's Richard Clarke, who have publicly criticized the prosecution of the war on terror have both been purged.[64] Paradoxically, this has not "militarized" intelligence but "corporatized" both defense and intelligence. The restraining influence of civilian leadership is lost when civilian leaders are no longer professionals but political appointees bought by industrialists and financiers, special interest groups, think tanks and lobbyists, one of the most influential of which has been the pro-Israel lobby. It was the number-three civilian official in the Pentagon, Douglas Feith, whose office sifted the raw intelligence from the different spy agencies to conjure up fictitious evidence of links between Saddam Hussein and Osama bin Laden.[65] It was Feith whose circumvention of the CIA and the Defense Intelligence Agency led Scheuer and others to charge that the war against Iraq was undercutting the "war on terrorism." And it was not coincidentally the same Feith who was responsible for the policy of detentions that led to torture at Abu Ghraib.

In another instance of executive power play, John Yoo, a lawyer from the Justice Department, authored a memo on September 25, 2001, authorizing the president to "deploy military force preemptively against terrorist organizations or the states that harbor or support them."[66] The memo came only two weeks after a joint congressional resolution passed on September 14, authorizing the president to respond to terror attacks but deleting a presidential request for broad preemptive powers. Yoo's memo calls the president's powers "unreviewable" and effectively destroys Congress's oversight function. What is especially pertinent to the torture debate is that the memo goes on to read "whether or not they can be linked to the specific terrorist incidents of September 11." In that one phrase, suspicion crystallizes. Under the guise of counterterrorism, the Promethean state reserves to itself the arbitrary right to pursue any group, anywhere, among any population. Counterterrorism is a license to attack the population. The appearance of the Yoo memos and the others two years earlier than the war in Iraq suggests powerfully that what happened in the military prisons in Iraq and elsewhere was anticipated if not planned, and was definitely not unintended.

With the executive so unified around and usurped by private business interests, the state's spy network unsurprisingly vanishes into private hands. The logic by which the invisible nerve center of information networks aligns itself with the indivisible carpace of the corporate total state is the logic by which at Abu Ghraib, with perfect symmetry, we find private contractors side by side with intelligence operatives. The limitless rationality of the Promethean state ends finally in an irreducible mass of flesh that will not submit. An intelligence contractor paid half a million a year, as many are, must produce information if the contract is to continue. Half a million requires a good deal of information to justify itself. Hence torture. With enough torture, the information flow improves and the corporate quota is met.

Financial networks that penetrate everywhere ultimately acquire knowledge about everything. What is present everywhere and knows everything becomes infinitely powerful. This trinity of omnipresence, omniscience, and omnipotence suggests that the inevitable goal of the collection and appropriation of information by the state is dominion, and in the case of a state so powerful as America, universal dominion. The Defense Advanced Research Projects Agency and the U.S. Air Force share a vision of a new transformational capability that aims to provide a means of delivering a substantial payload from within the continental United States (CONUS) to anywhere on earth in less than two hours.[67] That this hegemony is not everywhere and equally asserted is only from gaps in capability or necessity; the logic itself is relentless. The goal is "full-spectrum dominance," the denial of even regional aspirations to any other power. Thus the 2000 PNAC report that eventually became the basis for the White House National Security Strategy report (NSS) of September 20, 2002, "Rebuilding America's Defenses: Strategies, Forces, and Resources for a New Century," proposed an unprecedented increase in military spending, the opening of new American military bases in Central Asia and the Middle East, the overthrow of noncomplying regimes, the abrogation of international treaties, control of the world's energy sources, weaponization of outer space, total dominance of cyberspace, and willingness to use nuclear weapons to achieve American goals.[68]

In this context, even to think in terms of nation-states and national interests is an effect of propaganda, for if the market penetrates everywhere and its interests rule, then what we are talking about is transnational armies and transnational objectives. Far from protecting the interests of the population, the corporate state protects its interests *from* populations. The liberation of Fallujah entails the expulsion or massacre of its people; security demands the creation of a legal no-man's-land of nonpersons—enemy combatants who do not deserve the protection of law.

And since one cannot erase a population as easily as a law, one creates gray zones where people become diminished, less than human, where they fade into oblivion. In the empire, such gray zones multiply endlessly creating individuals who are neither terrorists nor innocents, civilians nor combatants, neither free nor sentenced. It is for them that the category of torture-which-is-not-torture is created to mask the absolute dominion that the state demands.

Civilizational War

But ideology prevents the questioning of the virtue of the state and its interests and rewrites the state's normalization of terror as a *war on terror*. It turns the cordoning and targeting of populations into a liberation theology of democracy, secularism, capital markets, and human rights battling the fascist forces of Islam.

Only nine days after the attack on the World Trade Center, for instance, Michael Ledeen, propagandist and middleman to arms dealer Manuchar Ghobanifar in the Reagan-era Iran-Contra scandal wrote, "We are the one truly revolutionary country in the world, as we have been for more than two hundred years. Creative destruction is our middle name."[69]

Despite the label of neoconservative, this is not and never has been the language of genuine conservatism, traditionalist, prudential, or libertarian. It is not even the language of the Cold War whose éminence grise, George Kennan, advocated an essentially defensive and reactive posture to the Soviet threat, in marked contrast to the belligerence advocated by the Prometheans.[70] Some have suggested that the export of democratic revolution to the Middle East, which Ledeen, like other Prometheans, advocates, descends from Trotskyism but only a few neoconservatives appear to have been explicit followers of Trotsky.[71] Moreover, there is an intrinsically anti-intellectual cast to neoconservatism, a romantic celebration of the unconstrained political will over the dry rationality of economic life. Thus to see in the neoconservative perpetual war only the logic of international capitalism working itself out is a misreading. That logic no doubt operates, but it is harnessed to a romantic and even messianic vision in which the technocrat and entrepreneur substitute for the proletariat as the heroic subject of history. The characteristic of neoconservatism is to wield a nationalist ideology that nevertheless puts the nation in the service of one class, the capitalist, and to employ the rhetoric of freedom to promote the spectacular achievements of "private" striving but do so through the channels of military and economic coercion.

The counterpart of the elevation of capital in the ideology of the Prometheans is the simultaneous degrading of labor to mouths that need feeding and bodies that need housing. This suggests why Islam especially must be seen as the enemy. Premodern, precapital, and fecund, the societies of the Middle East are made to appear to Israel and its allies in the West as the embodied threat of overpopulation. Islam, this inchoate mass of animality and breeding, must be spiritualized and rationalized. For public consumption and in government pronouncements a careful distinction is maintained between moderate and fundamentalist Islam, but among ideologues it is Islam itself that is the designated enemy. One could go further and say that it is traditional religion and the limits it sets on human striving and rationality that is the enemy, for the traditional understanding of Catholic teaching in the areas of war and economics have also come under attack.

Long before 9/11, the tocsin of crisis was sounded. There is a clash of civilizations, decreed Harvard's Samuel Huntington, one that positions Islam as well as Confucianism against Christianity, now unfailingly remade as Judeo-Christianity to emphasize the Hebraic rather than the Greek or medieval elements of the religion.[72] Rather fortuitously, this cultural divide also nicely parallels American global ambitious and interests. It was Bernard Lewis, a doyen of Middle Eastern studies at Harvard, who first coined the term in a 1990 essay titled "The Roots of Muslim Rage," from whom Huntington picked it up.[73] Osama bin Laden, Lewis argued, must be viewed as the last gasp of a losing cause still fighting the "Crusaders"; Islam, left behind by the Enlightenment, is in need of its own Reformation. For Lewis, Turkey's Kemal Ataturk with his vision of a secularized Westernized Arab democracy purged of Islam's medievalism is the ideal and Chalabi of Iraq is his Kemalist protégé.[74] But even before the Lewis-Huntington thesis, Rafael Patai in *The Arab Mind* conjured up these Orientalist fears and proposed the remedy—force and humiliation, sexual humiliation especially—physical violence against the body and psychic trauma to cripple the spirit.[75] It was sterile obsessions with fecundity that gave birth to the castrating formulas of Abu Ghraib.

Postcolonial critics, however, deny the thesis of an antimodern "origin of Islam," requiring for its remedy Western-style democracy. Instead, they diagnosis radical Islam as a modern pathology resulting from the trauma of colonial invasions—British, French, and Italian—and from CIA-backed proxy wars by the mujahideen in Afghanistan against the Soviets. The pathology of Arab states, they argue, is more symptomatic of the marginalization or perversion of Islam, a marginalization invisible to Lewis, who like Patai or Daniel Pipes or the other designated public experts on Islam, "does not like the people he is purporting to have expertise about," and "considers them to be good and worthy only to the degree they follow a Western path."[76] Patai's tract demonstrates that the psychological torture that shocks the psyche into abjection merely replicates in the microcosm of the human body the rupture of tradition and history that colonization perpetrates in the macrocosm of the nation. It is not by accident, then, that the public memory of Islam preserved in priceless manuscripts, artifacts, and relics was stolen, looted, incinerated, or sold openly at the same time that in secret acts of arson the memory of the population was erased by torture, then seared and branded with images of self-alienation and self-loathing.

Naturally, anyone who diagnoses the invasion and occupation as neocolonial must be stigmatized as inherently anti-American, for in public the language of the Promethean state articulates universal liberation and rights and strives to be studiously neutral to religion and race. Anti-Americanism, like anti-Semitism, thus becomes a way to foreclose critical thinking, a passive version of the kind of censorship practiced by Daniel Pipes' Campus Watch, which blacklists "pro-Arab" scholars who criticize Israel on American campuses.[77] Martin Kramer, another vehement critic of Middle Eastern departments in the United States and an ideological comrade of Pipes, has been quoted as saying, "Academic colleagues get used to it. You are being watched."[78] His preferred vision for Middle East studies would be to restore it to its roots as the handmaiden of American evangelism and British imperialism.[79]

The Promethean thesis today is of an America simply reacting, both ideologically and militarily, to the aggression of an enemy as total as the Soviet Union. History, after having just been pronounced dead by Fukuyama, revives and finds a new foe in Islamo-fascism, a phrase coined by Christopher Hitchens, left-wing enfant-terrible turned neoconservative militarati.[80] It acts as a convenient label that forestalls any real debate on what it is that actually threatens Western civilization and allows the defense establishment to ramp up spending that would otherwise have declined after the resolution of the Cold War. The label of fascism is also misleading in several ways. It links Islamism to a form of modern political organization that it only loosely resembles, obscures the nationalist element in it, and entirely overlooks its anticolonial and defensive nature.[81]

The oversight is meaningful. America has historically represented itself as a liberator of oppressed people, and while this has been dismissed by some as mere rhetoric concealing self-interest, it is also the case that American self-interest has frequently been an enlightened one, the post–World War II restructuring of Europe and Japan being cases in point. Not so with Iraq. To put it another way, one reason to deflect attention away from the anticolonial nature of Islamism is to obscure the frankly neocolonial nature of the American project in the Muslim world.

This does not trouble the ideologues of the *mission civilisatrice* for whom the American project is seen as a return to the pagan virtues of the Prince as well as a revisiting of the British empire, an uneasy ménage-à-trois of Victoria, Machiavelli, and Alcibiades that presents itself as benign, racially diverse, a champion of human rights, reason, and progress, and promises a universalist ethos to accompany the prosperity created by global capital.[82] It invokes a vision of peaceful, free-trading citizens, a multiethnic brotherhood of man. Under the mask, however, the reality is different. Under it, faceless mercantilism uproots communities and breaks apart nations; under it low-grade war masquerades as peacekeeping, conquest as liberation, detention and torture as law and order. The language of empire, petrified by dissimulation, masks a confusion of human meanings underneath.

It was perhaps for that reason that Nicholas Berg called the company he set up in Baghdad, Babyl Towers.[83] He knew better than most that his work was at the heart of the propaganda offensive of empire, the nerve center from where the land between the rivers would be monitored and controlled. From the great towers of New York, the eye of global capital falls on the ancient ziggurat of Nimrod. As the story is told in Genesis, shortly after the Flood, the inhabitants of Babel build a tower that reaches into the sky. For a nineteenth-century scholar, Rabbi Naftali Zvi Yehudah Berlin, the singular language of Babel was the language of social control as the great tower itself was a technology of control, spying on its citizens.[84] It becomes a new religion, a false god. An envious Jehovah intervenes, the linguistic mask is shattered, the tower is abandoned. In the ruins of the ancient city an hour south of Baghdad, the tower today is no more than rubble but next to it rises the palace of Nebuchadnezzar, rebuilt by Saddam Hussein.[85] Successor to Nimrod, giver of the laws and ruler of an unequaled global empire, it was Nebuchadnezzar who destroyed Jerusalem and brought the Jews into their Babylonian captivity. Saddam saw himself in his direct line of succession. Did Berg, the scholar of Torah, remember all this as he clambered up to repair the spy towers of the new global empire?

What is suggested in these synchronous meanings that uncannily emerge? The voices of empire speak a singular language, the civilizing language of human rights, law, and reason. But behind the mission of civilization the threat of force is never far. "Afghanistan and other troubled lands today cry out for the sort of enlightened foreign administration once provided by self-confident Englishmen in jodhpurs and pith helmets," writes Max Boot, a *Wall Street Journal* editorial writer now at the Council on Foreign Relations.[86] "Speak Victorian, Think Pagan," advises Robert Kaplan, arguing for the virtue of waging ruthless war for global order.[87] America needs to "whack bad guys quietly" under cover of humanitarian aid projects and elude congressional oversight by relying on small, autonomous units.[88] This is the Promethean note again, the call for defiance of the law in service of higher ends.

Dionysus

For many, the naked display of force, whether through terror or torture, is salutary in itself. For *Post* columnist Krauthammer, "Power is its own reward."[89] Since the defeat of the Taliban, he points out, "the psychology of the region is now one of fear and deep respect."

In challenging the Olympian—we might say Apollonian—gods of international law, diplomacy, and multilateralism, the gods of stability, the neoconservatives offer their own Dionysian principle, a principle of perpetual turmoil and dynamism institutionalized in restless mercantile capital and speculative finance, global military expeditions, and bellicose democracy. Thomas Barnett of the U.S. Naval War College in *The Pentagon's Wars* describes the the three-front war "where nothing is sacred and no one is ever absolutely safe," where the United States is forced to employ "System Perturbation" to destroy the other side's "rule sets," and where "America will resume its historical role as the most revolutionary force on the planet." [90]

This willingness to engage in open-ended wars—Barnett calls for the ability to fight three or four, the neoconservatives see five to six—and even nuclear wars has gone hand in hand with an unwillingness to allow America to be hampered in expanding its own arsenal of weapons.[91] Albert Wohlstetter, University of Chicago and Rand military strategist, is a leading figure behind this rethinking of the post-1945 Cold War theory of nuclear deterrence, known to the public as MAD (Mutually Assured Destruction).[92] The idea behind MAD was that the superpowers would be deterred from fighting a nuclear war by the assurance of an overwhelming response that would annihilate their respective populations. Wohlstetter claimed that this implicit threat was profoundly immoral. He was perhaps more disturbed that it tended to nullify the American superiority in arms. In the 1970s, Bush Sr. appointed others of the same persuasion, the right-wingers of the notorious "Team B," to contradict CIA analyses suggesting that the Soviet threat was being exaggerated to sabotage detente and increase budget appropriations for the Pentagon.[93] In his voluminous writing, Wohlstetter provided a rationale for fighting limited nuclear wars, a basis for withdrawing from any further arms control, and a justification for preemption, strategies that though first formulated in the 1970s had to wait on the sidelines in the think tanks and opinion journals for Wohlstetter's protégés—Khalilzad, Wolfowitz, Perle, and Chalabi—to come into power and implement them.

The Wohlstetter doctrine is now on the political stage in full dress; the Bush administration is working on such weapons as a "Robust Nuclear Earth Penetrator," and its January 2002 Nuclear Posture Review laid out a nuclear policy that called for the development of low-yield or so-called mini-nukes and integrates nuclear weapons with conventional strike options.[94] The review discusses possible first-use of nuclear weapons, even against non-nuclear countries. Bush has also opposed ratification of the Comprehensive Test Ban Theory and terminated the Anti-Ballistic Missile Treaty with Russia in 2002. The missile shield program Bush is proposing will add over 100 billion dollars in the next few years to the defense budget.[95] In the Bush second term, Stephen Hadley, a strong proponent of using nukes against non-nuclear nations, has been elevated to national security advisor.

Like Wohlstetter, Andrew Marshall, the other, perhaps more influential theorist of defense in the administration, was a Rand analyst who came to the Pentagon as a civilian specialist in 1973 and stayed on. Marshall, who heads the secretive work of the Office of Net Assessment (ONA), has played a major role in Bush's defense review and he too includes Cheney, Rumsfeld, Khalilzad, and Wolfowitz among his acolytes. Relatively invisible outside the defense world, Marshall and his devoted following—the "Church of Saint Andrew" as they are termed—have behind them key strategic decisions of the Reagan years including an early version of "Star Wars," or the Strategic Defense Initiative. The weaponization of space, the use of robot technology and new technologies from nonmilitary fields such as the pharmaceutical industry, and the exploitation of the psychological element of war are all conspicuous elements of the "Marshall Plan" under Bush.

An equally fierce proponent of nuclear war, Edward Teller, came into prominence in the 1960s and 1970s testifying before Congress and on television against the Partial Test Ban Treaty. In addition, he championed the development of an ABM system that would employ nuclear explosions to destroy incoming missiles and lobbied hard against the SALT treaties of Presidents Richard Nixon and Jimmy Carter. Teller, like many of the Prometheans, was a staunch supporter of "Star Wars."[96]

The work of these theorists off mass destruction underlies the Rumsfeldian transformation that more and more integrates the military into the civilian sector while expanding its targets into the general population. The theater of war is thus insidiously extending to include every part of the enemy's space, and the targets are increased to include every member of the enemy population. The stage is set for a policy of terrorizing the population. This is entirely in keeping with the historical evidence, which suggests that it has been the civilian, not the military leadership, that has always been the most eager to use weapons of terror. In the last hundred years, for instance, air power has been dissociated from the military and controlled by the civilian and it is airpower that has been the primary vehicle of mass destruction and terror. While Eisenhower and MacArthur both opposed the use of the atom bomb, the civilians in the administration pushed for it. It was civilians also who pushed for the terror bombing of Tokyo in which 80-100,000 people died in one night. In Iraq, it is the civilian leadership again—Cambone, Adam Shulsky, who headed Rumsfeld's disinformation campaign, Feith, Wolfowitz, Gonzalez, Yoo, Jay Bybee, head of Legal Council in 2002, Rumsfeld, and finally Bush—who have asserted the need, indeed the desirability and justice, of torture.

The message of all this is quite clear. It is the will of the U.S. executive and defense alone and not any prescription of domestic or international law nor any deference to domestic or international opinion that undergirds American foreign policy making. Donald Kagan, classicist, father of Robert Kagan, and a frequent collaborator with Bill Kristol, is blunt. "People worried a lot about how the Arab street is going to react," he notes. Well, I see that the Arab street has gotten very, very quiet since we started blowing things up."[97]

But it is not destruction so much as terror that is the common goal of the advocates of nuclear weapons and the apologists of nonlethal weaponry and psychological warfare. Prometheus's fire, after all, was not solely a technology to master the elements but numinous, an object of man's most primal fear. Thus, the "shock and awe" campaign against Baghdad, a city of five million inhabitants, tortured its residents into states of war psychosis, confusion, and paralysis as much as it killed them.[98]

To act with impunity, the total state indeed *prefers* a control that leaves no marks, operates through fear, that appears to its citizens as invisible satellite eyes in outer space, as robot sensors, as scanners that probe mechanically, as spy software that reads keystroke to keystroke the random fluctuations of inner space.

Through fear, control remains anonymous and invisible. Invisible, it becomes inevitable, virtuous, and complete.

In this fascination with collapsing the boundaries of spirit and body, with dynamism and flux, with probing the outermost and the innermost, the Promethean betrays itself as romantic in its aesthetic despite its rhetoric of reason and law. Entrepreneurship presents itself less as a necessity of capitalism than as a spiritual ideal of initiative and strife. The ethos of business and military blend into each other in the doctrine of "perpetual war," not merely to fatten defense budgets but to deplete the civilian, for populations present themselves to the Prometheans as recalcitrant flesh to be disciplined and spiritualized through strife. Under the rhetoric of democracy and egalitarianism, hierarchy is the reality, a hierarchy in which business elites, technocrats, and their ideologues control the masses with the wand of propaganda.[99]

The concept of space thus becomes central to the Promethean ideology, which articulates it through the ethos of competition and the survival of the fittest, the maintenance of distance between elites and mass. Space is the unifying concept in the expansion of the state territorially into the heavens and internally into the psyche. Everything outside the state is a lack needing to be remedied or filled, as failed states, regressed cultures, as gaps in order. Into these gaps, whether in the heavens or on earth, the state inserts its rationality through the stealthy monitoring of a robot technology that represents the elimination of the human. In so expressing rationality without the inconvenience of undisciplined flesh, the Promethean state articulates the demigod. Sensing its own robot impunity and limitless expansiveness, it arrives at that dangerous solipsism that is reflected in such statements as, "We create our own reality." In a world thus fashioned and driven from within, external constraints become not merely ineffective but irrelevant.

Why should one be surprised, then, that even though spokesman Boot has called himself a "hard Wilsonian," the Prometheans as a whole would undo the entire legacy of internationalism from Woodrow Wilson onward? Why should we be surprised that many members of the administration actually belong to the Federalist Society, which has a rabid antipathy to international law?[100] Those who wrote the torture memos, John Yoo, Viet Dinh, Jay Bybee, Attorney General John Ashcroft, Michael Chertoff, head of Homeland Security, and several other lawyers appointed to senior positions in the Bush administration at Defense, Justice, and the White House are intimately associated with it.

In that context, Abu Ghraib cannot be regarded as tangential or aberrant. Instead, it appears completely symptomatic of both ideology and organization at the highest levels. Abu Ghraib reveals that behind the rhetoric of the liberation of people lies the reality of the disciplining of populations—mass detentions, evacuations of cities, torture, and terror bombing. The military and civilian leadership are fully aware of this. If they rewrite and minimize the significance of Abu Ghraib, it is precisely to deflect attention from the confluence of developments in both government and military that have given rise to it, not by chance but deliberately. A state that strives for omniscience about populations, a state that seeks and creates gaps or provocations to justify its own limitless expansion, an ideology of a civilizing mission in a barbaric country, a culture of secrecy, the usurpation of total power by a handful contemptuous of existing laws, a theory of defense built on terror, a relentless rationality set apart from the flesh—how could torture not be the logical outcome?

8
Context III: Virtual Violence

What happened at Abu Ghraib was predictable, and the pornographic form it took was also predictable. The ideology that justifies it does so not only through a discourse of civilization in which Arab and Muslim culture is fundamentally sick but also through a discourse of gender that is intertwined with race and religion.

Since Muslim countries, as "failed states," are constructed as part of the "gap" the corporate state finds threatening to its order, we can expect that state propaganda will be active in supplying a rationale for intervention that is peculiar to the culture of Islamic societies. That is, we can expect to find the context of Islamic "failure" located not in politics or history but as before in essences; in a regressive Islamic anti-modernity whose particular symptom is the oppression of women. We can expect that this propaganda will not distinguish between Saddam's secular Iraq and the Taliban's Afghanistan, but will instead concoct an ahistoric narrative of culture and regression.

And that is exactly the case. As a neutral bureaucratic language effaces Abu Ghraib as a crime and reinstates it as an administrative issue and rewrites the massacre of Fallujah and air strikes in no-fly zones as policing operations, it also whites out the torture and killing of Iraqi women under the occupation. Instead, it dwells at length on the tribal practice of beheading to create and sustain the illusion of a humanitarian intervention *on behalf of* women.

This makes sense since the "old order" against which the Promethean state rebels is not simply that of the international legal order but also that of traditional religious teaching as instantiated in Islam. The administration's use of religious rhetoric or its support of some right-wing Christian positions are actually of relatively parochial import and are calculated to play to the domestic cultural divide. On more essential matters, the Prometheans betray a neo-pagan exultation in the uninhibited exercise of power that makes it perfectly consistent for them to demonize Islam under the banner of women's rights while fighting those same rights at home.

So, to observers in traditional religious societies, a Western claim to liberate women through the mechanism of the corporate state rings hollow and suggests the replacement of one form of anti-individualism, springing out of oppressive tribal structures, with another, more virulent one arising out of the modern state, even one limited by a constitutional system. But since the restriction of women's rights in Islamic societies is not different from that in traditional Christianity or Judaism, against which the modern state and economy are also ranged, we have to ask how it is possible for the state to rally its domestic religious constituency against values such as sexual abstinence, a more traditional role for women, and opposition to pornography and abortion, to which that constituency is somewhat sympathetic in principle.

The answer is that nationalism trumps the values debate. The "culture war" between the policies of the rational progressive Left and those of the conservative religious Right is easily manipulated and converted by state propaganda into one between what is routinely derided as anti-Americanism and its opposite, which is taken by default to be patriotism but is easily shown to be simply an unabashed support of corporate-state interests abroad and at home. This "patriotism" feeds a type of radicalism that uproots, shatters, homogenizes, and perverts the traditional values of community and individual and replaces it with values of the mass, that is, human beings taken not as the totality of their intact individualities but as incoherent economic and biological drives fragmented by commerce and advertising and then reconstituted by bureaucratic administration and the apparatus of ideology into an object of manipulation.

In place of the propaganda "culture war" foisted on us by the state, in which the freedom of individuals, the Republican "red state" ideal of liberty, is pitted against the social needs of groups, the Democrat "blue state" ideal of equality, we should substitute the real war between the corporate total state and the mass on which it feeds on one hand and the community and individuals of the limited republic on the other. In both red and blue states, therefore, the real struggle is between corporate interests and the mass culture they propagate and the rights and values of individuals and the communities to which they belong. It is a struggle that crosses party lines. It is from this perspective that we ought to view the story of the women of Abu Ghraib, or, more accurately, the absence of a story about them, one of those singular absences that more than any misstatement reveals the falsity of the propaganda of liberation.

Rumors of Rape

When the story first broke, no one appears to have found it peculiar that there were only male prisoners in the pictures, even though Taguba had reported an MP "having sex" with a female prisoner, a peculiar phrasing that contrives implausibly to suggest consent. The only reports were of American female soldiers, in Kuwait, Afghanistan, and Iraq, who had been assaulted by GIs. One report buried in the GI rape article was of three U.S. Army MI soldiers accused of assaulting a female inmate at Abu Ghraib who were subjected to an administrative review, fined "at least five hundred dollars," and demoted in rank.[1] Also in that article was a brief but chilling reference to the rape of a young Iraqi boy by American soldiers. On all this, the mainstream domestic outlets were largely silent except for a piece in the *Christian Science Monitor*.[2]

A rough timeline of abuse, put together from the alternative press, activist sites, and foreign newspapers such as the *Guardian* and the *Scotsman* suggests, however, a widespread problem:

September 2003: Nagem Salam interviews a former Abu Ghraib detainee, Umm Taha, with two small children at home, who alleges she was shoved into an old, very hot bathroom with clogged toilets and infested with insects. Kept there 22 days, she slept on the floor and was allowed out only to drink from a dirty barrel, relieve herself, or clean toilets in front of the men. She vomited so frequently she had to be given fluid, which was done with a dirty IV. In Tikrit, she was kept in a tent with another woman and ten children between the ages of ten and fourteen years, forced to separate feces from urine in a waste bucket and stir the mess after it was burned. She recalls another woman who had a black eye and bloody lips who told her she was put into a wooden cage and beaten.[3] Iman Khammas, head of the International Iraq Occupation Watch Center, reports that a middle-aged woman was sexually assaulted after she was detained at Baghdad airport.[4]

October–November 2003 (especially November 8): The Taguba report finds that an American MP "had sex" with an Iraqi woman; Iraqi women were forced at gunpoint to bare their breasts (according to some reports also their genitals); and naked female prisoners were videotaped.[5] The evidence was shown to Congress but not deemed suitable for the public.

November 2003: A woman at al-Kharkh prison in Baghdad tells Amal Kadham Swadi, an Iraqi woman lawyer investigating the abuse, that she was raped by

American soldiers and shows the stitches in her arm from injuries she received fighting them off. [6]

December 2003: The anonymous letter writer "Noor" claims that she and others were stripped, raped, and impregnated by American soldiers. The lawyer Swadi investigates and finds her case credible and representative of systematic abuse and torture by U.S. guards "all across Iraq."[7]

December 2003: David Enders writes of nearly 1,000 prisoners in Al-Rusuphah in December 2003, 54 of whom were women (a huge divergence from the number given by Khammas), held in cells as at Abu Ghraib. Prison officials insisted that none of the women were pregnant, but according to Enders, at least one was seven months pregnant. Another had given birth while incarcerated. He reports that there were others all across Iraq including a fifty-year-old economist, a former bank director who had only one leg and had been held since August 11 for being a member of the Ba'ath Party, and a lawyer over fifty who had been arrested at her house during a wake for her brother and had been made to stir human feces in front of male prisoners. Also imprisoned were psychologically disturbed women and three juveniles, one fourteen years old.[8]

In another account, Daham al-Mohammed, head of the Union of Detainees and Prisoners, also reports a case of a mother of four who killed herself after being raped by American guards in front of her husband at Abu Ghraib. The story was related by the woman's sister, who assisted with the suicide. Khammas describes the abuse of several women including Um Tai, the wife of an ex-official, who was arrested as a hostage to force her husband to give himself up. Over sixty, with liver and kidney ailments, she was kept in solitary confinement in a tent the size of a mattress, not allowed water and food for two days, and forced to relieve herself in her room. Khammas also describes eyewitness accounts from Abu Ghraib that women had given birth in prison or had been arrested while pregnant. Khammas, Daham al-Mohammed, and Hoda Nuaimi, a politics professor at Baghdad University, all separately said that three young rural women had been killed by their families after leaving Abu Ghraib pregnant.[9]

One prisoner in Baghdad described rooms with cold draughts, little or no hot water, and twice-daily meals consisting of a handful of rice and vegetables so bad that diarrhea was widespread. A prisoner was raped seventeen times by Iraqi policemen with the knowledge of American guards. An older woman was beaten in the genitals by a female soldier in full view of male detainees. Three women were forced on their backs and beaten on their feet.[10] Khammas cites a second report of an older woman forced to stir feces in front of male prisoners.[11]

February 2004: Professor Huda Shaker and a colleague are sexually assaulted at a checkpoint. She reports numerous accounts of rapes and impregnation by American soldiers.[12]

March 2004: When Swadi complains about lack of access, American guards threaten arrest.[13]

April 2004: Three soldiers are fined and demoted for sexually assaulting a female detainee.[14] According to a Reuters cameraman held at Abu Ghraib, a twelve- or thirteen-year-old girl is stripped and paraded before male inmates.[15]

May 2004: British Labour Party MP Ann Clwyde investigates and finds accurate a story that a woman in her seventies, held for six months without charges, was mocked and then ridden like a donkey.[16]

May 2004: At Abu Ghraib, a handful of middle-aged women were held until this month in solitary confinement for 23 hours a day with windows boarded up in cellblock 1A, where the torture photographs were taken. None had seen their families since arrest earlier in the year. Swadi finds the charges of anti-coalition activities against them "absurd." They were arrested to coerce their spouses and for potential intelligence value.[17]

A fifty-five-year-old divorced mother of five, accused of supporting insurgents, is dragged, beaten, and stripped by American soldiers.[18]

Former detainees report that several women have committed suicide following rape.[19]

Some of these real instances of sexual assault are only allegations, many are corroborated, but all are credible and several are supported by other evidence. Yet none have been investigated seriously or reported widely in the domestic press. The media silence was so deafening that it prompted the activist group International Women Count to send an open letter to U.S. congresswomen in May 2004 to ask why, though IWC was "reliably informed by religious supporters of President Bush that photos of rape and other sexual torture of women in Iraqi prisons are commonly used as pornography among U.S. troops," allegations about the torture of women at Abu Ghraib were not being covered or investigated.[20]

Clearly, one reason for the silence is the resurgence of traditional "shame culture." Before the sanctions in the 1990s, Iraq actually had one of the most advanced constitutions in the Arab world, with mandatory education and equal pay for equal work. But the economic chaos following Gulf War I and the resulting increase in sex trafficking led Saddam to revive religious and tribal practices like honor killings both to preserve the social fabric from complete disintegration and to broaden his constituency in the Islamic world.[21] Women, fearful of dishonor, are now reluctant to speak out.

Another reason is the overwhelming nature of the violence in Iraq—"a total of 506 violent deaths in under three weeks in Baghdada alone,"according to veteran journalist Robert Fisk.[22] In the four months after the war, more than 400 women were raped, kidnapped, and even sold in Baghdad alone, according to the Organization for the Freedom of Women in Iraq.[23] In this chaos, violence on the street against women cannot get enough attention, let alone hidden violence in the prisons. According to a Human Rights Watch report published in mid-July 2003 there were at least twenty-five rapes and kidnappings of women in Baghdad between the end of May and the end of June 2003, compared to only one a month on average before the war.[24] But while under the Geneva Conventions this is the responsibility of the occupying force, the American public, conditioned to believe in the unrelieved oppression of women in Islam, blames the violence on Muslim culture and considers Iraqi women in rape-torn, occupied Iraq liberated. Actually, even in conservative Wahhabi Saudi Arabia, rape is a rare crime.[25] Under Saddam, before the invasion, rape was a capital offense and ordinary Iraqi women were relatively safe from street crime.[26] It was Saddam's pre-invasion amnesty for criminals, wartime devastation, and the postwar disbanding of the police force by the Americans that caused the crisis of abduction, rape, and killing in which the prison abuse of women is overshadowed.[27]

Rapes and kidnappings are also grossly underreported and do not take into account either bungled attempts or other lesser crimes. Sexual abductions are, after all, only a fraction of the kidnappings police have to deal with, most of which are for ransom. The chaos is compounded by house raids and checkpoint searches where women are frisked by males because of a shortage of female soldiers for the job. As Middle Eastern experts like Brown University's William Beeman point out, for Muslims such practices violate a woman's honor so seriously that in some conservative families, it is the equivalent of rape and renders women who are not married unmarriageable.[28]

Assaults, rapes, abductions, body searches, prostitution, honor killings, stripping and photographing in detention, torture—together these make a picture of extraordinary and random sexual violence ravaging the country. If anything, observers have not adequately grasped the depth and extent of the suffering of Iraqi women, a suffering equal to that of the men. The average journalist, relatively safe in the armored Green Zone in Baghdad, is likely to have been overwhelmed by it. Unfamiliar with the language and history of Iraq, unable to safely travel around a country the size of California, indoctrinated by Pentagon news briefings, and with few sources besides Western human rights groups and Westernized Iraqis in the affluent areas, reporters become trapped by their own cultural preconceptions and retreat defensively into agnosticism about what can be known, blaming the unreliability of Iraqi reports of prison rape.[29] This is not to suggest that the Arab media does not propagandize. Nor is it to suggest that every allegation made has been credible. However, given murderous conditions and the breakdown of communications, the indisputable fact is that many Iraqi accounts have proven far more credible than accounts by the American government and press.

Yet, looking through an archive of articles specifically on Iraqi women on the website Peace Women, there are fewer than thirty from major American news outlets, mostly from the *New York Times* and the *Christian Science Monitor*. Only seven pieces focus on the endangerment of women's lives, of which one describes the death of an American activist.[30] A March 7 article in the *Times* raises the first hint of concern about the women whose fathers, brothers, and sons have been snatched from them and who crowd the prisons frantically waiting for any word about them. One mother searching for her son charges that she was shoved and chased with dogs.[31] There are two other articles about the possible abuse of women in Iraqi jails, both of them after the story went public on CBS at the end of April.[32] Even an otherwise well-written article in the *Boston Globe* about the dramatic increase in street crime manages to insert a comment on "exaggeration," even though it concedes that activists and officials concur in believing that rates of rape are greatly underreported because they are not tracked and women are too ashamed to speak up.

All this suggests that the silence over the abuse of Iraqi women has as much to do with the ideology of Western journalists as it has to do with Iraqi culture. Western gender feminism, for instance, predisposes reporters to color accounts of rape with hostility to any cultural move suggesting patriarchal attitudes. Thus, several reports dwell on the mandated covering of the head and as many as four focus on restrictive clothing and lack of makeup.[33] The women described are usually well-to-do and Westernized, hardly representative of most of the population. And often, bias is disguised as journalistic skepticism, as in this gingerly worded article in the *Christian Science Monitor*, one of the few on the subject in the mainstream press:

> Rumors of prison rape have been eddying for months. They started with a letter, allegedly smuggled out of Abu Ghraib by a female prisoner. Passed from one person to another, the letter and the photos are being used by anti-US clerics and militants to stir up outrage against the occupation. . . ."Please, bomb us with bombs, and even with nuclear weapons, because we are all pregnant by American soldiers," reads one version of the letter. "Every day they walk us naked in front of soldiers and other prisoners. We want you to know that if you have a daughter in here, or a mother, or a sister, that she has been raped and is pregnant by these American soldiers." . . . The letter might be fabricated—different versions of it crop up, and no one has been able to find the girl who wrote it. But to most Iraqis, it doesn't really matter: the real photos of abuse at Abu Ghraib gave all rumors, both true and false, instant credibility.[34]

Here, rape becomes a matter of perception. The photographic evidence of rape is less important than the "Arab rumor mill," a phrase whose convenient introduction into the article subtly undermines the real evidence. As much as one-tenth of the 1,344 words in the article either suggest falsity—e.g., rumors, not real, counterfeit, fakes, blurry, allegedly, fabricated, whether true or false, it scarcely matters if (Azzawi's mother) was raped or not, the rumor was out, no one has been able to find (the girl who wrote it), a whisper of rape—or focus on honor killing and the way rape allegations are manipulated by "anti-U.S." forces. Even the subtitle, "Photos—even if fake—spark rumors that hit family honor," is misleading because there *is* photographic evidence for the rape, but it is cited only briefly in an article more concerned with the cruelty of honor killing, as if to make us aware that a much worse fate awaits Iraqi women than rape. But of course the whole point of honor killing is that there is no worse fate.

Statements by American authorities are presented without qualification or irony. Statements by Iraqi women, unless Westernized, are qualified with commentary. We are invited subtly to put aside the claims of rapes not only because they are "rumors" and therefore insubstantial; not only because the photographic evidence is misleading and therefore insubstantial; not only because violations less than rape—virtual rape, like imprisonment or stripping—have become proxies for it and diminish the substance of the claims, but because in comparison with the "honor" society's lethal punishment for even "virtual" violation, real rape becomes something less than substantial.

Consider the public reaction to the picture of the female soldier mocking the genitals of an Iraqi man. One of several defenses was that no real harm was inflicted except to the sensibilities of Muslim men, who, it was suggested, did not have a right to take offense since their patriarchal culture encourages the killing of women, something much worse than "abuse."[35] Many commentators refused to call what happened torture and argued that simulation of pain was not "real," a position not supported by the Geneva Conventions, which consider mock executions and degrading treatment as forms of torture. These defenses are exactly paralleled in the two subtextual moves made in the *Christian Science Monitor* article: Arab/Muslim patriarchy with its honor killings is the real violator of women, not rape, which in any case Muslim culture construes too broadly; it's more than likely that these alleged rapes are therefore only rumors, not real, and even the photographs of rape are false, not real.

Cultural myopia estranges and exoticizes the patriarchal representation of "woman's honor" and "virtual" rape from the vantage point of the only world whose representations really do matter, ours. Exoticizing allows us to dismiss torture allegations as exaggerated and documented torture as unimportant next to honor killings. Exoticizing Muslim culture also prevents us from seeing the similarity of Iraqi responses to our own. While American women may not have become less marriageable as a result, there were nevertheless some 300 complaints over the pat-down security searches that have been introduced at airports since 9/11.[36] Apparently, Americans, too, object to being asked to remove clothing, expose private parts, and even duckwalk during security screenings sometimes conducted in areas accessible by others. In cases that mirror reports of prison abuse at home and abroad, female passengers with large breasts were reportedly targeted for screening by supervisors who intentionally set off magnetometers, and in some cases photographed or monitored the stripping.

Both the exotic nature of Muslim representations and the unproblematic nature of ours are thus questionable propositions. Cultural conservatives in America, like many Muslims, argue that public representations of nudity, sexuality, and violence have an effect on levels of real sexual violence. In modern American legal culture, by contrast, an image that assaults the mind is not regarded as also assaulting the body. Maintaining an inflexible distinction between the real and the simulated, it refuses to accept that the latter may have as much of an impact as the former. For American culture, at least in relation to women, the physical limit of the body is the boundary within which sexual violation must be measured. But that may not be as clear-cut as we assume, which is why constitutional theory that deals with verbal or visual representations—the First

Amendment laws of free speech and exercise of religion as well as privacy laws—are especially self-contradictory. While religious and ethnic groups can decry public representations, such as the lurid depiction of the torture of Jesus in the film *The Passion of the Christ*, or the depictions of lynching in *Birth of a Nation*, those who claim that violent or degrading pornography should be restricted in the public domain are resisted with cries of censorship.

This ambiguity in our ideas of representation lies at the heart of Abu Ghraib and prevents us from recognizing that photographing naked prisoners is a violation tantamount to rape. The use of such photography in the interrogation techniques that CIA trainers passed on to intelligence agencies like the Shah's notorious Savak in Iran makes it only too credible that at Abu Ghraib prisoners were being blackmailed with the threat of public exposure of photos or their publication on porn sites.[37] If, as the evidence suggests, that was the case, then it is our distinction between literal and "virtual" rape that may be questionable.

Furthermore, since photographic representations lend themselves to multiple reproductions and transformations, it is no longer a question simply of whether they are genuine or not, but of the purpose they are put to once they enter the public realm. If false, are they designed to mislead or cast doubt on what is real or instead designed to bolster what is real? If genuine, are they intended nevertheless to promote something false? Things are no longer what they seem but what they can be made to seem. What we are talking about is psychological manipulation, the operation of power through images. Abu Ghraib is one locus of such manipulation, the center where several dynamics of power meet like spokes in a wheel—that of a conquering and a conquered people; an expansionist state and a defensive one; the active gaze of the male and the passive objectification of the female; the producer of information, pornography, or violence and its consumer. To sustain these dynamics, one needs images; for the images to have effect, the dynamics need to be in play.

Violent Pornography

As violence operates pornographically in the visual pyrotechnics of "shock and awe," pornography operates violently, erasing the boundary between simulated and real, not simply by mimicking the effects of the real but by tarnishing the status of real rape as an act of violence. Violent crime is now passed off as "consensual" theater. State propaganda easily exploits this disappearance of the boundary between real and simulated, and, consciously or unconsciously, nebulous stories about prostitutes and hoaxes start to creep into the media and confuse reports of real rape by invoking the mitigating notions of consent and intent.

Al-Wasat, a London-based weekly, describes "Nadia," who was beaten, stripped, raped repeatedly, and photographed during six months at Abu Ghraib. Dumped along the highway with 10,000 dinars to "start a new life," she was too ashamed to return home and became a housemaid.[38] In "The Cost of Liberty," the *Washington Post*, otherwise indifferent to Iraqi women, paints a glowing picture of a young American soldier who slips an extra hundred dollars to a prostitute, Nada, and treats her gently.[39]

The similarity of the names may be a coincidence. But if "Nada" is the same as "Nadia," what are we to make of the enormous differences in the two accounts? Is "Nadia's" case concocted to fit into "anti-U.S. sentiment"? Or is "Nada" suspect? Why is a case so unrepresentative of the experiences of Iraqi prostitutes highlighted? The *Al-Wasat* article is a graphic first-person account in incorrect, emotional English with few corroborating details, but its substance is in keeping with scores of reports. The *Post* article is dispassionate, with corroborating detail and nuances of thought and analysis. Yet being anomalous, it conveys an entirely misleading picture of the situation of Iraqi women. The two stories illustrate the perversity of the new media war—the theatrical can be accurate while the coldly factual can propagandize.

In similar fashion, hoaxes and allegations of hoaxes emerge to confuse the story of Abu Ghraib. In July 2003, just as the stories about women began surfacing, the *Washington Post* published its heartrending front-page story about an Iraqi woman, Jumana Hanna, under the headline, "A Lone Woman Testifies to Iraq's Order Of Terror." *Post* reporter Peter Finn had been led by Hanna on a tour of Al Kelab al Sayba, Loose Dogs Prison, and he turned her into a heroine in his article. Fearful that the publicity would endanger her life, American authorities moved Hanna, her seventy-two-year-old mother, and her two young children out of a homeless shelter and into a trailer in the Green Zone.[40] Since then, it has turned out that crucial parts of Hanna's story were concocted out of whole cloth. But for some time it served to distract from the real story that was percolating in the media.

On May 4, 2004, just when evidence of the rape of Iraqi women threatened to become public, a BBC report described graphic photographs circulating on Arabic-language websites that showed two Iraqi women being raped at gunpoint by men in American army uniforms. The report claimed that the photos were inauthentic, suggesting that the uniforms did not look genuine.[41] The *Boston Globe*, however, published them.

When a conservative American site was allegedly led by antiwar Iraqi sources to the porn sites from which the photos originated, the Arab-language sites and the *Globe* removed the photos, but another website, Jihad Unspun, insisted that they portrayed actual rapes caught by pornographic filmmakers. To complicate the matter, a group that monitors Islamist sites believes that Jihad Unspun is a CIA creation intended to track those who visit or order Bin Laden videos.[42]

We are left with several possible explanations—lacking proof or unwilling to compromise victims, someone used preexisting porn to bolster their case; or antiwar groups concocted the story to add to the scandal; or American intelligence planted the photos to undermine the real rape stories about women; or the photos were home movies by soldiers in Iraq or Eastern Europe, where there is also widespread sex trafficking.[43] Even more troubling is the possibility that the pictures weren't hoaxes at all, but photos of actual rape planted on porn sites by a commercial ring. Coincidentally, DynCorp, the private corporation that now holds the contract to train Iraqi police, was sued successfully by employees for its involvement in a sex-slavery and pornography ring in Kosovo where it was providing security to UN and American forces.[44] The ring victimized Bosnian women who were raped or imprisoned by Serb forces, and one employee pled guilty to photographing himself raping a fourteen-year-old girl.

The *Globe* hoax story illustrates why it's no longer possible to judge the authenticity of an image by its appearance or even its venue. Wartime rape can surface on porn sites and commercial or homemade porn can be created on the battlefield. When websites like SexinWar, for instance, advertise themselves as having "exclusive rape hard-core content" drawn from the Iraq war, can we be entirely certain that the contents are staged?[45]

Yet while caution about fraud may be one explanation why journalists have been reticent about Iraqi women at Abu Ghraib, it seems an unsatisfactory one, given that they have avidly covered the abuse of men. Unsatisfactory, that is, unless for some reason the abuse of women has a significance that the abuse of men does not.

That significance can be understood only from the liberal ideology shared by journalists, for whom the torturers of Abu Ghraib acted alone, untouched by the political culture that encouraged them or the military hierarchy, which suggested every torturous act even if it did not explicitly enumerate it. And here is the root of the problem. In the exercise of its power, the corporate state makes full use of the way in which perceptions influence actions, intentions, and consent; it makes full use of powerful imagery to exploit the porous boundary between the spiritual and the physical through advertising, propaganda, and psy-ops. Yet, in the liberal ideology of law that the state imposes on its citizens, that boundary is rigidly maintained. According to that ideology, only the stated intention of the abusers counts, not the innumerable effects that reveal entirely contradictory intentions. The thread that runs from Justice Thomas's ruling through the sentencing of the reservists to the demonizing of terrorists is this: the corporate state is never accountable for the contexts it creates, the political culture of duplicity and violence, the pornographic violence of the desires it drives in prison cells and army barracks, in free-fire zones, and snuff movies. The state is never responsible for creating the torturer or the terrorist. The punishing weight of the law falls only on individual flesh and blood.

But if context is eliminated in law, it is not eliminated in public perception. It is context that makes the photographer's intent fluid, the subject's consent uncertain, and leads to the Iraqi perception that the photographing of naked female detainees is not simply a violation of privacy but rape, and depending on the use made of the pictures, even worse than rape The visual, textual, or audio recording that makes an act pornography powerfully changes how the act and its participants are perceived, not merely by outsiders but by themselves. A woman caught undressed on camera can be represented as a prostitute to her community and, most damagingly, to herself. The intent and will of the photographer, ineluctably printed on top of her own absence of intent or will, becomes an act of force nothing short of a violation of her identity. While a physical rape ends with the act, this virtual rape can continue for the life of the image. Knowledge that such photographs existed would have been enough of a threat for most Iraqi women to keep silent about their abuse, even without the additional threat of blackmail, for the "consent" of a participant, like the "intent" of an author—both staples of feminist defenses of pornography—can be easily misrepresented.

But the liberation theology of the Prometheans that sends universal rights to the four corners of the globe fails to consider the vehicle through which it does so, a sociopolitical culture that liberates sexual practices from social constraints only to better exploit the commercial potential of desires. Formed through social dialogue and construction, such desires are not freely chosen in the first place and may even be compulsive. Circulated as images through networks of representation and commercial exchange, they become subject to market forces that guarantee that at any moment after their insertion into circulation, the link between the representation and the original intent or consent involved will be transformed and even contradicted. In a global business worth $57 billion, of which the U.S. share is $12 billion and expanding, AT&T, "Ma Bell," the prime distributor of pornography on cable television, has one in five broadband customers paying to see "real, live all-American sex—not simulated by actors."[46] For corporate culture, if not for the law, there seems to be no firewall between the real and the simulated. With the advent of the Internet, a digital camera makes mere consumers of pornography into producers and suppliers, who in order to compete with the big players turn to where they can most easily find violence and degradation ready-made—war zones. There, desperate women fleeing economies shattered by military intervention and neoliberal policies participate in "needle torture," "pregnant bondage" and "toilet-drinking," titles that recall details in the accounts by Iraqi detainees. This new violence makes up an ever-increasing proportion of marketed pornography, is far more easily accessed, and operates through interactive formats whose graphic effect is far more powerful. This thin or at times nonexistent line between genuine and simulated degradation and violence that commercial smut peddlers encourage us to ignore not only makes the sexualized torture of Abu Ghraib more possible, it also makes it more permissible.

Sex crimes surge in wartime, around military bases and in the aftermath of the "structural adjustments" of globalization.[47] They also flourish in peacetime in the militarized underbelly of society, its prisons. The armed services are not the only place where sexual abuse is pervasive in the United States. In jails throughout the country, the rape and physical torture of men, women, and teens are well documented.[48] A study of male rape cited by a 2001 Human Rights Watch report showed that 21 percent of male inmates in seven midwestern prisons had been sexually assaulted in some way by another prisoner and blamed prison officials for negligence and callousness in preventing or punishing the crime. Extrapolating these findings to the national level gives a total of at least 140,000 inmates who have been raped.[49] Male staff members are the primary abusers of female prisoners at rates that vary from 7 to 27 percent, well above those in other industrial nations. The abuse includes rape, voyeurism, and the photographing of naked prisoners, as well as assaults and verbal abuse; it takes place during confinement as well as during routine frisking; and it is strikingly similar to the complaints made by Iraqi women about their American captors at Abu Ghraib and elsewhere.

The Propaganda of Gender

Unpunished or underreported though it may be, rape is thus never invisible in war, either in reality or in imagination. The sexualized torment of Abu Ghraib provoked a greater outcry than the carnage of war and occupation. Jessica Lynch may have contradicted the story about her rape, but the story itself raced through the Net and the army. A largely fictitious account of Saddam's invasion of Kuwait that included the now debunked story of Iraqi soldiers tossing babies out of incubators was called "The Rape of Kuwait."[50]

The feminization of the invaded nation in this metaphor of rape is paralleled in the feminization of its men in the photos from Abu Ghraib, which are homoerotic images calculated to simultaneously evoke our homophobia and brand our enemies emasculated. They evoke egalitarian feminism, but only through an inversion of the pornography of hierarchical masculinity. In these rapid sleights of hand, the face of Jessica as captive femininity, which evokes patriarchal protection, is quickly shuffled under the face of Lynndie, the femininity that humiliates and avenges itself on the alien male. And that male himself is constructed as both the extreme of heterosexuality—oppressor of his own women—and the extreme of homosexuality—enslaved to ours. Allegations and falsifications of rape circulate deftly alongside real instances of it and throw all into question. Besides medical reports, there is little to betray the existence of the crime unless it is photographed, and if photographed, the veil of silence envelops the victim again. In this interplay, the rumors of rape, fed by the stripping and photographing of prisoners, point to the way in which power is employed not simply in the traditional methods of war—from bombing to torture—but also in the creation and imposition of imagery that effaces and replaces the subjectivity of the defeated people with a new subjectivity, one that defines them both to themselves and others as abject and dispossessed of their very selves.

The silence over the abuse of Iraqi women cannot be rooted simply in reporters' fears of being inflammatory, for in Islamic as in many societies, the sexual molestation of men is regarded as more aberrant than the rape of women. It cannot be because there have been many more males detained and tortured than females, for it should still be possible to report on those who were victimized, few or many.

Instead, it is to ideology that we again have to look for an explanation. With none of the justifications for war made before the invasion remaining, human rights have taken center stage in revisionist histories. The abuse of women is flagged as not just one among many abuses but the quintessential failure of Islam, the one that most conclusively defines the regressive nature of Islamic society. The brutality of Saddam tells us nothing about Islam.[51] However, the treatment of women goes to the heart of Islamic culture in Saudi Arabia, Iran, and Afghanistan—all places of interest to American foreign policy. Many prominent members of the administration have made that case in virulent sophistries about Muslim culture. But it is conservative women who have been especially vocal in support of feminist interventionism.

"Under the Saddam Hussein regime Iraqi women were not allowed to work outside the home," writes Lisa DePasquale, apparently unaware that until the Gulf Wars women played a major role in the country's political and economic development.[52] And Kay Hymowitz issues this challenge: "Where are the demonstrations, the articles, the petitions, the resolutions, the vindications of the rights of Islamic women by American feminists?" And then answers herself, "Too busy ... contemplating their own victimhood, gender feminists cannot address the suffering of their Muslim sisters realistically, as light years worse than their own petulant grievances."[53]

She criticizes postcolonial feminists like Gayatri Spivak and Leila Ahmed for "condemning Western men for wanting to improve the lives of Eastern women," refusing to indict Islamic society for misogyny and instead focusing on the trivial problems of women in the West. This misreads postcolonial feminism, which in no way supports the patriarchal misogyny of non-Western cultures but does delineate the historical context in which practices like polygamy or veiling arise and the purposes they serve. Ahmed can recognize misogyny but can also recognize when the language of women's rights is being hijacked by an imperial agenda.[54] "White men saving brown women from brown men," to use Spivak's phrase, is a rhetorical tactic that allows conquerors to pose as liberators abroad while cutting off feminist opposition at home.[55] This happens in two ways: by both appealing to a universalist ethical imperative—Don't Muslim women deserve the rights and freedoms of Western women?—and disparaging particular socioeconomic needs—Don't Western women understand how good they have it compared to other women?

And sure enough, when we scratch the surface of Hymowitz's concern, we find something a little less benevolent, captured in this piece of doggerel by

Rudyard Kipling, which she quotes approvingly in criticism of the gender feminist notion of a universal feminine nature that is "peaceful": "When you're wounded and left on the Afghan plains/And the women come out to cut up your remains/Just roll to your rifle and blow out your brains."

So we return again to the colonial discourse in which a knife in self-defense is savagery, but imperial bombs are civilization. It is finally a question of the level of technology involved. But if we use cultural or ethical norms as a pretext for war, are we in any way different from the Taliban?

What these embattled feminists ultimately have in mind becomes clear in an attack by one of them, Susan Okin, on arranged marriage, which has certainly been part of most cultures for most of history. Okin, from the Olympian view of the modern American female, feels confident that some women "might be better off if the culture into which they were born were ... to become extinct."[56]

Although she softens her tone midstream, the quick reach for force and the *veiled*, as it were, bigotry betray the essential illiberalism of her position, dutifully one step behind male neoconservative hawks who want to bomb Afghan women out of burqa. One can be pretty certain that once the "liberated women" have served their temporary use as the pretext for the destruction of their nation, their welfare will be of little interest to their benefactors. One can be as certain that once the war is over, the liberators will show equally little interest in the conditions of women in their own countries. In any case, the feminist argument for war in the Muslim world is seriously crippled by the facts about U.S. intervention there. In Afghanistan, when fundamentalists revolted against the Communist government's attempt to extend education to girls in March 1979, it was the United States, along with Saudi Arabia and Pakistan, that supported the fundamentalists.[57]

The same is true in Iraq. Despite Saddam's torture, rape, and killing of political opponents, women in Ba'athist Iraq were educated, had the vote, and occupied important positions in government. The Iraqi constitution once enshrined equality for women. But under the sanctions, over a half-million war widows supplied the only boom industry in Iraq—prostitution. There were only three women on the U.S.-appointed Iraqi Governing Council, only one woman in the Iraqi cabinet, and no women among the eighteen provincial governors. The committee charged with drafting the interim constitution was all male. Iraqi women had to demonstrate in the streets to have their demands met.[58] Temporary marriages, the Islamic version of prostitution and a rare custom before the war, became widespread among impoverished widows.[59] Neither former consul Bremer nor the Governing Council, including the women, suggested any amendments to the articles supporting honor killings and abuse by male relatives.[60] "We don't do women," was the reply from the Ministry of the Interior when asked to explain the indifference of both imperial and native overlords to Iraqi women.[61] So much for empowerment.

The welfare of women is even more besieged. A tally by an Iraqi human rights group based on thorough investigation of hospital figures and reports runs as high as 37,000 for the period between March and October 2003, and a study by the British *Lancet* found 100,000 fatalities.[62] *The Lancet* estimate gives a wounded figure of 2,497,139 for the year.[63] That number will be even higher when the full impact of the war on health is accounted for. Since more than half the number is female, and given that men in Iraq have been fodder for war for several decades, we end up with a reasonable estimate of tens of thousands of female deaths from the war and occupation alone, excluding the deaths during Gulf War I and the sanctions, which would run the number into the hundreds of thousands. Add to this the suffering of families destroyed, homes blown to bits, rapes, assaults, abductions, malnutrition, injuries, lost wages and possessions, the rise of reactionary religious laws, and can we still say that we have improved the lives of Iraqi women? Will we, like Madeleine Albright justifying the deaths of Iraqi children under sanctions, claim that their suffering was "worth it"? And should we call ourselves civilized for dealing so generously in other people's pain and death in the name of liberating them?

While mouthing the rhetoric of feminism, American policy has been as inimical to the welfare of women as it has been to the welfare of the whole country, and it is this finally that explains the silence on the abuse and torture of Iraqi women. Were we to have the same sort of photos of women on the front pages as we did of the men, what would become of the mask of the liberator?

9
The Torture Trompe l'Oeil

In the summer of 2004, the facade of the occupation was crumbling in Iraq. The Berg beheading drew fire away from the administration over May until the first impact of the torture scandal died down. By the end of June, under cover of the furor, the administration handed over power to the Iraqi interim government, hoping to disguise the rapid escalation in the violence of the occupation. A trompe l'oeil was in place. Though story after story about prison abuse surfaced, none gained traction as the public turned from prison abuse to the Democratic and Republican Party conventions. Election politics at home distracted activists. The eight military investigations dealing with intelligence, policing, and detention reported their findings duly in the fall, but the results were so uncoordinated and selective that when Chip Frederick was sentenced in October to eight years for his part in the torture, a casual observer might have concluded forgivably that justice had been more than adequately served.[1]

Yet this was far from the case. In an e-mail in June, one of the agents assigned to investigate the prison abuse scandal pleaded that his case load was "exploding" and that high visibility cases were on the rise.[2] At year end in 2004, the number of soldiers charged had ballooned into twenty times the original number and a total of 130 American troops had been punished or charged, of whom about thirty were Marines and Navy Seals.[3]

Moreover, since these charges stem from the government's own investigations they are likely to represent only a fraction of the problem. With every month bringing fresh charges, new tapes, or documents, the evidence is overwhelming that a mass crime has been committed, a crime that reaches back to the earliest days of the occupation and extends to facilities on three continents.

***Cuba: September-October 2002, Camp X-Ray, Guantanamo Bay*:** FBI agents saw a dog used "in an aggressive manner to intimidate a detainee," and a month later saw the same detainee "after he had been subjected to intense isolation for over three months ... totally isolated in a cell that was always flooded with light. By late November, the detainee was evidencing behavior consistent with extreme psychological trauma ... talking to nonexistent people, reported hearing voices (and) crouching in a corner of the cell covered with a sheet."[4]

Iraq: April 2003, Al Rutba: A Saudi national traveling from Syria to Baghdad, Abdallah Khudhran al-Shamran, told Amnesty International that he "was subjected to beatings and electric shocks," suspended from his legs, and had his penis tied.[5]

***Iraq: August 2003, Kirkuk*:** Fifty-five-year-old Sadiq Zoman Abrahim, detained during a house raid that produced no weapons was returned to his family in a permanent coma with signs of massive head trauma and electrocution. [6]

***Iraq: September 2003, Mosul*:** British troops beat and killed a hotel worker, Baha Mousa, while five others were left with massive kidney damage, broken ribs, organ damage, severe bruising, and permanent scarring,[7]

***Iraq: September 2003, Camp Redemption (Abu Ghraib)*:** Amnesty informant "H," a fifty-five-year-old woman, claims that Americans brought in fourteen male inmates naked and handcuffed, spread their legs and beat them in the genital region until they collapsed. She claims that interrogation sessions always included an ice block and were followed, a few hours later, by a visit by two doctors, an American and an Iraqi. The prisoners were always taken away unconscious.[8]

***Iraq: April 13, 2004, Al-Mahmudiya*:** A witness saw a marine "shock an Iraqi detainee with an electric transformer," holding "wires against the shoulder area of the detainee (who) danced as he was shocked."[9]

***Afghanistan: December 2003, Bagram*:** Mullah Habibullah, about twenty-eight, died of "pulmonary embolism due to blunt force injuries to the legs," according to doctors. An Afghan, Dilawar, twenty-two, died from "blunt force injuries to lower extremities complicating coronary artery disease."[10]

***Indian Ocean: Camp Justice, Diego Garcia*:** Interrogation techniques used on Diego Garcia reportedly followed prescriptions given in a secret CIA manual with sections on "Threats and Fear," "Pain," "Narcosis," and "Heightened Suggestibility and Hypnosis."[11]

In a Christian Peacemaker team's summary of 72 detention cases, not once was the detainee allowed legal representation, tried, or convicted for a crime, and in no case did coalition authorities on their own initiative inform relatives of a detainee's whereabouts. In ten cases, there was abuse ranging from beatings and electrocution to deprivation of food and water.[12]

By 2004, there were around 12,000 and probably many more prisoners held at one time in custom-made U.S. military prisons, including shipping containers and prison ships, such as the USS *Bataan* and the USS *Peleliu*.[13] The majority were held in Iraq in thirteen large and many smaller disclosed detention centers and in perhaps others yet undisclosed; 300 were held in railroad boxcars at Bagram, north of Kabul, and hundreds others elsewhere in Afghanistan. What the CIA manual denotes as "the most difficult" were sent to Diego Garcia. Some 3,000 suspected Al Qaeda members were held in Bagram, Diego Garcia, and Guantanamo Bay, where approximately 600 detainees have been held without charge for two years; approximately 150 captives have reportedly been "rendered," that is, illegally transported to third countries that permit torture and "have cultural affinities" with the prisoners.[14]

Reports on this can be heard regularly on the BBC, read in the *Guardian*, the *Toronto Star*, and several other foreign English language newspapers of repute, as well as in the reports of the major human rights organizations. But not in the American mainstream media.

Where in all this were American journalists? The activist website Iraq Occupation Watch contains a few articles on prison abuse in the major newspapers in the years before the CBS Abu Ghraib exposé. On March 11, 2002 the *Washington Post* wrote about renditions of terror suspects to foreign countries for torture in which U.S. intelligence continued to be involved.[15] In December 2002, it ran an excellent front-page article on the CIA' s involvement in interrogations in Afghanistan in which an official who had witnessed the transfer of Al Qaeda prisoners to countries known for brutal torture, like Jordan, Egypt, and Morocco, noted, "If you don't violate someone's human rights some of the time, you probably aren't doing your job."[16] In January 2003, *The Economist* described the involvement of American intelligence in torture.[17] In March a cover story in *The Nation* suggested that torture was being mainstreamed and discussed the cases of suspects killed by blunt force injury or hung from the ceiling by chains at Bagram, Afghanistan.[18] In May and August, the *New York Times* and the *Los Angeles Times* had pieces on torture at Basra and elsewhere.[19] In November, AP ran a major story about abuse at Abu Ghraib, Camp Cropper, and Camp Bucca that included prisoner deaths involving marines. Their Pulitzer Prize–winning reporter Charles Hanley described six corroborated cases of torture, including deaths, substantiating reports that summer from Amnesty International. When Hanley asked U.S. Command directly about these reports, however, he was neither answered nor refuted and his story was not pursued at all. [20]

After that, we hear from only a few alternative outlets. Even when the government released its January 16 brief on the abuse charges, the major newspapers paid little attention. The *New York Times*, *Philadelphia Inquirer*, *Dallas Morning News*, and *Boston Globe* published short inside reports while the *Washington Post* and *USA Today* did not run stories at all. Only CNN, Fox News Channel, and NBC mentioned it on television.[21] There was nothing more on prison abuse except for a piece in the *LA Weekly* in February that described the flouting of the Geneva Conventions. It was only when Hersh's article came out in April 2004 that reporters began to make up for lost time. There are around seventy articles each in the month of May and June in the Occupation Watch archives (including foreign and alternative English media), but only about half that number in July, about a third that number in September and October, and only two in November. Prison abuse is now on the back burner in American politics, even though Iraq and the war of terror continue to command headlines.

There are, of course, good reasons. Journalists forced to rely on secondhand government briefs and embedded in the military are often unable to see the facts on the ground as they really are. Danger exacerbates the difficulty. The Committee to Protect Journalists lists Iraq as the most dangerous place in the world to cover news, and in 2004, according to the International Federation of Journalists, 49 journalists and support staffers were killed there and many others kidnapped, detained, or shot at by Iraqi insurgents.[22] Suicide bombings, surprise attacks, and oil-field sabotage make it risky and expensive to pursue a story in Iraq.

Another part of the problem is the government's policy of embedding reporters and vetting reports, part of an intense scripting of the war. Roughly 650 journalists were embedded in Iraq during the war in 2003.[23] The "embeds" are reporters selected by their editors to spend weeks or months as part of a unit under a plan centrally managed by Public Affairs at DOD. The program is intended to "shape perception of the national security environment" for a decade, according to a military brief, which eagerly anticipates that most coverage will be positive. The brief offers samples of headlines that meet the embed standard: "'Club 32' eliciting smiles from troops missing home," "It really does rain in Kuwait," "Marines try to streamline mail," and "Marines, sailors seek a higher power."[24]

In keeping with this, after the terse January brief in which the charges of abuse were first announced to the public, there was a clamp-down on information. Prison camps in Afghanistan and Iraq became off-limits. "I have never seen greater news management in thirty-plus years in this business," says Loren Jenkins, foreign editor for National Public Radio.[25] One instance of this is that media reporting of combat deaths was delayed by law for twenty-four hours. The lawmaker responsible for this is now also pushing for camera crews to be banned from covering direct combat actions.[26]

In its effort to manage perceptions, the military often bypasses conventional channels and gets news directly to the public where the focus is kept insistently on the barbarism of the opponent, making torture on the American side harder to criticize publicly. The media war in this respect has been completely unscrupulous. False statements appear on the front page while retractions are buried weeks later in the inside pages. For instance, the "murder" of aid worker Margaret Hassan was trumpeted on front pages in October 2004 on the strength of an ambiguous video and an unrecognizable mutilated body, but in December when dental records revealed that the body was not hers, there was silence except in the foreign press.[27] Meanwhile the story deflected from the findings of the various investigations of the abuse and provided the necessary cover of righteous blood-lust under which Fallujah could be razed. Hassan's disappearance also diluted the impact of a report in the British medical journal, the *Lancet,* that the war and occupation had produced some 100,000 or more civilian deaths. While the Hassan story covered the front pages, the *New York Times* and *Washington Post* both carried the *Lancet* story inside without editorial comment or follow-up.[28]

Sometimes news is leaked out in drips to minimize public reaction. The one ghost detainee that Rumsfeld originally admitted to has now expanded unobtrusively into thirty (the Church report by the navy Inspector General) "dozens or hundreds" (the Fay-Jones report on the role of military intelligence), a number that may never be definitive since the CIA claims it does not keep records of its detainees. Information has been withheld or has mysteriously disappeared. The Taguba report reached the Senate hearing with at least 2000 pages missing and Reed Brody, a lawyer for HRW, has complained that DOD documents released in June 22, 2004, were incomplete. They only went up to April 2003, did not cover

Abu Ghraib and other Iraqi prisons, and were missing Sanchez's crucial September and October 2003 memos.[29] It has taken a year and a lawsuit against the Pentagon as well as other agencies before the ACLU has been able to access documents that their original Freedom of Information request in October 2003 was unable to produce. The new papers have turned out to contain radioactive material—the mock execution of juveniles, electrocution, several literal executions conducted by marines under threat of death, and a number of incidents of racial and sexual torture.[30] The documents convey powerfully the official culture of censorship that cloaks what is going on. In one email, an officer suggests that the bodies of prisoners should not be autopsied in the US "for legal reasons." Other documents show that several officials in the intelligence agencies were aware of what was going on, had questioned it, and were told to keep quiet. A Navy corpsman, for instance, is quoted as saying, "There was a lot of peer pressure to keep one's mouth shut."[31] In January 2003, the FBI complained about sexual torture at Guantanamo, claiming that they had observed incidents as early as 2002 but had not been given any assurance that their concerns were being taken to DOD. In a memo on June 25, 2004, the head of the Defense Intelligence Agency (DIA), Vice Admiral Lowell Jacoby, complained in a memo to Under Secretary of Defense Cambone that a photo taken by a DIA agent of a special operations interrogator punching a prisoner hard enough to make him require medical attention was confiscated. There was no reply.[32]

The government also uses the opposite strategy, swamping investigators with information or allowing intentional misstatements to stand uncontradicted in order to destroy the credibility of reporters. In this way, too much disclosure does the same work of disinformation as too little. For instance, at one point, the Pentagon turned over 21,600 pages of documents in two months, after having already made 16,600 pages available on the Internet—far too much for the public to digest at one time.[33] Another tactic used has been to undermine the substance of criticism by character assassinations of the critic. UN weapons expert and war dissenter Scott Ritter, for instance, was caricatured as a male "Hanoi Jane" Fonda and personally savaged with charges that he had had sex with teenagers.[34]

In more abstract terms, the Promethean tendency toward invisibility translates into a culture of unparalleled secrecy. Alien terrorists are covertly deported, immigration hearings are closed to the public, and federal court records are sealed and blanked off the docket. Information about Guantanamo detainees and thousands of immigrants supposedly detained under the Patriot Act is hidden, while private information about citizens is surreptitiously harvested under the data-mining system, Matrix. In its first two years, the administration has doubled the number of documents classified (44.5 million) and made it easier to reclassify previously declassified information.[35]

But secrecy is not the only technique of this trompe l'oeil. Behind a public face of contrition the government actively thwarts public interest in the crimes committed in the prisons and endorses the culprits. The disconnect between language and action is profound. After all the public talk of "holding people accountable," Rumsfeld finally rewarded General Geoffrey Miller by putting him in charge of all military prisons in Iraq in April and is said to be keen to pin a fourth star on General Sanchez. Alberto Gonzales, the author of one of the most notorious "torture memos," has become attorney general in the Bush second term. White House counsel Haynes, who developed and defended three of the most egregious policies—the denial of Geneva protection to prisoners at Guantanamo, the plan to try suspected war criminals in military tribunals, and the incarceration of U.S. citizens without counsel or judicial review—has been nominated to be a judge on the U.S. Court of Appeals for the Fourth Circuit.[36] Major General Barbara Fast, who served as chief of intelligence for Sanchez, has been given command of the U.S. Army Intelligence Center at Fort Huachuca, Arizona.[37] Michael Chertoff, the head of the criminal division of the DOJ who authorized the Bybee torture memo, is now director of the entire complex of Homeland Security.

Not only international law but international human rights organizations are held up to derision by neoconservatives. For instance, longtime cold warrior and nuclear hawk Frank Gaffney has labeled the International Red Cross, which is composed of leading Swiss government officials, an "agitation operation against American interest."[38] There have been threats, some direct, others indirect. General Fay warned whistle-blower Samuel Provence that he could be punished for not having spoken out earlier about the abuses. Provence charges that there has been a sustained effort to cover up the involvement of senior officials.[39] According to the documents uncovered by the ACLU, DIA officials who complained about interrogation methods they had witnessed had the keys to their vehicles confiscated, were instructed "not to leave the compound without specific permission even to get a haircut," were threatened, and were told that their e-mail messages were being screened. Major General Thomas Fiscus, judge advocate general of the U.S. Air Force who opposed the approval of harsh interrogation techniques, has since been publicly reprimanded for "fraternizing"—in his case, a dozen consensual sexual affairs during the last decade—and was retired at the permanent rank of colonel.[40]

The conclusions of the supposedly independent investigations also demonstrate why relying on government investigations is fruitless. A December 2003 report on intelligence-gathering in Iraq criticized the treatment of high-value prisoners at Camp Cropper and disclosed that CIA officers in Iraq were ordered away from an interrogation center operated by a secret Special Operations unit, Task Force 121, because agency officials suspected there was abuse.[41] Yet an investigation in February still concluded there was *no* evidence of abuse. Though the December report was included as a classified annex to the Fay-Jones report, the ultimate finding was that Sanchez, although responsible, was not culpable.[42] This type of semantic whitewash repeats itself in other investigations. Despite eyewitness accounts by an FBI agent and a marine that sexual abuse was committed at Guantanamo, Navy investigators found the charges "unsubstantiated," while examples of less serious abuse were found accurate. "We were gravely informed about cold water being poured on a detainee and the American flag being draped over another. ..." The technique is adroit—admit to lesser infractions to create credibility but dismiss more serious cases as unsubstantiated, although they might fit in very well with medical evidence and similar substantiated claims elsewhere.

The language of normalization even extends to academia. In response to "trophy photos" showing SEALs posing with abused prisoners, Gary Solis, a former Marine Corps prosecutor and judge who teaches at the United States Military Academy, insisted that they showed "stupid" and "juvenile" behavior but not necessarily a crime.[43] Showing a level of secrecy unprecedented in military law, the Navy has refused to identify the SEAL lieutenant who beat the detainee Jamadi, referring to him as well as all other SEALs in the courtroom only by the first letter of his last name.[44]

In the familiar strategy of the forensic drama, when senior personnel are involved blame is not attached to individuals but to procedures. There is criticism of the "flawed interrogation policies" and the breakdown in "good order and discipline," but no finding that any senior Pentagon or White House official pressured interrogators to use abusive tactics. Even low-level cases have taken their time—it has taken two years for the two homicides at Bagram to be addressed.[45] There are several hundred investigations of individual cases under way in the military or the federal process and more than fifty broader assessments by the

Pentagon, starting with the Miller and Ryder reports, of which the Formica report on the special operations was still unavailable in April 2005. Yet this welter of investigation has only diffused responsibility and obscured the most essential aspects of the story.

The end result is that soldiers or interrogators have taken the rap for the policymakers, although they too have, in general, suffered few consequences. In one instance, a SEAL who beat a detainee so badly that he later died was acquitted in a nonjudicial hearing closed to the public.[46]

There are conflicts of interest. The Army Criminal Investigation Division investigation is headed by a provost-marshal, General Ryder, who is also responsible for setting policy for the MPs. That is the same Ryder whose report on Abu Ghraib in the fall of 2003 failed to unearth abuses happening literally under his nose when he visited. Although he was apparently alerted to the problem by the FBI as early as January that same year, he still did nothing about it.[47] That he was then put in charge of the CID investigation is conclusive proof of the government's bad faith in the matter.

Conclusions are cooked. The Church Report by the Navy Inspector General on global detentions found that by January 2003 military interrogators in Afghanistan were using techniques similar to those that Rumsfeld had approved for use only at Guantanamo. Still, it managed to conclude that despite their similarities, "these techniques did not migrate from Guantanamo Bay to Afghanistan," as the Schlesinger report had suggested in August. Instead, it claimed that the techniques were developed independently by interrogators in both places who took a broad reading of the U.S. Army field manual.[48] The Mikolashek report by the Army Inspector-General, which Democrats in Congress branded a whitewash, found 94 cases of abuse in Iraq and Afghanistan but again blamed them on individual soldiers rather than policymakers.[49] According to Physicians for Human Rights, even the key Schlesinger report is a charade. While it nominally places the blame on the civilian leadership, the actual wording it uses calls into question the prohibition on torture, condones the abuses, and strongly advises against Rumsfeld's resignation.[50] The Church report concludes that Pentagon policies "did not authorize or condone abusive treatment" of detainees and that there was "no single overarching explanation" for the abuse.[51]

In this farcical justice, outright cronyism plays an important part. Appointed to his role as investigator by his colleague Rumsfeld, Schlesinger is also a former defense secretary, and a member of the Homeland Security Advisory Council as well as the Defense Policy Board. Perhaps of all the reports, the Fay report on military intelligence gets closest to the truth when it traces the harsh "nondoctrinal methods" at Abu Ghraib to the CIA, but Fay, like Schlesinger, is also in the sticky business of investigating colleagues, including Sanchez and Sanchez's top MI subordinates, Barbara Fast and Pappas. In a culture of such collegiality, it would be naive to expect anything but a whitewash of government wrong-doing.

In addition, Human Rights First has faulted the investigations on a number of other key points: lack of subpoena power, misuse of security classification to withhold information, and lack of real independence. Human Rights Watch notes that while reports and testimony have shown the involvement of Feith, Cambone, Boykin, Miller, and Rumsfeld, not one of the five has been investigated or charged.[52] Most crucial to the failure of the investigations has been their limitation to the military and their inability to tackle the role of the CIA, a role that is absolutely central to uncovering the real nature of Abu Ghraib. Church, for instance, interviewed no detainees or key officials involved with the interrogations, and completely ignored interrogations by the CIA. He did not interview Paul Bremer, who headed the CPA from July 2003 until late June 2004, and admitted that he did not even know that Bremer reported directly to the Pentagon not the State Department. Church also failed to interview the FBI officers who complained about abuses at Guantanamo, as his investigation was over before the e-mails surfaced in December.[53]

The strategy of alternating forensic and pulp dramas has succeeded. On one hand we have reports, so numerous, detailed, and specialized that public attention has been lost among them; on the other, singular acts of hostage-taking and beheading, which portrayed violence inundating the country whose victims most of all are Iraqis themselves, create the illusion of symmetry in suffering and turn the victimizer into the victim. Abu Ghraib is seen in split screens—one limited and lurid, finding its way to well-publicized courts-martials, and the other so encumbered with legal documentation that it seems arcane and politically motivated. What is finally obscured is the broad outlines of a deliberate criminal policy.

Yet, there is a puzzle in all this. The torture did not make the headlines until the major papers came to the story in 2004, almost two and a half years after the earliest evidence of the government's new approach to detentions first came out. But if we look through the reporting, we find that practically every angle of the story has, at some point, made it into the major newspapers, even if rather cursorily.

Reviewing the record: the *Washington Post* ran a three-part series about a secret CIA center in Kabul nicknamed "The Pit," and described "ghost detainees" in secret prisons flown to and fro by a covert airline[54]; ABC reported the threats made by Fay against Provance;[55] Reuters wrote about the abuse of journalists;[56] NBC described the involvement of elite Delta forces in drugging, smothering, and water torture of prisoners, methods intended to be carried over to other sites;[57] the *San Diego Union Tribune* also reported on the involvement of marines in abuse;[58] the use of dogs was addressed by several papers;[59] the *Christian Science Monitor* and ABC described how Pentagon political appointees like Feith marginalized military lawyers;[60] "Roots of Torture," an important *Newsweek* piece, demonstrated how Bush, Rumsfeld, and Ashcroft signed off on directives that circumvented the Geneva Conventions and enabled torture;[61] the *New York Times* reported that Rumsfeld issued orders, later rescinded, that deprived prisoners of clothing;[62] the *Washington Post* described explicit attacks on prisoners' religion and the abuse of children.[63]

Yet for this breathtaking litany of defiant lawlessness, where is the public outrage, where is the outcry from journalists?

And what is even more remarkable is that even earlier than the Seymour Hersh exposé, there were journalists who had asked the right questions. Abu Ghraib and even the 320th Military Police Battalion had already figured in those questions. The renditions, after all, were widely known; "torture lite" was official policy, and the approximate nature of what was happening at the prisons, down to the nude photographs, had been reported. First, there was a CNN report shortly after the noncommittal January brief; later in March, there was one in the online journal Salon.com.[64] Yet for some reason, all these early warning signals came to nothing.

Why? There is a "culture of intimidation" of the media, suggests Katrina vanden Heuvel, editor of *The Nation*. "Journalists are afraid not to be patriotic."[65]

There is some evidence for this. On December 6, 2001, for instance, appearing before a Senate committee, Attorney General John Ashcroft chastised critics of the administration's terrorism policy for giving "ammunition to America's enemies."[66] In another instance, when a *New York Times* reporter vented her real feelings about the war and what was happening in Baghdad, she found herself quickly reassigned, even though what she reported was in a personal e-mail circulated among friends. A reporter videotaped a marine in the act of shooting in the head a wounded Iraqi lying in a mosque and found himself the target of denunciations and death threats. Immediately after the beheading of Nick Berg, Mike King, editor of the *Atlanta Journal-Constitution*, began receiving angry calls and e-mails from readers demanding coverage equal to Abu Ghraib. King says, "It was like a mantra: 'We're watching to see how you treat it.' ... This was going to become the litmus test for fairness."[67]

More controversially, there have been charges, denied by the government, that reporters have actually been targeted on the battlefield. When U.S. forces invaded Baghdad in April 2003, all unembedded journalists were urged to leave the city, but some chose to stay, with deadly results. On April 8, an American aircraft bombed Al-Jazeera's Baghdad offices, killing reporter Tareq Ayyoub. Unintentional, claimed the military, but Al-Jazeera's documentation proves that the Americans received the coordinates of the office's location before hand.[68] On the same day, an American tank also fired on the Palestine hotel, killing José Couso from Telecinco, a Spanish network, and Taras Protsiuk from Reuters.[69] Earlier during the war, Human Rights Watch visited three media facilities in Baghdad hit by U.S. air strikes: the Ministry of Information, the Baghdad Television Studio and Broadcast Facility, and the Abu Ghraib Television Broadcast Facility. The last two were completely destroyed.

Were such acts simply accidental as the government insists? Recent events suggest otherwise. In November, when U.S. troops again laid siege to Fallujah, the attack included a new tactic—eliminating all those who had publicized civilian casualties during the first attack in March. This time at Fallujah, Al-Jazeera was absent, banned from reporting in Iraq indefinitely. Al-Arabiya's unembedded reporter, Abdel Kader al-Saadi, was arrested by American forces and held for the length of the siege.[70] Fallujah general hospital was stormed, doctors arrested, and the mobile phones stolen to prevent communication with the world. During the invasion of Mosul, similarly, the United States immediately seized control of Al-Zaharawi hospital. Clerics who spoke out against the occupation were arrested or killed. No witnesses, no casualties.

But while all this is powerful evidence of a military culture hostile to media coverage, something of the kind is surely to be expected in wartime. Can we blame the lack of interest in the torture story entirely on it or is there something else at work?

The *New York Times*' Elizabeth Bumiller thinks journalistic convention is responsible for the media failure on Iraq in general.[71] For her, asserting that a government claim is false, even when it is so, can make a journalist seem unbalanced. Objectivity often perversely demands that reporters make both sides of a story seem balanced, in many cases by treating even something known to be false with a certain gravity rather than refuting it point-blank. Bumiller presents this tendency almost as an aesthetic preference, as a matter of style, a distaste for strong emotion.

But this is rather indulgent to American journalism. Analysis of the general coverage of the war shows that this preference for the neutral works usually to benefit the official version of events. The convention of neutrality is only a version of the bureaucratic language which normalizes government violence and falsehood. The apparent "value-neutrality," the pretense of nonpolitical objectivity, is simply a mask for a deeply political and completely amoral genuflection before power. This is exhibited in a general credulity toward official sources and a pervasive distrust of nongovernment sources. Thus, government explanations of civilian deaths are treated as objective despite routine contradiction from video footage and independent sources, while international human rights reports are automatically dismissed as biased. There are even obvious instances of outright censorship by editors or publishers. Reporting on Osama bin Laden's videotaped speech in late October, the *New York Times* ran six paragraphs of the speech on the front page, while burying on page 9 the key point made early in it that 9/11 was motivated by Bin Laden's reaction to American-Israeli "tyranny" in Palestine and Lebanon.[72] The finding of the prestigious Defense Science Board panel that groups like Al Qaeda were driven by opposition to U.S. foreign policy—specifically to its Israeli bias—rather than generalized anti-Americanism was delivered to the secretary of defense on September, two months before the 2004 election, yet the *New York Times* broke the story only on November 24, weeks after the election, when it would not hurt either of the two pro-Israeli candidates for president. The *Times* also redacted a crucial sentence referring to "one-sided support in favor of Israel and against Palestinian rights."[73]

Self-censorship, then, is the real problem. Not only this explicit kind but a more general blindness that compels us finally to return to ideology as the best explanation for the media's failure on Abu Ghraib. If the media coverage has not added up to outrage it is because reporters have faltered in drawing the necessary conclusions and calling things by their true names. Take, for example, the two stories most thoroughly blanked out this summer in domestic coverage.

1. In July, the German TV news magazine *Report Mainz* cited ICRC reports of over 100 children in U.S. custody and eyewitness accounts of soldiers abusing children, including an account by Sergeant Provance that interrogators molested a fifteen-year-old girl and physically abused a sixteen-year-old boy.[74] Sy Hersh mentioned in a lecture to the ACLU that he had heard tapes of children screaming as they were being sodomized in front of their parents.[75]

2. In August the British medical journal *Lancet* reported on medical complicity at Abu Ghraib. Dr. Steven Miles, professor of bioethics at the University of Minnesota, charged that in direct contravention of the Geneva Conventions, medical personnel allowed interrogators access to medical records, helped design and implement psychological and physical torture, revived patients in order to continue torturing, and falsified death certificates and medical records, such as those of Iraqi Major General Mowhoush.[76]

Compare the attention given to the torture photos with the complete silence shrouding these two explosive pieces. Was the overexposure of some crimes meant to distract from the existence of others? Was the stripping and humiliating of adult males seen as more publicly defensible than the abuse of children? Male rape, after all, can be used manageably in a partisan attack, but child abuse might be ammunition strong enough to blow up both sides.

Or were the torture photos leaked intentionally in a calculated damage-control effort as some have suggested? There is a documented history of ties between the CIA and the major media—from CBS to *Newsweek* and the *New York Times*. Reaching far back to the Cold War, this record makes it impossible to discount the possibility of a damage-control campaign.[77]

But even if some such manipulation did take place, the largest part of the media failure had to do with internal not with external constraints. Stephen Hess, a former analyst at the Brookings Institution, believes that government intimidation might have been a factor shortly after 9/11, but the real problem since then has been journalists simply finding the torture stories "too unbelievable."[78] Charging a few "bad apples" with individual crimes is one thing because they do not represent the state; charging the government with procedural error, wrong judgment, carelessness, or cultural insensitivity is also permissible, because the underlying "intention" and morality of the state is not called into question. But charging the government with the abuse of children and medical complicity in torture ruptures the facade of the liberal state and the ideology that journalists themselves share too deeply to undermine. So we find a *Post* article, for example, trying to minimize the use of dogs in terrorizing prisoners. It suggests in frankly racist terms that the animals simply disliked the Iraqis because of their smell and appearance.[79] So also Jonathan Alter, who approvingly cites Harvard law professor Alan Dershowitz's endorsement of torture warrants, proposes that suspects be extradited for questioning to countries not as squeamish about torture as we are.[80] In his prescription, we sense palpably the contradiction of liberal journalism—it closes its eyes to what it is too good for, but holds out its hand for what it is not good enough to do without.

It closes it eyes and it forgets. And what it forgets returns in jail cells and police stations at home. The meaning of Abu Ghraib is ultimately not to be found in isolation but in acts elsewhere and at other times, which unfold from opaque depths that are at first strange but then completely familiar. The water tortures that American forces used in the Spanish-American War come home to American police stations.[81] The electric torture used in Vietnam reappears in Arkansas prisons in the 1960s and in Chicago squad rooms in the 1970s and 1980s.[82] Torture continues today in American prisons where guards wear and use electric stunguns routinely. Reiterating these meanings not differently but only more completely, Abu Ghraib is the externalized heart of an American gulag no different in kind if not in degree from that of the Soviets, no different from the carceral systems of any empire. Susan Sontag suggests that in failing to charge prisoners or sentence them for determinate lengths, it may even outdo many of them.[83] The inexorable link between bases multiplying abroad and jails proliferating at home, between CIA manuals and Super Max at home, the secret and total complex of military, industry, and prison—this is the repressed of liberalism.

In the 1960s Dan Mitrione, an employee of the Agency for International Development, advised Brazilian police on electroshock and trained Uruguayan police in psychological techniques of torture, such as playing tapes of women and children screaming to convince the prisoner his family was being tortured.[84]

Following the research of brainwashing expert Edgar Schein of MIT, several leading psychologists, as well as federal prison psychiatrist Dr. Martin Grode, suggested in the 1960s and 1970s that the federal prison system was the perfect place for experiments with brainwashing unruly or litigious prisoners.[85] Suspected militants were to be sent into solitary confinement until they complied.[86] Dr. James V Bennett, who was director of the U. S. Bureau of Prisons, had this to say about the new techniques: "In my judgment the prison system will increasingly be valued, and used, as a laboratory and workshop of social change."[87]

In the 1950s and 1960s, as part of the general funding of the behavioral sciences, the government sponsored research into torture, beginning with captured German POWs, employing Nazi collaborators, and following up on Nazi research into methods of information extraction from hypnosis to electroshock therapy.[88] LSD and other hallucinogens were administered to unsuspecting American soldiers, over a thousand of whom developed psychiatric illnesses. As part of its MK-Ultra project, the CIA funded Dr. Ewan Cameron at McGill University, who was later to become the first chair of the World Psychiatric Association as well as president of the American and Canadian psychiatric associations. Through a front-group operating secretly out of Cornell University, Cameron conducted research on mind control through "terminal" experiments that went far beyond legal and moral bounds.[89] Included in testimony on March 15, 1995, before the President's Advisory Committee on Human Radiation Experiments, are statements by victims of this and related programs that they were subjected to trauma-based mind-control programming to mold them into "robot" spies, assassins, and sexual blackmailers.[90] In other widespread experiments, children, allegedly retarded, were administered LSD.[91] MK-Ultra work was contracted out to numbers of prestigious institutions such as the University of London, Harvard University, McGill University, the National Institutes of Health, and the Rockefeller Foundation among dozens of others.[92]

It was out of these billions of dollars of research that the "no-touch torture" that we believe to be so civilized was developed to add to the repertoire of the state. Using disorienting techniques and self-inflicted pain to make the subject responsible for his own suffering, the new psychological torture removes the visible insignia of external control. Thus, from the Cold War funding of the sciences of society and psyche, we get the two monstrous weapons of invisible control in the total state, the bureaucratic language that perpetuates social control through its domination of discourse and the psychological torture of individuals which that discourse permits.

Are we still shocked at Abu Ghraib? Can we still suggest it is an aberration? The truth that liberal journalism will not concede can be pieced together easily from the reports placed haphazardly before us. This is what we can conclude from what we know so far:

Abu Ghraib is part of a deliberate policy. Seymour Hersh reports on Copper Green, a Special Access Program that allows special forces to "grab whom you will, do what you must."[93] But the SAP is only one of several programs. The FBI memos also describe Wolfowitz's order to interrogators to masquerade as FBI agents they could then later scapegoat. The memos hint at several similar clandestine operations intended to escape legal accounting and there is oblique evidence of these operations elsewhere—in January 2004, the respected think tank, Global Security, wrote that the Bush government had filtered more money into their "black budget" than any other administration in American history, some $30 billion that month. Black budgets usually fund black ops—highly sensitive and secret projects, such as assassination squads. Another item, a proposal to prevent intelligence agents from torturing prisoners, was dropped when it was adamantly opposed by the House, which also refused to include it in any form in the intelligence overhaul bill in January 2005. [94]

The policy is organized and secret. "The entire operation was so mysterious that all persons involved in the operation, including US troops, were wearing masks." The *New York Times* describes how a Yemeni student suspected of links to Al Qaeda, is bundled aboard a jet to Jordan by white men wearing masks; the student has since disappeared.[95] Hidden railway cars, far-off tropical islands, ships isolated at sea, private jets flying between continents, prisoners packaged and bound with duct tape, gagged and hooded—this is the global mini-gulag of empire. At Camp Echo, the CIA facility built in 2003 at Guantanamo, a secret site, unmentioned in public, holds dozens of "ghost" detainees, unregistered and unregulated.[96]

The CIA has at least one jet of its own for whisking prisoners around the globe—"a Gulfstream V turbojet, the sort favored by CEOs and celebrities [that] ... since 2001 ... has been seen at military airports from Pakistan to Indonesia to Jordan, sometimes being boarded by hooded and handcuffed passengers." Registered to a fictitious corporation and directed by fictitious humans, it has "permission to use U.S. military airfields worldwide." Its travels give us a glimpse of the boundaries of the mini-gulag: "Since October 2001 the plane has landed in Islamabad; Karachi; Riyadh, Saudi Arabia; Dubai; Tashkent, Uzbekistan; Baghdad; Kuwait City; Baku, Azerbaijan; and Rabat, Morocco. It has stopped frequently at Dulles International Airport, at Jordan's military airport in Amman and at airports in Frankfurt, Germany; Glasgow, Scotland; and Larnaca, Cyprus."[97]

The policy is part of an international criminal effort. Bob Baer, a former CIA operative in the Middle East, suggests, "If you want a serious interrogation you send a prisoner to Jordan. If you want them to be tortured you send them to Syria. If you want someone to disappear . . . you send them to Egypt."[98] Among the countries where prisoners are sent is Uzbekistan, a dictatorship notorious for police torture that reportedly includes immersion in boiling water.[99]

Maher Arar, a naturalized Canadian citizen on a Canadian flight, was arrested at New York in September 2002 by U.S immigration, made to sign a document permitting his deportation to Syria where he was held in a "coffin" (a hole in the ground) and tortured with metal whips. Arar was proved to have no ties whatsoever to terrorism, yet it was only a Canadian police raid on a veteran journalist who had written about the affair that provoked public outrage and finally led to an investigation.[100]

Abu Ghraib is the export of America's internal gulag. In May 2003, Ashcroft appointed an envoy to help "restore law and order in Iraq" by remaking Iraqi prisons on the American model. Through the International Criminal Investigative Training Program (ICITAP), the envoy decided on everything from the number of bunks per prison to the training of Iraqi prison guards. Since its inception in 1986, ICITAP has been on numbers of missions from Haiti to Indonesia, a successor to the U.S. AID training programs that trained police and prison officials around the world in techniques of murder and torture, mostly against leftist insurgencies.

On the Iraq team were a group of Republican-appointed prison bureaucrats turned private managers with dismal histories of prisoner abuse. As director of the Utah Department of Corrections in the 1980s, Gary DeLand was charged repeatedly with denying prisoners adequate medical treatment and subjecting them to cruel and unusual punishment. In 1981, DeLand was sued by a mentally ill prisoner charged with disorderly but nonviolent conduct who was kept naked for 56 days in a "strip cell," described in court documents as having "no windows, no interior lights, no bunk, no floor covering, and no toilet except for a hole in the concrete floor which was flushed irregularly from outside the cell." John Armstrong, the assistant director of operations of American prisons in Iraq, was once commissioner of Connecticut's Department of Corrections. In a 2001 Amnesty International report on abuse of women in prisons, Connecticut was used as an example of how not to treat female prisoners. The allegations against the prison system there included sexual assault and voyeurism by male guards.

With these veterans of the state prisons go the history of American prisons, from Chicago in the 1970s and 1980s, where electroshock, oxygen deprivation, hanging on hooks, the bastinado (beating of the soles of the feet), and genital assault were used—principally on black or brown prisoners—to facilities today, where prisoners are confined 23 hours a day in concrete boxes for years and are electroshocked with 50,000-volts administered through a belt they are forced to wear. One prisoner in California's Pelican Bay State Prison was even thrown into boiling water.[101]

Rape, especially sodomy of male prisoners, is endemic. According to Terry Kupers, a psychiatrist who testifies about human rights abuses in U.S. prisons, "The plight of prisoners in the USA is strikingly similar to the plight of the Iraqis who were abused by American GIs. Prisoners are maced, raped, beaten, starved, left naked in freezing cold cells and otherwise abused in too many American prisons."[102]

Abu Ghraib repeats systematic torture practices used by foreign militaries and intelligence services. Forced standing, "the crucifixion," was prevalent in Western European armies in the early twentieth century and was also used by the police in the United States, by Stalin's NKVD, and the Gestapo. It blows up extremities to twice their size causing blisters, fainting, and kidney failure. It was the third most common torture during apartheid, after beating and electricity.[103] Hooding was a common feature in Brazilian and South African torture. The Brazilians also used a technique called "the Vietnam," which combined the tortures of the North Vietnamese—forced standing—with those of the United States and South Vietnam—electrical torture using field phones. At Abu Ghraib, the "Vietnam" reappears. Israeli torture also replicates the experience of Iraqi prisoners. Overhead cameras continuously monitor torture sessions and photographs of the raped women are circulated among the victim's neighbors to humiliate and coerce.[104]

Abu Ghraib repeats systematic practices used by the CIA earlier and elsewhere. After it was codified in the CIA's Kubark Counterintelligence Interrogation manual in 1963, "no-touch torture" was disseminated globally to police in Asia and Latin America through USAID's Office of Public Safety (OPS). Among other techniques enumerated in KUBARK, prisoners are photographed in humiliating postures to disorient and control them. The manual was widely disseminated in Central America during the 1980s even after OPS was shut down by an angry Congress in 1975.[105] The infamous CIA-run School of the Americas in Fort Benning, Georgia, which trains Latin American military personnel, has also advocated the use of torture and disseminated manuals teaching torture methods, as the Pentagon admitted in 1992.[106] Ostensibly, the CIA no longer does so, but changes made to the school since then appear to be cosmetic, and since 9/11, additional funding and students have reportedly been flowing in.[107]

Elite forces have been trained to use some of the worst techniques. At a top-secret site near Baghdad's airport, in six interrogation rooms at the battlefield interrogation facility (BIF), Delta Force soldiers routinely drugged prisoners, held them under water to mimic drowning, or smothered them almost to suffocation. The techniques were intended to be used elsewhere. It appears that some of the worst incidents of torture involved special forces. At Mahmoudiya, "a Marine guard squirted alcohol-based sanitizer" on a prisoner, lit a match and ignited him, leaving second-degree burns and blisters on the back of the hand.[108] The Army unit that set interrogation guidelines for Abu Ghraib, 519th Military Intelligence, came there from Kabul, where it had worked closely with the CIA in learning torture techniques that left at least one Afghani prisoner dead.[109]

The torture policy uses Israelis agents and trainers. Before the invasion, U.S. forces were sent to Israel to train for urban warfare and intelligence, reportedly studying Israeli tactics in the assault on the Palestinian refugee camp in Jenin in 2002.[110] Methods studied included targeted assassinations and collective punishments, both forbidden under international law. In late 2003, the United States also brought urban warfare specialists from the IDF to Fort Bragg, North Carolina, the headquarters of Special Forces.[111] Modifications made by Israel and clearly adopted by the United States for interrogations of Arab captives include constant references to sex, forced nude role-play as dogs, and simulated sex. These acts were apparently photographed and shown to the detainee or to family.[112] Israeli officials, however, have denied involvement at the Abu Ghraib prison. Foreign Minister Silvan Shalom dismissed the claims by Brigadier General Janis Karpinski that Israeli soldiers were there as "completely baseless."[113] However, Seymour Hersh's reports as well as a photograph of an IDF soldier at the prison that was widely published on the Internet, appears to contradict him.

It repeats Cold War justifications to escape legal or moral constraints. In the 1950s, when the Pax Americana demanded that any Soviet challenge anywhere be met with "genocidal atomic warfare" because "hitherto acceptable norms of human behavior do not apply," espionage and torture were, of course, de rigueur.[114] But at the end of the Cold War, despite the disappearance of the Soviet KGB and the East German Stasi, the United States still managed to hang on to its spy agency. It exempted the CIA's psychological torture methods through intricately constructed reservations to the UN Convention Against Torture, which

Congress had ratified.[115] Once the war on terror started, these so-called "stress and duress" techniques reappeared and have now expanded to include extended food, sleep, sensory, or water deprivation, exposure to extreme heat or cold, and "position abuse" designed to cause pain or humiliation. "Torture lite," with its pretension to scientific precision and avoidance of obvious brutality, simply normalizes the "third degree" of earlier American police practice. Relevant to this stealth resumption of torture is the fact that America's close ally, Israel, has also recently reinstated it. Although Israel's Supreme Court ruled that torture was illegal under any circumstances in 1999, its security agency, Shin Bet, returned to it as policy after the second Palestinian intifadah against the Israeli occupation in September 2000. Israel used an authorization similar to the Justice Department memos to the Pentagon that claimed anti-torture international laws "may be unconstitutional" as they relate to the war on terror.[116]

It targets Muslims with religious and sexual torture meant to destroy the psyche. In late 2002 an FBI agent at Guantanamo observed a female interrogator, Sergeant Lacey, whisper to and caress a handcuffed and shackled detainee during Ramadan, Islam's holy month when contact with females is particularly offensive to a Muslim man. The agent saw the interrogator squeeze a detainee's genitals and bend back his thumbs. Her treatment of other detainees left them curled in fetal positions on the floor crying in pain.[117] In October 2002, another FBI agent saw a detainee "gagged with duct tape that covered much of his head" because he would not stop chanting from the Koran.[118] Also in September or October of 2002, FBI agents saw a dog used "in an aggressive manner to intimidate a detainee." Dogs are considered impure by many traditional Muslims who do not keep them in the house. About a month later, agents saw the same detainee "after he had been subjected to intense isolation for over three months ... totally isolated in a cell that was always flooded with light." By late November, he was "talking to nonexistent people ... hearing voices (and) crouching in a corner of the cell covered with a sheet."

One of the Guantanamo detainees, a Yemeni Muslim named Fahmi Abdullah Ahmed, had the hair on his head shaved in the shape of a Christian cross. Ahmed believed it to be a religious taunt by his captors.[119] Detainees who seemed religious were forced to endure aggressively sexual behavior by provocatively dressed female interrogators or by alleged prostitutes. Female interrogators have even smeared "menstrual blood" on some detainees to break them.[120]

Systematic targeting of Islam was the charge in a *Newsweek* article, denounced by the government and later retracted by the magazine, that the Koran had been mishandled, and in one instance, flushed down the toilet.[121]

Yet none of this has provoked anything like a public outcry or a demand for investigation, even though the Koran is seen by Muslims as the physical embodiment of divinity, not merely a transcription of religious truth. It is regarded in the same way as the Communion host is by Catholics. Its desecration is thus the literal desecration of the divine.

This intentional nonchalance betrays a selective amnesia. In failing to acknowledge the systematic and purposive nature of such violence, we unwittingly expose the dark underbelly of our own rationality, as fundamentalist as any fundamentalist religion. In reality, the terror that haunts America, that appears to it as nightmarish threats from abroad, flaunts itself in these acts in cells hidden from the public gaze as the repressed of the liberal democratic state. Here the shock of violence that is sent abroad in aerial bombardment returns in the awe of what reveals itself uncannily in scenes emerging from an *abaissement du niveau mental*. They flood the consciousness with their unassimilated and terrifying psychic content, showing us again in the heart of rationality the seeds of the irrational; displaying to us tattooed on the sinews of the corporate state the insignia of religion. Abu Ghraib is the *return of the repressed*.

10
Ideology II: The Tower of Babel

Like the repressed, history returns. Self-directed, self-interested man looks into a warped mirror and finds *homo religiosis*. The sublime of religion that appalls us, also fascinates. What shows itself in the scenes of prison abuse does not appear as only defensive, the planned, rational response of threatened modernity but as something more burdened with emotion, something that simmers under the glassy surface of "no-touch," something sharp, frenzied, even exhibitionistic. It calls attention to itself. Underneath the neoliberal rhetoric of a defensive war of modernity against the rise of a new barbarism, we must ask if we find instead a war of religion, an aggressive war against an ancient enemy, a new crusade.

General William Boykin has described the battle against Islamic terrorists as a clash between Christianity and "a guy named Satan" and has suggested that Christians need to support the divine plan that has put Bush in office. In January 2003 Boykin remarked publicly that "Allah" was an idol. In June 2002 he showed a congregation photographic evidence of what he considered a demonic presence in Mogadishu, the capital of Somalia.[1] It was Boykin who briefed his boss, Under Secretary of Defense Stephen Cambone, on Miller's visit to Abu Ghraib. It was Boykin who encouraged the directive to change policy there along the lines that had proved so effective at Guantanamo.

Boykin represents the enormous influence of fundamentalist Christians, many of whom have made a significant contribution to Bush's election. Religious language seems to drench the administration. For instance, "Rods from God" is the name for the bundles of tungsten rods fired from orbiting platforms that hurtle down to earth at 3,700 meters per second and destroy even underground targets anywhere on the planet in a few minutes.[2]

Christian Zionists constitute a vocal 3 million of America's 98 million evangelicals and with the 30 million other Christians who have Zionist beliefs have long been the mainstay of U.S. support for Israel,[3] operating through such political groups as the powerful Council for National Policy, which has included John Ashcroft, Pat Robertson, Jerry Falwell, and Oliver North among its members.[4] The only non-Jew ever to receive the Jabotinsky medal for services to Israel, Falwell was permitted by President Reagan to attend NSC briefings, while best-selling Armageddon author Hal Lindsey was allowed to speak on nuclear war to top Pentagon strategists. Lindsey's 1970's best-seller, the *Late Great Planet Earth*,[5] is responsible for bringing to worldwide fame the dispensationalist view that since the return of the Jews to Israel, history has been unfolding according to Revelations.[6]

Apocalyptic millennialists like Tim LaHaye, one of the authors of the *Left Behind* novels, believe that a worldwide conflagration centered in the Middle East will be the prelude to the return of Christ.[7] Other fundamentalists like the dominionists focus on the present world, seeking to remake the United States as a country under biblical law. In recent years, some evangelicals have targeted as their priority a swathe of the world dubbed "the 10/40 window" (North Africa, the Middle East, and Asia between 10 degrees and 40 degrees north latitude) for conversion.[8]

What all these groups have in common is support for the Iraq war, a belief that Islam is false, and faith in Zionism. Christian Zionists advocate the unconditional support for Israel, the return of all Jews to Israel, the legitimacy of the West Bank settlements, a greater, *Eretz*, Israel that spreads from and includes Jerusalem, and the rebuilding of the Temple of Solomon on the present site of the sacred Al-Aqsa mosque. The power of this pro-Israeli lobby ensures that Israel receives $3–8 billion annually from the United States in aid and military assistance and that House members of both parties are neutered on the subject of Israel. In March 2002, Senator Inhofe stated in a speech on the Senate floor that he supports Israel because God said so.[9] It was the same Inhofe who claimed that he was more outraged by the outrage over Abu Ghraib than over the treatment of the prisoners. "They're murderers, they're terrorists, they're insurgents. Many of them probably have American blood on their hands. And here we're so concerned about the treatment of those individuals."[10] Should we draw a connection between Inhofe's Zionist beliefs and his view of Iraqi prisoners?

Franklin Graham, whose father, Billy, converted Bush, has called Islam evil, and fundamentalists routinely mischaracterize Islam as idolatry, paganism, or a cult.[11] One former leader of the Southern Baptist Convention has even called the prophet Muhammad a "demon-possessed pedophile."[12]

Is it too much to suggest that some evangelicals' beliefs about Muslims might coincide with those of politicians who for other reasons might find detention and torture the best response to a recalcitrant population? When terrorism is seen as either religious extremism or violent heresy, the rooting out of that heresy may take such medieval forms as the scourging of the body in which the heretical spirit lodges. In this way, apocalyptic Christianity joins with the corporate state in the disciplining of flesh and the prisoner posed in the "Vietnam" like a hooded Christ recalls us uncannily to both the Inquisition of Catholic Spain and the witch-hunts of the Puritan forebears of America.

Israel First

But while it is true that Christian Zionists are numerically powerful, their rise in importance in American politics has only coincided with the rise of Jewish Zionists in the late 1960s and '70s. During the Yom Kippur War in 1973, an oil crisis was caused by the oil cartel OPEC's embargo of the Western nations that supported Israel in the war, sending shock waves into the Western economies and acquainting them with the power of Arab nationalist sympathy for Palestine. Other new intellectual currents were also strengthening support for that power—feminism, third world nationalism, anti-colonialism, environmentalism, and a peace movement aimed at de-nuclearizing the world. Under the impact of these, Western Europe, the U.K., and Japan began to rethink their reflexive support for Israel. The Soviet Union, long sympathetic to the Palestinian cause, clamped down on its Jewish population, which was by then openly demonstrating for Israel.[13] In 1975, the UN General Assembly passed Resolution 3379 condemning Zionism as "racist" by 72 to 35, and it became transparent that Israel's time as a race-based settler state was marked.[14]

Only at this point did neoconservatives make their transition from left to right, claiming they had seen the light on the need for US military muscle to keep the world safe from communism. More accurately, they had come to realize that American military and financial aid, as well as a favorable population ratio, was the best bulwark against any future transformation of Israel from a Jewish state into merely a state for Jews. The Arab womb was the real weapon of mass destruction they feared. [15]

Threatened by the fledgling power of the Arab states, Israel began systematically organizing the influential and wealthy diaspora in the West, labeling any perception of similarity between Nazi and Zionist policies as "communist" and fostering a general intellectual reaction against the emergence of the postcolonial world.[16]

It is this secular history that provides the context for the emergence of the anti-Arabism whose visible face we see in the extraordinarily demeaning images of Abu Ghraib. Through Hollywood, the media, government-related lobbies, law firms and academia, the diaspora began a campaign to dehumanize the Arab and sought to make common cause with other constituencies, the defense industrial complex, and then the Christian Right. In 1980, the wooing of the Right received the official sanction of the Israeli government, and an "International Christian Embassy" in Jerusalem was established whose function was and remains to coordinate worldwide Christian support for Israel and for Jewish settlement of the West Bank.[17] Enter Christian Zionism to the center stage of American politics.

Jewish Zionism

But reading history in these terms lays one open to the charge of anti-Semitism, for why should one see in Zionism anything anti- Arab unless the intent were to de-legitimize the Jewish homeland?

That objection is not tenable on several counts. First, the record indicates that on certain issues the American media apparently acts in a prearranged concert on cue from the Israeli lobby.

Edward Herman, author of several influential works on the American media, describes how in 1979, when Israel was under world pressure to end the "redemption of the land" program, the Jonathan Institute in Israel brought U.S. officials and journalists like Bush, Will, Senators Jackson and Danforth, the historian Paul Johnson, and others together to script their response—the PLO was to be labeled a terrorist group tied to Moscow, and Israel was to be portrayed as the victim. In Washington in 1984, the same script was reiterated to Secretary of State George Shultz, ambassador to the UN Jean Kirkpatrick, Senator Moynihan, Daniel Schorr, and Ted Koppel of NBC. Herman argues that the Israeli lobby in America, no longer satisfied with the pro-Israeli slant of the *New York Times, Washington Post,* and CNN, would now like to actually black out inconvenient facts with the countercharge of anti-Semitism.[18] Thus, elected officials who have dared to criticize Israel, such as Republican Senators Percy and Findley and Democrat Representatives, Hilliard and McKinney, have been thwarted in their bids for office.[19] On campus, the campaign for divestment of stock in Israel has been dubbed "anti-Semitic in effect, if not intent" by Harvard president Lawrence Summers.[20] Pro-Israeli watchdog groups, CAMERA (Committee for Accuracy in Middle Eastern Reporting in America) and FLAME (Facts and Logic About the Middle East) intimidate print or TV journalists who contradict the official line, attacking even the *National Geographic* and the *Encyclopedia Britannica* for "unabashed inventions." The influence of the Christian Right can be denounced—and is so routinely—without heads rolling, but any imputation of a pro-Israeli bias is liable to call down an avalanche of letter writing orchestrated by the Anti-Defamation League, the B'nai Brith, and a host of Jewish groups whose influence on Capitol Hill is the elephant in the room that everyone acknowledges and no one talks about.

The second reason why the anti-Semitism charge founders is evident from the nakedly racial language of some influential Zionists in Israel. Jewish ultra-nationalists like Gush Emunim are not simply nationalists. They assume that the Jewish people "are not and cannot be a normal people," because the covenant God made with them at Mount Sinai transcends the "human notions of national rights."[21] This refutes entirely the classical Zionist claim that only by emigrating to Palestine and forming a Jewish state could the Jews become like any other nation. According to Rabbi Aviner of Gush Emunim, "while God requires other normal nations to abide by abstract codes of 'justice and righteousness,' such laws do not apply to Jews." When the Israeli Haredim (ultra-Orthodox) refused to donate or receive blood transfusion from non-Jews, because their blood was "impure," they were supported by many distinguished Israeli rabbis, including former chief rabbi Mordechay Eliyahu.[22] Ultra-nationalists and fundamentalists heavily influence the Israeli government, especially Ariel Sharon's right-wing Likud. Gush Emunim members, who constitute a significant percentage of IDF's elite units, reportedly exhibit greater brutality toward Palestinians, a brutality justified by the twin senses of historical persecution and incipient crisis that characterize Jewish exceptionalists for whom criticism of Israel inevitably invokes the Holocaust.

Zionism is an ideology of blood and soil, for the ideology of even secular Zionism involves "Jewishness," even though there is no racially pure separate group of Jews.[23] You would not know these things from the American media, however, which characterizes Israel as a Western liberal democracy and treats Zionism as any other nationalism. Charles Krauthammer describes Israel as "the world's one Jewish state, and the only democratic state in the Middle

East,"[24] while the *Los Angeles Times* editorializes that "Israel must remain a Jewish state."[25]

And what are the policies of this bulwark of secularism, human rights, and democracy? Employment, housing, and access to services follow a discriminatory pattern with the best going to Ashkenazi Jews from Europe and the worst to "Israeli Arabs," that is, Palestinians within the 1948 borders. By the Law of Return, Israel must accommodate any Jews from anywhere who might at any time migrate to Israel. But it cannot accommodate the indigenous Palestinian population that fled Israeli terror in 1948 if they wished to return. Israeli identity cards can list the official ethnicity of a person but not the nationality. Since 1967 to date, Israel has arbitrarily detained over 630,000 Palestinians. In 1989 alone, Israel detained 50,000 Palestinians, representing 16 percent of the entire male population of the West Bank and Gaza Strip between the ages of 14 and 55. By contrast, that same year, out of a total African population of 24 million in South Africa, no more than 5,000 or 0.2 percent were detained for security offenses under apartheid.[26] Palestinians have the highest rate of incarceration in the world—approximately 20 percent of Palestinians in the occupied territories have, at one time, been arbitrarily detained by Israel.

Without knowing this history, we cannot follow the trail of blood that leads from Iraq to Palestine, from the torture at Abu Ghraib to the practices of the IDF. And not seeing that trail, we think of Abu Ghraib as error, or incompetence, or folly when it was none of these. It was not a matter of "security" or "law and order," but a part of a war on the population, a war in which torture had a specific role, the same role it has in Gaza, to intimidate the population into submission.

Yet having said this, it is also true that Zionism as an analytic tool is somewhat elusive. It explains why some of the prominent players act as they do but does not fully explain why what they do is effective. The real question is why the language of religious chauvinism and superior civilization has such purchase with the American public.

American Exceptionalism

If Zionism finds a responsive chord, it is because America itself is convinced of its unique national destiny—a belief that powerfully influences its foreign policy. "Manifest destiny," as it is termed, ultimately has religious roots that can be traced to the Calvinist doctrine of the elect, the 144,000 souls who are predestined for salvation not because of their inner righteousness but because the worldly success that accompanies their deeds is seen as a mark of providential favor.[27] This exceptionalism is no more purely religious but secular; it is the American civic religion.[28]

In this secular religion, to believe oneself "favored" rather than "blessed" is to believe that one's status as the chosen is derived from the success, not the rightness, of one's acts; from the power that makes one's representations alone real and others' unreal. It is this power, to which the will of our enemies is irrelevant, that is behind both the "shock and awe" bombing of Iraq and its "virtual" counterpart, the pornographic torture of prisoners. Thus, a senior Bush aide states in a much quoted exchange, "We're an empire now, and when we act, we create our own reality. ... We're history's actors ... and you, all of you, will be left to just study what we do."[29] Abu Ghraib is the end result of this solipsism of the Promethean state that is shared by both Zionist as well as non-Zionist actors.

Both also share a unique relationship to the law that suggests why it may not be possible to look to the law and legal institutions alone as the answer to Abu Ghraib. Both groups share the heritage of covenant theology that reads Holy Scripture as the record of legal contracts between God and man, a heritage that both privileges the law while simultaneously promoting a sense of not being subject to it.[30] The written contract binds us, but the interpretation of that contract is not left to us but to the state whose authority is granted by the law. Take for instance a Justice Department memo dated January 9, 2002. It refuses to find international law applicable to President Bush in his detention of Al Qaeda or Taliban members but finds the same law applicable to terrorist suspects and insists that they can be prosecuted under it. Perhaps this is only common hypocrisy, but one can also see it as inextricably bound up with the Promethean doctrine of an American state beyond specific laws because it embodies the very contract between God and man that undergirds all particular laws. We can see in it the legacy of the doctrine of Sola Scriptura, resonant in American religious history, which recognizes the Bible as the Word of God not primarily because of logical or historical arguments but by the enlightenment of the Holy Spirit's "internal testimony," a mystery that is ultimately impenetrable to rationality.[31] In the Promethean state the thin veil of reasoning that the law normally draws over state action has been rent and power radiates alone. Unchecked by any countervailing force, it is by virtue of that fact touched with the divine.

From covenant theology also derives the literalism of the brand of nineteenth-century evangelism—dispensationalism—that Falwell and Roberts practice, which permeates even secular culture. Dispensationalists read the final book of the Bible, Revelations, as a literal account of a postwar progression to a world-consuming conflagration, Armageddon. In doing so, they discount the importance of reason, learning, or social consensus in their interpretations in favor of what they see as a literal reading of the biblical text. Parallel to this is their reading of human history as a literal record where that text transparently reveals itself. Dispensationalists, like Fukuyama, see history winding down, although in their version the denouement ends in apocalypse.

From fundamentalism also comes another trait of secular culture, a distaste for any mediation between man and God, whether through priesthoods of men or through the elaborate rationality of philosophy. This distaste would lead one to infer that Americans would also have an aversion for the regulations of contracts and laws. But, paradoxically, in a popular culture filled with anti-intellectualism, the written Constitution like the written Scripture holds a privileged position. The paradox might only be apparent. Just as fundamentalism disdains mediation, an anti-intellectual culture might find an oral tradition based on a continuing interpretative dialogue between past and present actually less attractive than the fixed guidelines of a written contract, whether made between one nation and another or between nations and God. In other words, the mechanism of the Constitution, like the text of Scripture or the language of law, could actually become a convenient tool to avoid working out the ongoing difficulties of the political world and to elude rather than meet its demands. Politics ultimately demands mastery over reality whereas the law requires only external conformism to certain specified criteria. So, the mechanism of the law not only tends to relieve us of the burden of competence, it ultimately fails to check aggression. Instead, aggression expresses itself not outside law, but through it. Scriptural and legal limits come to mark the boundary beyond which feelings of empathy or compassion need not run. Those not chosen become, in Kipling's words, the "lesser breeds without the law."[32] The literalism of the Armageddonists, their faith that the biblical text translates directly into events unfolding in history, is bound up completely with this sense they have of enacting history as subjects and being set apart through history and law from those whose histories and beings are objects to be written or acted upon.

It is this sanctified contempt for the Other that is at the heart of Abu Ghraib and militates against any reading of it as a war crime of errant individuals. The half-dozen reservists are no more than scapegoats in a program of racial and religious abasement that was conceived as completely legitimate. The photographs horrify us precisely because they express this sense of legitimacy, much as the postcards of the 1920s depicting laughing crowds watching Negroes being lynched conveyed acceptance at the time.[33]

Such sanctified terror is rooted not only in Zionism, then, but in the sectarian beliefs of fundamentalist Christians from which many elements of the Promethean ideology are drawn. From biblical righteousness, the Promethean sense of the state as virtue incarnate; from Christian dominionism, the impetus to expand; from apocalyptic ruminations, the Promethean obsession with terror.[34] And through all of these runs an unexamined sense of supreme moral satisfaction, a Puritan certainty about the nature and precise physical location of evil in the other that is translated not simply in the messianic language of Americanism but even in the shibboleths of liberalism. Evil is outside, out there in the world, radically disordered, deserving of eradication. To fully understand Abu Ghraib, therefore, we need to shatter the linguistic policing behind which torture masquerades as "national security," "necessity," and "protecting our freedoms"; we need to free ourselves from the control of the singular language of Babel, the empire of universal law and reason. We need to comprehend the extent to which the totalizing discourse of reason itself masks those local meanings and sufferings in which humanity resides.

When we do so, what appears behind the mask is a confusion of meanings that evades easy categorization. A study of hundreds of communications by Bush, Ashcroft, Powell, and Rumsfeld between September 11, 2001, and May 2003 found four characteristics common to them—a set of Manichean distinctions between good and evil and security and danger, a description of the war on terror as a "mission," conflation of the will of God and the export of freedom and liberty by America, and claims that dissent is a national and global threat.[35] Quasi-religious language is deployed on behalf of exceptionalism, but the exceptionalism is only superficially crafted to appeal to religious sentiment. Underlying the veneer, the language is intensely inflected with attachment to the soil and fear of its violation and echoes the Zionist ideology of soil. We find repeated terms and phrases, such as "homeland," with its distinctly Germanic flavor, and "we fight them there so we don't have to fight them here." This is not the language of ethical or spiritual religion, but that of the religion of the state, of territory and power.

I have termed this ideology Promethean for its refusal to submit to objective criteria of the good or the just while claiming to represent them. Not so much abrogating law as assuming the function of law-giver, the new messianism uses the language of law for its content—human rights, justice, liberty—in order to press its claims, but its framework is intensely revolutionary. This is understandable. Overtly religious rhetoric has a poor chance of success in a country whose self-image is of a melting pot. Those who believe in the unquestioned "goodness" of American force have included not only Zionist neoconservatives —and Israel is the non-negotiable heart of neoconservatism—but Cold War hawks who once saw in the spread of communism an equally radical threat to the West.[36] Despite its religious overtones then, the rhetoric of American empire is fundamentally neither conservative nor religious in the conventional sense but expressive of an ideology of power in which religion has been consciously deployed. Under the rubric of civilizational conflict, a war of religion is invoked, but the rhetoric of religion itself conceals the more familiar language of territory and resources, the struggle of political interests.

What interests and for whose benefit? The Americanist language would suggest American national interest; the pervasive influence of Zionism would suggest Israeli. Of course, publicly if not privately, Zionists like to argue that there is no difference between the two. Ideology, which grows more powerful as the total state accelerates, smoothes over these discrepancies in words, these failures of meaning. It throws out vague threats to the "national interest" and postures aggressively behind the official narrative of a global war on terror by the universal empire. This is the propaganda discourse of Babel but what does Babel conceal? When the propaganda narrative of terror is pierced, what lies behind?

The Globalists' War

Again, it is Abu Ghraib which points us in the direction of the answer. Despite academic scorn, the book that proposed the religious and sexual torture there, Rafael Patai's *The Arab Mind*,[37] has remained "the most popular and widely read book on the Arabs in the U.S. military" in the training of special forces.[38] Since Rumsfeld has made such secret and elite units central to both the Iraq war and the "War on Terror," the popularity of the book demonstrates how crucial the torture at Abu Ghraib is to both.

Delta Force, Navy SEALs, Airforce Special Ops, Rangers, Civil Units, and Psychological Operations—the whole panoply of special forces have now become the critical heart of military operations through key appointments—U.S. Army

Chief of Staff Peter Schoomaker, a member of Delta Force whose appointment marks the first time a special forces commander has controlled the military; civilian Assistant Secretary for Special Operations Thomas O'Connell, late of the Phoenix program in Vietnam, who in the early 1980s ran the army's secret intelligence unit Grey Fox; Cambone, the ballistic missiles hawk; and Boykin, the Christian warrior.[39]

As the torture investigations expand and we find that the role of the reservists has been less significant than that of the CIA, military intelligence, and special forces, it becomes plausible that special forces have become central precisely for their unaccountability both to budgets and laws, precisely to facilitate greater brutality in interrogations, precisely to put into practice the techniques advocated by Patai. No surprise, then, that besides using shadow forces, Rumsfeld has also been intent on skirting the public sector altogether and using private contractors, accountable only to hidden cliques in the government, transferring the state's most essential function to big business.[40]

In direct contradiction of the patriotic rhetoric of Americanism, public money is siphoned off to increasingly bloated defense contractors, domestic and foreign, an outsourcing of security and intelligence that casts a dubious light on the role of Rumsfeld's ominously titled Proactive Preemptive Operating Group (P2OG). A highly classified addition to Grey Fox created in 2002, its stated aim is to "improve information collection by stimulating reactions" among terrorists, that is, by provoking terrorism.[41] To what purpose? What ends are served, when as Rumsfeld has stated publicly, victory in the war on terrorism now consists in convincing the American people that it will be a long war, or when a former CIA officer refers to counterterrorism as a "growth industry"?[42]

Cui Bono? The inexorable relationship of corporate greed to espionage and of espionage to torture demonstrates that behind the virtuous rhetoric of universal law and reason and the nationalist language of state interest and security, the Promethean state is run by transnational private interests in effective control of ideology and arms, bending both to their purposes. It is within this secretive corporate matrix, hidden from the official channels of government, deeply implicated in American and foreign intelligence operations, that we find the key to Abu Ghraib. Precisely for that reason, official investigations of abuse are likely to prove completely and deliberately ineffective, for judge and jury are drawn from the very mesh of media, industry, and military from which the problem arises.

The truth the liberal media will not acknowledge is that Abu Ghraib is the unveiled face of American empire, and that it is the financial interests of empire that the CIA and its agents serve, whether in prison or in the press. To accept this truth means derailing the comfortable locutions in which America is the exceptional superpower, an essentially righteous nation, and a force of unmitigated good in the world. It means accepting a darker vision of the country as one corrupted initially by its postwar hegemony and now slowly descending into the same abyss out of which its twentieth-century enemies have crawled. It means once and for all abandoning the ideology of exceptionalism that has kept the media and the public blinkered through revelation after revelation, not merely of individual atrocities and war crimes, but of the essentially illicit nature of the Iraq war itself and American foreign policy over Israel-Palestine, which makes it *prima facie* a crime against humanity. To be understood fully, Abu Ghraib must ultimately be seen as an integral part of that larger crime.

But for that to happen, America must first be willing to accept that it has pursued a Janus-faced approach to torture, condemning human rights abuses of which it is also systematically guilty. American torture is no less torture, especially as, even by its own admission, the new sophisticated forms are profoundly damaging because they are hidden and therefore more persistent than the older ones. While the KGB and Stasi have disbanded since the end of the Cold War, the CIA has kept its archives sealed and off- limits, and when Congress finally ratified the UN Convention Against Torture, it did so only with intricate reservations that exempted psychological torture.[43]

These reservations and exceptions in the legal edifice betray the law of the Promethean state for what it is—the means to shore up an increasingly remote elite ruling class that appropriates the machinery of government to its own ends. Despite the generous use of patriotic American rhetoric, the networks of power through which the Prometheans operate demonstrate that in the pursuit of the "global war on terror," it is transnational business and third-country interests that prevail over any legitimate national interest.

That being so, the law cannot be the answer to Abu Ghraib, and for that reason the media's insistence on the legal aspects of the issue is both irrelevant and counterproductive, for it reinforces the facade behind which the state persuades its citizens that it is just and democratic. We do not need any more self-serving trials of individual perpetrators orchestrated to serve that facade. We do not need the charade of government self-regulation. What we need instead is a broad, popular investigation of the actions of the hidden business and political elites whose bidding is done by armies and governments and who through private armies and private espionage, paid for by the public, turn the instruments of the public welfare against that welfare. We need a revelation in naked terms of the matrix of financial, racial, and religious interests from which the policies of torture emerged. Since those policies were conceived deliberately outside the regular channels of government, their investigation cannot be left to a government body or a corporate media intimidated by the business and political leadership. It must be conducted by independent media and citizens' groups. To avoid this and continue to think of Abu Ghraib as simply a war crime to be prosecuted on a case-by-case basis by the military is to surrender to the propaganda of Americanist ideology, which insists that the language of law alone is sufficient to address inequities in the structure that undergirds the law.

We have to recognize that Americanist ideology itself is possible only because there continues to exist an extreme differential in power in the world of nations. And it is that differential in power that must first be addressed. Political and economic disequilibrium has been the prerequisite for the cultural and religious chauvinism of a Rafael Patai, as in the past the pseudoscientific formulations of racism were made possible only when indigenous power had been thoroughly eroded and the European empires had arrived at the zenith of their might. Racism, while no longer overtly possible in the multiethnic empire that America is today, is still evoked subliminally through media symbolism, through the blond Jessica—and not the black Shoshana—who becomes iconic; through the golden boys of the elite special forces who are Caucasian, not colored.[44]

As such, if it needed the fall of the Soviet Union to create the power vacuum in the Middle East out of which the virulently anti- Arab formulations of the neoconservatives arise, it will need the rise of an equal countervailing force before American empire and its accompanying ideology are thwarted. Against the power of capital and technological might, new forms of power will have to be wielded—the protean power of organization and information offered by the Internet, which alone can consolidate world public opinion. It will need the rise of a new global journalism, of media voices outside empire, of critics who know their own histories and will not submit to having them rewritten by the legators of empire. Until then, the establishment media—the Western news feeds like AFP and Reuters, the media conglomerates like CBS and Fox—will continue to erase the colonial legacy of the modern world and present Abu Ghraib ahistorically as an aberration, and yet present the policy behind it as somehow vital to a righteous "war on terror." The past history of CIA covert actions in Iraq and elsewhere demonstrate how false the first assumption is. The second assumption is also a fiction created by the media. The artificial linking of Abu Ghraib to the war on terror and the linking of Israel's "terrorist" problem to America's ignores or conceals both Israel's participation in and interest in the Iraq war and the similarity of Israeli colonial practices against Palestinians and American practices against Iraqis. In other words, the media narrative is disfigured fundamentally by a refusal to admit that Abu Ghraib is not limited to the here and now but has taken place elsewhere and at other times, because to admit that would be to admit that what took place at Abu Ghraib was systematic, planned, and consistent with the ideology of the American ruling class. The roles of both Israel and the CIA immediately link Abu Ghraib to a persistent and lengthy history of Anglo-American neocolonialism in the Middle East. Israel and the CIA are the red flags that signal the imperial nature of what is taking place in Iraq.

The failure of the media on Abu Ghraib is thus a result of an erasure of history. Behind the pretense of transparency, the American media constructs the viewpoint through which we read its account of the world, omitting from that account the past that would make sense of it. Journalists subtly impose on their readers a worldview that is indebted to a position of unparalleled power while feigning ignorance of that position, the bloody history behind it, and their own complicity in that bloodshed.[45] In doing so they only reflect the autism of Western historians who continue to look at the twentieth century through the parochial lens of European fratricidal struggles and ignore the mammoth awakening of the former colonies to their own destinies. Perhaps the autism serves a purpose. A narrative in which the West wrestles first with the lesser evil of the fascist right and then the greater evil of the totalitarian left and does so on behalf of "humanity" and "human rights," that is, supposedly on behalf also of those awakening masses in the colonies, enables one to quietly erase the savage economic reality of colonialism and substitute for it the colonizer's comforting vision of the export of law to the lesser breeds.[46]

Democracy, human rights, rule of law—this is the rationale and justification of economic expropriation and it has always been so, since the earliest years of the expansion of European capitalism. Consider this chilling passage from one of the most influential early modern works of political theory, the sainted Thomas More's *Utopia*, which describe how the Utopians treat the native "other":

> But if the natives refuse to conform themselves to their laws, they drive them out of those bounds which they mark out for themselves, and use force if they resist. For they account it a very just cause of war, for a nation to hinder others from possessing a part of that soil of which they make no use, but which is suffered to lie idle and uncultivated; since every man has by the law of nature a right to such a waste portion of the earth as is necessary for his subsistence.[47]

Crudely put, this is no more than an early version of PNAC's justification of American global domination Yet the neoconservatives manifesto is only the most frank and radical exposition of a posture that the United States has held to more or less consistently, especially in its covert actions, since the end of World War II under both Democrat and Republican administrations. "Torture-lite" and the outsourcing of intelligence were after all initiated under President Clinton, not President Bush. But the blunt language of the Bush administration has this advantage that it makes it possible for us to put aside all quibbling and name Americanist ideology for what it is—the resurrection of nineteenth-century imperialism.

Consider the justifications used by the European colonists as they divided up Asia and Africa among themselves in the nineteenth century. Then, as now, the world was split into those with us and those against us; then, as now, the West, or as it is termed today, the international community, was threatened by the awakening masses; then, as now, civilization was ranged against barbarism, the democratic productive West ranged against the despotic unproductive East—then Eurasia, now West Asia; then, as now, our freedom and the "American way of life" demanded that world resources flow easily in our direction; then, as now, politicians played on vague fears of cities inundated by the tides of the poor or poisoned by mushroom clouds, subtly confusing cultural and physical annihilation.

Now, as then, the empty language of law is orchestrated with imagery and symbolism that evokes deep-seated racial anxieties; now, as then, the state-corporate complex masks its own drive for resources and markets with an ideology of moral and cultural superiority that permits conquest and dispossession of one people in the interests of another favored people.

Yet there is one important difference from the colonialisms of the past, foreign or American, nationalist and chauvinist or internationalist and universalist. There is an essential difference between empire today and the jingoism of Teddy Roosevelt or the liberal interventionism of Wilson, both great heroes of today's neoconservatives.[48] Neither Wilson nor Roosevelt operated unconstrained. America, however powerful, was still in its affinities a republic among some notably bloody empires—the British, the French, the Russian. To much of the colonized world, to whom the Great War and its successor were less anti-fascist than they were inter-imperialist and a squabble among fellow despoilers, Wilson alone seemed to champion, at least verbally, the self- determination of people and the priority of international law. Perhaps his internationalism was only a realistic assessment of how best to negotiate American power in a world where direct claims to hegemony might provoke rival powers. Perhaps the international institutions he set up were only moral and economic force-multipliers. Nevertheless, Wilson operated with constraints that the Prometheans entirely lack.

Wilson still operated in a world of limits. The Prometheans of today acknowledge no limits except of their own imagining, and at least for now the world they find themselves in allows them the self-indulgence of that imagining. With such absolute power comes absolute corruption, only not the corruption that the law easily unmasks, the simple corruption of bribery and chicanery. The occupation of Iraq displays ample evidence of that as well, but the deeper corruption that rots the institutions of America today is one legitimated by law, whose presence is revealed not in the courthouse but in the solitary recesses of prison cells hidden from the light. Torture is the insignia of this corrupt power. Torture is the deadly proof of the metastasizing cancer of American empire.

For those who recognize this, the Promethean nostalgia for pith helmets and the white man's burden betrays a dangerously aestheticized view of war and power.[49] Beneath their self-proclaimed conservatism, the new imperialists show little affinity with the original republican tradition of noninterventionism and states' rights championed in the American Constitution. Instead they display an insidious fascination with the sublime, scorn the classical libertarian tradition of rational self-interest as decadent, and mock its fear of the welfare-warfare state as isolationist. Intoxicated with their vision of Rome redux, the Prometheans remember the glories of empire and forget its other face.

But for the past victims of empire, that other face is unforgettable. To the past victims of empire, it is precisely the colonial savagery of the Iraq invasion, the colonial exploitation of the occupation, the colonial contempt of the torture and dehumanization, that cry out. And when neoconservatives idolize Churchill as the hero of Western freedom in their amnesiac tributes to the British Empire, the former colonies remember the Churchill who thought chemical gassing a fitting means to control tribesmen.[50] While neoconservatives credit him with ending the Holocaust, former colonies remember that he created another when he commandeered Bengal's harvest and starved three million.[51] When neoconservatives thrill to the heroic promise of Winnie's "blood, sweat, and tears," the former colonies recall that "Bomber" Harris began the savage fire-bombing of Dresden *before* the London Blitz, not in response. The former colonies recall that it was the British, not the Nazis, who created the earliest concentration camps during their wars against the Boers. Before the torture chambers of Saddam and before the American Phoenix program, it was in British cells that rape and electrocution were employed on the IRA.[52] Long before the CIA rendered its suspects to others for torture, the British were rendering Indians to other Indians to be tortured.[53] The former colonies know that colonialism corrupts the colonist and the colonized. But the citizens of empire today are prevented from recognizing this by an ideology that marries unfettered power to an unparalleled sense of righteousness and entitlement. We rule, it seems, not from lust for power but from the imperative of destiny.

In Sven Lindqvist's *A History of Bombing*, Lieutenant Giulio Cavotti, "leaned out of his delicate monoplane and dropped the bomb—a Danish Haasen hand grenade—on the North African oasis Tagiura, near Tripoli. Several moments later, he attacked the oasis Ain Zara. Four bombs in total, each weighing two kilos, were dropped during this first air attack."[54]

That first attack, a collective punishment of Arabs "who were resisting the advanced rationality (and occupying spirit) of the Italian army" demonstrates what that imperative is. The words of General for Allied Land Forces Thomas Blamey, printed in the *New York Times*, spell it out boldly for those who turn squeamishly away from the raw truths of power: "You know that we have to exterminate this vermin if we and our families are to live. ... We are not dealing with humans as we know them."[55]

Yesterday's vermin are today's insurgents and terrorists, and the advanced rationality that is so irresistible turns out to be technological superiority and overwhelming might.

The differential in power between the developed and developing world has been the impetus behind the frank colonialism of the post–Cold War world. At the very moment that the postcolonial world showed its strength, the terror-masters of the Pentagon—Wohlstetter, Teller, Marshall, the Team B agitators—seized the helm. The CIA, forced into making cosmetic changes to assuage the public, resurfaced with a new repertoire of nonlethal weapons and no-touch torture perfectly adapted for use by a powerful minority of elites against vast populations—silent, invisible, and acceptable to a democratic state with its innumerable internal constraints. The dominant narrative of the West describes postwar history in the Manichaean terms of the Cold War, but another narrative suggests that the Cold War may have been no more than a facet of the West's resurgent colonialism. Similarly, in the raucous domestic landscape of postwar America, the "culture wars" may only recapitulate internally the same story. On closer examination, the culture wars turn out to describe the battle between the traditional constituencies of the ruling elites and the new demographic sectors—women, blacks, gays, immigrants—whom those elites alternately seduce and coerce.

Friction between immigrants and natives, the bleeding of jobs overseas, a public humanistic culture on the East and West Coasts at odds with the Christian culture of the Midwest and the South, great swathes of the cities in a chaos of drugs and crime, fear among white men of competition from women and ethnic minorities, an anxiety about declining white birthrates and burgeoning colored ones—with the disappearance of the Soviets, a besieged America discovered itself in talk-show radio and cable and was led by them through the wilderness of the Clinton years to the promised land of Bush. The internal fears of this fractured America were carefully orchestrated and projected out as terror, the terror whose raison d'être is to permit us to terrorize. The collapse of the Soviet Union created the vacuum for Amero-Israeli expansion but the impetus was delivered from turbulence within. Fear propels American state-terror, but it is not the fear of external threat so much as fear that is stoked and fed assiduously within the state.

All that was needed was an opportune moment. A change of regime in Iraq was planned even before Bush took power in January 2001, and at that point, conveniently, history intervened and created the very circumstance that allowed that ambitious project to be put in motion.

At every turn there is unmistakable evidence of something amiss. A secret 32-page FBI report concluded recently that there were no known Al Qaeda concealed networks in the United States.[56] This conclusion was markedly at odds with testimony given by FBI director Robert Mueller in 2003 before the Senate Select Intelligence Committee in which he claimed that terrorist "sleeper cells" were the "greatest threat" to U.S. security and that several were probably in place. This sudden *volte-face* acquires a meaning when placed next to other peculiarities—remarks by President Bush and senior officials de-linking the war on terror from

Al Qaeda; the puzzlingly frequent escapes that Bin Laden seems to have engineered;[57] Rumsfeld's rapid and nonchalant admission shortly after 9/11 that it might not be possible to catch Osama;[58] the inescapable fact that almost all of the arrests of important or allegedly important Al Qaeda figures post–9/11 have been by local authorities and very few by the American military.[59] Consider that of the 120 terrorism cases reported on FindLaw, the major database for important legal cases, there have been only two actual terrorism convictions, both in the case of Richard Reid, the shoe-bomber. Consider that of eighteen charges of "terrorism" brought between September 2001 and October 2004, fifteen are still pending and one was dismissed; that of six "terrorism convictions" hailed by the president, five resulted from questionable plea bargains involving lesser charges not necessarily related to terrorism and one has not yet been tried. In only one case was there an actual conviction, not for terrorism but for the much more elusive charge, "material support for terrorism," and even that has since been overturned.[60] Consider that since September 11, 2001, deaths from terrorist attacks that could conceivably be related to the global war on terror have amounted to around a thousand or less, hardly a figure that supports the existence of a war on the scale of World War I and II as it has been constructed in the public imagination.[61]

Instead, it is at the public's imagination that the new war is directed, with its black psychological operations that erase the boundary between civilian and military, war and peace, state and non-state. Civilizational war is a literary creation, a narrative spun out of the whole cloth of psychological operations by spy agencies whose masters stand to benefit from such a war. The circumstantial evidence is overwhelming that Abu Ghraib was such an operation. The pervasive influence of the CIA, the telltale FBI memos, the opportune leaks, the convenient scapegoats, the publicizing of select photographs, the methodically calibrated torment.

Return again to the pictures from Abu Ghraib. What if Al Qaeda is only a pretext? What if the war *on* terror is really a war *of* terror? Who would benefit? What if Abu Ghraib were not the anomalous exception in an open society but a gathering shadow of darkness that creeps day by day over a society that was really never as open as it claimed to be? What if a society that has wrestled with one too many demons has come to resemble some of them?

To finally expose the truth behind Abu Ghraib, this unarticulated darkness that breathes in the heart of American politics must be expressed. The shadow culture hidden through the long years of the Cold War must at last be confronted and exorcized, not in legal inquisitions or judgments, not in prison terms or sentences, but in open hearings and relentless investigation. For a media tainted by ideological and institutional corruption, that may no longer be a task that is possible. If the coverage of Abu Ghraib demonstrates anything, it is the almost complete corruption of the establishment media into a court press, servile to power, enslaved by privilege, reluctant to challenge official lies and disinformation. It may ultimately remain to the media of the future, to Web-based activists, citizen-journalists, and people of conscience to uncover the whole truth of the imperial conquest of Iraq and the overt and hidden savagery on which it rests, for which Abu Ghraib is the deepest and truest emblem. The underrated masses of the third world, those dismissed as too poor, too ignorant, too broken by work or oppression, and the ordinary citizens of the West, those who are presumed to have succumbed to the bludgeoning of lies and calumnies of their rulers, will have to join forces, for it is ultimately they who must educate themselves and others about the reality of the global empire under which we all live and for whose actions we too are finally responsible, if not guilty. The day that citizen-army rises we will have the media we need and which every honest and just society deserves, a media that works for the welfare of all rather than a few and which puts its faith not in the duplicitous truisms by which power coerces us but in the power of truth itself, which needs no force beyond its own to win its supporters.

Notes

1. Graphic Evidence I: Photographs

1 CBS, "Abuse of Iraqi POWs by GIs Probed," April 29, 2004.

2 CNN, "Shock, outrage over prison photos," May 1, 2004.

3 Paul Majendie, "Iraqi Prison Photos Mar US Image," Reuters, April 30, 2004.

4 Amnesty International, "Iraq: Torture not isolated," amnesty.org, April 30, 2004.

5 Majendie, "Iraqi Prison Photos Mar US Image."

6 BBC/UK, "UK troops in Iraqi torture probe," May 1, 2004.

7 Ibid.

8 Andrew Woodcock, "Troops Swapped Hundreds of Torture Pictures," *The Scotsman,* May 2, 2004.

9 "In Washington, Annan voices hope that US and UK will discipline soldiers who beat Iraqi prisoners," statement of the UN Secretary General, New York, un.org, May 2, 2004.

10 "Angry Ex-Detainees Tell of Abuse," *Washington Post,* May 3, 2004.

11 Leon Worden, "Karpinski Interview Sparks New Call for Rumsfeld Testimony," *The Signal* (Santa Clarita, CA), July 13, 2004.

12 Sandra Laville, Richard Norton-Taylor and Helena Smith, "Inquiry into 'torture' pictures: Mirror stands firm as doubts raised over images of British abuse," *Guardian,* May 3, 2004.

13 Ibid.

14 Scott Wilson, "Angry Ex-Detainees Tell of Abuse," *Washington Post,* May 3, 2004.

15 Ibid.

16 Robin Wright, "In U.S., Seeking To Limit Damage," *Washington Post,* May 4, 2004.

17 Seymour Hersh, "Torture at Abu Ghraib," *New Yorker,* April 30, 2004.

18 Quoted in ibid.

19 CBS, *Face the Nation,* May 2, 2004.

20 Sewell Chan and Michael Amon, "Prisoner Abuse Probe Widened," *Washington Post,* May 2, 2004. The emphasis is mine.

21 "Karpinski Says She Had Warned Her Superiors About the Treatment of Iraqi Prisoners at Abu Ghurayb Detention Facility," *Newsweek,* May 2, 2004.

22 Associated Press, "Soldier's Journal Details Prison," April 30, 2004.

23 Hersh, "Torture at Abu Ghraib."

24 Reed Brody, "What About the Other Secret U.S. Prisons?" *International Herald Tribune,* May 4, 2004.

25 "A System of Abuse," *Washington Post,* May 5, 2004.

26 Mark Matthews, "Powell: Bush told of Red Cross reports," *Baltimore Sun,* May 12, 2004.

27 Associated Press, "Army says 20 prisoner abuse inquiries are under way," May 4, 2004.

28 Human Rights Watch, "A Timeline of Torture and Abuse Allegations," Counterpunch.org, May 4, 2004.

29 Human Rights Watch, "Iraq: US Treatment of Detainees Shrouded in Secrecy," hrw.org, April 21, 2004.

30 Luke Harding, "Bremer knew, minister claims," *Guardian,* May 10, 2004

31 AFP, "Former human rights minister told Bremer about Iraq detainee abuse," May 3., 2004.

32 Nermeen Al Mufti, "Bremer knew," *Al Ahram,* May 19, 2004.

33 Christian Peacemaker Team, "Report and Recommendations on Iraqi Detainees," January 2004.

34 Ben Knight, "Claims of torture in Guantanamo Bay," ABC, October 8, 2003.

35 CNN, "Doubts over UK abuse pictures," May 3, 2004.

36 Christian Davenport, "New Prison Images Emerge," *Washington Post,* May 6, 2004; Luke Harding, "Torture commonplace, say inmates' families," *Guardian,* May 3, 2004; Baumont, Bright, and Harris, "British quizzed Iraqis at torture jail," *Observer,* May 9, 2004.

37 Miles Moffeit, "Sex-assault cases from Iraq often stall," *Denver Post,* April 12, 2004; "Iraqi Children among Abused Prisoners at Abu Ghraib," *The Scotsman,* May 7, 2004.

38 Julian Borger, "Private contractor lifts the lid on systematic failures at Abu Ghraib jail," *Guardian,* May 7, 2004.

39 CBS, "Bush: Abuse is Abhorrent," May 5, 2004.

40 "Resign, Rumsfeld," *The Economist,* May 6, 2004.

41 Editorial, *St. Louis Post-Dispatch,* May 6, 2004.

2. Framing a Narrative I: Politics as the Personal

1 "America's Shame," *Guardian,* May, 2004.

2 Newt Gingrich, "Double Standards on Abu Ghraib," *Wall Street Journal,* May 7, 2004.

3 Editors, "Abuse and the Army," *Wall Street Journal,* May 6, 2004.

4 Jed Babbin, "Post Saddam Crimes At Abu Ghraib," *National Review Online,* May 3, 2004.

5 Victor Davis Hansen, "The Western Disease," *National Review Online,* December 30, 2003.

6 Victor Davis Hansen, "Abu Ghraib," *Wall Street Journal,* May 3, 2004; Seymour Hersh, "Torture at Abu Ghraib," *New Yorker,* May 10, posted online, April 30, 2004.

7 James Taranto, "Why Abu Ghraib Matters," Opinion Journal.com (*Wall Street Journal*), May 3, 2004.

8 James Taranto, "Abu Ghraib and the Academic Left," Opinion Journal.com, May 6, 2004.

9 Midge Decter, "If Rumsfeld Is Driven Out, We All Lose," *Los Angeles Times*, May 7, 2004.

10 Ann Coulter, *Hannity & Colmes*, Fox News Channel (FNC), May 5, 2004

11 Ann Coulter, "This Is War: We Should Invade Their Countries," *National Review Online*, September 13, 2001.

12 Linda Chavez, "Sexual Tension in the Military," Townhall.com/*Baltimore Sun,* May 5, 2004; Peggy Noonan, "A Humiliation for America," Opinion Journal.com, May 3, 2004.

13 Kate O'Beirne, "Kate's Take: Congressional Abuse," *National Review Online,* May 7, 2004.

14 Charles Krauthammer, "Abu Ghraib as a Symbol," *Washington Post*, May 7, 2004.

15 Tony Robinson, *Hannity & Colmes*, FNCs, April 30, 2004. Former U.S. Army sergeant and interrogation instructor Tony Robinson stated that "frat hazing is worse" than "what [was] happening in these pictures." Jonathan Last, "Paternalism and Abu Ghraib," *Weekly Standard*, May 11, 2004.

16 Rush Limbaugh, "It's Not About Us, This Is War," *Rush Limbaugh Show*, May 4, 2004.

17 Oliver North, *Hannity & Colmes*, FNC, May 11, 2004: "Obviously twisted young people with leashes and weird sex acts, the kind of thing that you might find on any college campus nowadays."

18 Scott McClellen, White House Press Conference, May 6, 2004, cited in Media Matters for America, mediamatters.org, May 7, 2004. See also, "Torture Party," Kurt Nimmo, Counterpunch.org, May 9, 2004.

19 *Rush Limbaugh Show,* May 6, 2004.

20 "Babes Doing the Torture in Iraq," *Rush Limbaugh Show,* May 3, 2004.

21 Sewell Chan and Michael Amon, "Prisoner abuse probe widened: Military Intelligence at Center of Investigation," *Washington Post*, May 2, 2004.

22 CNN, "Rumsfeld tells Congress of his failure," May 10, 2004.

23 Cal Thomas, "Sorry Spectacle," *Washington Times*, May 12, 2004.

24 Don Feder, "Iraqi Abuse?" *Front Page Magazine,* May, 2004.

25 "Jessica Lynch Story is Turning 'Into a Monster' for the Bush Administration," Linda Hurst, Common Dreams, November 16 , 2004. See also Lynch's own recollections in Rick Bragg, *I Am a Soldier, Too: The Jessica Lynch Story* (New York, Knopf, 2003). Mark Morford, in a September 5, 2003 article in the *San Francisco Chronicle*, "The Big Lie of Jessica Lynch: A $1 Mil Book Deal, Zero Memory of Any "Rescue and the Worst Book You'll Read This Year," describes the discrepancies in the account written by Bragg, who left the *New York Times* for questionable reporting.

26 Anthony Harwood and Mark Ellis, "U.S. Soldier Hits Back in Torture Storm: I Only Obeyed Orders—Lynndie England," *Mirror* (UK), May 13, 2004.

27 Tom Regan, "Six morons who lost the war," *Chrisian Science Monitor*, May 4, 2004.

28 CBS, *The Early Show,* May 6, 2004.

29 Report of the International Committee for the Red Cross, February 2004.

30 Geneva Convention relative to the Treatment of Prisoners of War, Office of the High Commissioner for Human Rights, Geneva, Switzerland. Entry into force, October 21, 1950.

31 Alberto Gonzales, Memorandum to President Bush, January 25, 2002.

32 Cofer Black, director of the CIA's Counter Terrorist Center in testimony at a joint hearing of the House and Senate Intelligence Committees, September 26, 2002. This was dated incorrectly as early 2002 in John Barry, Michael Hirsh, and Michael Isikoff, "The Roots of Torture," *Newsweek,* May 24, 2004.

33 David Enders, "Searching for Yunis—and how many others?" Iraq Occupation Watch Center, occupationwatch.org, November 28, 2003.

34 John Woestendiek, "W. Va. reservist caught up in a storm of controversy," *Baltimore Sun,* May 6, 2004.

35 David Finkel and Christian Davenport, "Records Paint Dark Picture of Guards," *Washington Post,* June 5, 2004.

36 Ibid.

37 Dennis Cauchon, Debbie Howlett and Rick Hampson, "Abuse scandal meets disbelief in hometowns," *USA Today*, May 6, 2004.

3. Framing a Narrative II: Politics as Law

1 "Rumsfeld Testifies Before Senate Armed Services Committee," *Washington Post,* May 7, 2004.

2 USCENTCOM, news release, January 16, 2004, Centcom.mil.

3 Michael Hirsh, John Barry, Daniel Klaidman, "A Tortured Debate," *Newsweek,* June 21, 2004.

4 Laura Parker, "The Ordeal of Chaplain Yee," *USA Today,* May 16, 2004.

5 Seymour Hersh, "Chain of Command," *New Yorker,* May 17, 2004.

6 "General to testify on abuse probe," CNN, May 11, 2004.

7 "Transcript: Taguba, Cambone on Abu Ghraib Report," *Washington Post,* May 11, 2004.

8 108th Congress, Senate Armed Services Committee, Hearings on prison abuse in Iraq, May 11, 2004.

9 "Is He To Blame?" *Newsweek,* May 9, 2004.

10 Human Rights Watch, "A Timeline of Torture & Abuse Allegations and Responses," Antiwar.com, May 8, 2004.

11 NBC News, Investigation of the 800th Military Police Brigade, Article 15-6, Maj. Gen. Antonio M. Taguba, Findings and Recommendations, No. 16, May 4, 2004.

12 "U.S. News obtains all classified annexes to the Taguba report on Abu Ghraib," *US News & World Report,* July 9, 2004.

13 Hersh, "Chain of Command."

14 Anthony Harwood, "Lynndie England's Jail Orgies," *Mirror*, May 15, 2004.

4. Graphic Evidence II: Video

1 Andrew Miga, "Prisoner abuse Iraq style," *Boston Herald,* May 12, 2004.

2 Sewell Chan, "Berg mystery grows murkier," *Washington Post,* May 13, 2004.

3 Jay Rosen, "News judgment old and news judgment new," PressThink.com (blog), May 16, 2004.

4 "Nick Berg's murder," *New York Post,* May 12, 2004.

5 Greg Weiher, "The Purloined Letter: The Zarqawi Gambit," Counterpunch.org, February 26, 2004.

6 See for instance, Soj's analysis on May 20, 2004, on DailyKos.com.

7 Sandy Bauers, "A life lived fearlessly, but lost too soon," *Philadelphia Inquirer*, May 16, 2004; "Berg: Timeline," *Philadelphia Inquirer,* May 12, 2004.

8 AP, "Berg's final days still a mystery," May 14, 2004.

9 Ritt Goldstein, "Berg Beheading No Way, Say Medical Experts," *Asia Times,* May 22, 2004.

10 CNN, "Berg Family Has Questions," May 12; AP, "CIA: Berg killed by al-Zarqawi," May 13, 2004.

11 "CIA: Zarqawi Behind Beheading," Fox41.com, May 14, 2004.

12 Weiher, "The Purloined Letter—the Zarqawi Gambit."

13 Rod Nordland, "Is Zarqawi Really the Culprit?" *Newsweek,* March 7, 2004.

14 "CIA: Zarqawi Behind Beheading," Fox41.com,; Katherine Shrader, "CIA Says al-Zarqawi Beheaded Berg in Iraq," AP, May 13, 2004.

15 "Video shows beheading of American captive," Bill Nichols, *USA Today,* May 11, 2004.

16 Anthony Gregory, "The Unanswered Questions of Nick Berg's Murder," Antiwar.com, May 15, 2004.

17 Andrew Buncombe, "The story of Nick Berg—the tale that haunts America," *Independent* (UK), May 13, 2004.

18 "Time Stamps on Nick Berg Videos, 2 Cameras Used," Truthteller.com, May 12, 2004.

19 DrudgeReport.com, May 10, 2004.

20 Jason Straziuso, "Diplomat's e-mail shows Berg in custody," AP, May 14, 2004.

21 Jonathan Kent, "Berg video website shutdown," BBC, May 13, 2004.

22 Lawrence Smallman, "Bloggers doubt Berg execution video," Al Jazeera, May 14, 2004.

23 CNN, "Nicholas Berg: A Life of Adventure," May 11, 2004.

24 Toby Harnden in Baghdad and Marcus Warren in West Chester, PA, "Beheaded American was arrested as a spy 'because of his Jewish name,'" *Telegraph* (UK), May 13, 2004.

25 CNN, "Nicholas Berg: A Life of Adventure," May 11, 2004.

26 "Beheaded Hostage Had Been Warned to Leave Iraq," *Guardian*, May 12, 2004; see also Sewell Chan, "Beheading victim loved adventure," *Washington Post*, May 14, 2004.

27 Straziuso, "Diplomats e-mails show Berg in custody"; "Beheaded Man's Kin in Pennsylvania Learns of Video," AP, May 11, 2004.

28 Richard Jones and Jill Capuzzo, "Slain American's family says U.S. didn't protect him," *New York Times*, May 12, 2004.

29 Deborah Horan, "Details of Berg's detention remain murky," *Chicago Tribune*, May 12, 2004.

30 Jason Straziuso, "Berg's emails reveal dangerous travels," AP, May 12, 2004.

31 Robert Reid, "Questions surround slain American in Iraq," May 12, 2004.

32 Jon Hurdle, "Berg Died for Bush, Rumsfeld 'Sins'—Father," Reuters, May 13, 2004.

33 Sandy Bauers, "Parents agonize over their son missing in Iraq," *Philadelphia Inquirer*, May 8, 2004.

34 Goldenberg and Harding, "Shock in suburbs at restless son's death," *Guardian*, May 12, 2004.

35 R. Jonathan Tuleya, "State has no records of Berg's firm," *Daily Local News*, May 14, 2004.

36 Robert Reid, "Questions Surround Slain American in Iraq," AP, May 12, 2004.

37 Harnden and Warren, "Beheaded American was arrested as a spy 'because of his Jewish name.'"

38 James Risen, "U.S. Officials Failed to Protect Slain Civilian (Nick Berg), Family Says," *New York Times*, May 13, 2004.

39 Kevin Johnson, "FBI: Agents Advised Berg to Leave Iraq," AP, May 12, 2004.

40 CBS/AP, "CIA: Top Terrorist Executed Berg," May 13, 2004.

41 AP, "Pro-war Iraqi figure may be deported from United States," *Pittsburgh Tribune-Review*, April 5, 2003.

5. Context I: The Violence of Virtue

1 Jay Rosen, "News Judgment Old and News Judgment New: American Nicholas Berg Beheaded," PressThink.com, May 6, 2004. PressThink won a freedom of expression award from Reporters Without Borders in June 2005.

2 Liberty Forum, Post 1488534, June 1, 2004.

3 Liberty Forum, Post 1488471, June 1, 2004.

4 "Jennings Spikes Beheading Culprit al-Zarqawi's Ties to al-Qaeda," Media Research Center, MRC.org, May 13, 2004.

5 Rumsfeld, DOD daily briefing, June 17, 2004.

6 Jamie McIntyre, "Rumsfeld: Al Qaeda comments 'misunderstood,'" CNN, October 5, 2004.

7 Glenn Reynolds, "Hey, the Holocaust wasn't all that bad! Look what the Americans did in Abu Ghraib!" Instapundit.com, June 25, 2004.

8 Neil Boortz, "American's Beheading Old News for Media Elite," *Washington Times*, May 22, 2004.

9 Tim Graham, quoted in Chad Groening and Jody Brown, "Media, Liberal Pols Charged with Painting One-Sided Picture of Iraqi War," AgapePress.org, May 18, 2004.

10 Jennifer Harper, "American's beheading old news for media elite," *Washington Times,* May 2004, May 14, 2004.

11 Brent Bozell, "The Media on Nicholas Berg: So What?" Town Hall.com, May 19, 2004. Town Hall is an influential website for conservative public policy organizations, congressional staff, and political activists.

12 "CBS Skips Own Poll on Prison Photo Over-Coverage, NBC Takes Up," MRC.org, May 13, 2004.

13 Dana Blanton, "Little Movement in Bush-Kerry Match-up," Fox News poll, May 20, 2004.

14 Alyssa Rubin, "Carnage Dims Hopes for Political Way in Iraq," *Los Angeles Times*, April 19, 2004.

15 Dahr Jamail, "Americans Slaughtering Civilians in Fallujah," NewStandardNews.net, April 13, 2004.

16 Rahul Mahajan, "Report from Fallujah: Destroying a Town in Order to Save It," CommonDreams.org, April 12, 2004; Helen Williams, "Fallujah: An Eyewitness Account," News Wales.com, April 14, 2004; Dan Murphy, "Siege of Fallujah Polarizing Iraqis," *Christian Science Monitor*, April 15, 2004.

17 Daryn Kagan, interview with Al Jazeera editor Ahmed Al Sheikh, CNN, *Wolf Blitzer Reports*, April 12, 2004.

18 "The Trouble with Civilian Casualty Stories," *Washington Post,* April 15, 2004.

19 Mike Whitney, "Blood Will Have Blood," Counterpunch.org, March 3, 2004.

20 Jeffrey Gettleman, "As U.S. Detains Iraqis, Families Plead for News," *New York Times*, March 7, 2004.

21 Reuters, "US troops shoot three-year-old boy," March 28, 2004.

22 Quoted in Erin Olson, "Why Doesn't the U.S. Press Quote Iraqi Papers More Often?" *Editor & Publisher,* December 1, 2004.

23 "Australian PM retracts Hassan body statement," Ireland Online, November 18, 2004.

24 Tom Englehardt, "Icarus (Armed with Vipers) Over Iraq," tomdispatch.com, December 5, 2004.

6. Context III: Theater of Pain

1 Adam Liptak, Micahel Moss, and Kate Zernike, "Accused G.I.'s Try to Shift Blame in Prison Abuse," *New York Times*, May 16, 2004.

2 Al Tompkins, "The Story Behind the Lynndie England Interview," PointerOnline.com, The Pointer Institute, May 17, 2004.

3 Bradley Graham and Josh White, "Top Pentagon Leaders Faulted in Prison Abuse: Oversight by Rumsfeld and Others Inadequate, Panel Says," *Washington Post*, August 25, 2004.

4 William J. Haynes II, Pentagon's general counsel, memorandum, "Working Group Report on Detainee Interrogations in the Global War on Terrorism," March 6, 2003.

5 Joan Dayan, "Cruel and Unusual: The End of the Eighth Amendment," *Boston Review*, October–November, 2004.

6 One inmate's account is found in Timothy Greenlee, "The Walk of Shame," Timothy's Diary, March 25, 2003:

> "Officers Horton and Baum came to my cell and told me to "strip"! I complied. Officer Horton said: "Back up into the center of your cell and turn around. Arms in the air. Bend over and spread your cheeks. Put on a pair of underwear only." I said: "I have none." He said:

"You'll have to go naked then." And smiled an evil smile. I said: "I'm not leaving this cell naked. I want to speak to a Sergeant." Glaring at me Officer Horton walked down the 600 range and came back with Sergeant Merrit. I heard Merrit say: " … he'll have to just go naked then!" Sergeant Merrit then glared at me and said belligerently: "Turn around and cuff up!" I warily complied. I had no idea what was going on! It's always like that around here. They treat me like a mushroom—Keep me in the dark and feed me bullshit! So, naked as I came into this world, I was led down the top range, then down the stairs, then out cross the bottom range with crazy men screaming and laughing and whistling, making fun of me. I was led out into the B-East core area, out into the B- end main hallway, and into B-West core area and then onto 1100 range, up the stairs, down the top range and was then placed inside the shower stall, once again listening to the offenders screaming obscenities, jeering and making fun of me. After about an hour or so, officers Wright and Stifal came and got me and led me back, naked as before, the same way I'd come, out of 1100, B-West, across the hall and then back to my cell in B- East 611, again the object of jeering and catcalls from other offenders because I was naked. My cell had been absolutely trashed, yet again. All of my pitiful belongings had been searched and then unceremoniously dumped into a pile in the center of the cell."

7 "Background on Super Maximum Security (Super Max) Isolation Units," Everett Hoffman, Executive Director, American Civil Liberties union of Kentucky, *The Advocate*, Vol. 21, No. 1, January, 1999.

8 Cited in Mike Walsh, "Black Hoods and Iron Gags: The Quaker Experiment at Eastern State Penitentiary in Philadelphia," Eastern State Penitentiary official website. The Pennsylvania model, as it was called, was originally felt to be more humane and thought to encourage introspection and remorse among inmates.

9 Jessica Mitford, "The Torture Cure: In Some American Prisons, It Is Already 1984," *Harper's*, August 1973.

10 Fox News, "White House: Berg's Killers Will Face Justice," May 21, 2004.

11 "Will We See Beheading of Nick Berg?" *Rush Limbaugh Show*, May 11, 2004.

12 Sen. Joseph Lieberman, "Let Us Have Faith, Why Rumsfeld Must Stay," Opinion Journal (*Wall Street Journal* editorial page), May 14, 2004.

13 Dr. Walid Phares, "The Beheading of an Innocent," Front Page Magazine, frontpagemag.com, May 12, 2004. "There are many reasons why now is an opportune time for the Christians of the Middle East to consolidate their relationship with the American Jewish community," Dr. Phares said at a press conference in New York on December 11, 1994, to mark a joint declaration between several Middle Eastern Christian groups and far-right pro-Israel Jewish organizations, such as Likud America and the Jersualem Reclamation Project (website of the Manfred and Ann Lehmann Foundation, New York).

14 The *Jerusalem Post* of June 10, 1999, reported that Etienne Saqr, head of the Guardians of the Cedar, is a "leading member" of Phares' WLO. A Congressional Research Service report called The Guardians of the Cedar an "extremist Maronite militia and terrorist organization." John Creed, Congressional Research Service Report Lebanon 85-885-F, July 31, 1985, appendix.

15 David Thibault, "Berg's Killers Are Right about One thing," CNS News, cnsnews.com, May 11, 2004.

16 Niles Lathem, "US Hostage Screams in Horror as He Is Beheaded," *New York Post*, May 12, 2004.

17 Cited in "Press wrestles with grim clips," Randy Dotinga, *Christian Science Monitor,* May 13, 2004.

18 Cited in Peter Johnson, "A death caught on tape: should it run or not?" *USA Today*, May 11, 2004.

19 Jonah Goldberg, "Media Missteps," National Review Online, May 7, 2004.

20 Joel Mowbray, "John Kerry: the Sunshine Soldier," Front Page Magazine, frontpagemag.com, February 24, 2004. Richard Gibson, "Getting Away with Murder," Counterpunch.org, May 18, 2001. *Newsweek*'s Gregory L. Vistica established that one night in 1969 in Thanh Phong, Navy

SEALs led by Kerrey knifed or gunned down an elderly couple, women and children for which he was awarded a Bronze Star for killing 21 Vietcong.

21 Michael Tackett and Tim Jones, "Vietnam War Service Lifts Kerry's Run," *Chicago Tribune,* February 8, 2004.

22 Paul Crespo, "The media's double-standard on Iraq abuse," Town Hall, May 17, 2004.

23 Jonah Goldberg, "Media Missteps: Context gets lost in hysteria and grandstanding," National Review Online, May 7, 2004.

24 Leo Lacayo, "Tell Me, Where Is the Liberal Anger About Nick Berg," ChronWatch.com, May 12, 2004.

25 Howard Kurtz, "Beheading Adds News Twist to Scandal," *Washington Post*, May 12, 2004.

26 Ralph Waldo Emerson, *The American Scholar: An Oration delivered before the Phi Beta Kappa Society at Cambridge*, August, 31, 1837, in *Nature; Addresses and Lectures* (Boston: Munroe, 1849).

27 Richard Hofstadter, *Anti-Intellectualism in American Life* (New York: Knopf, 1963).

28 Also see Frederick Jackson Turner, "The Significance of the Frontier in American History," lecture to the American Historical Association, Chicago, 1893.

29 Andrew D. Grossman, *Neither Dead Nor Red: Civilian Defense and American Political Development During the Early Cold War,* chap. 3 (New York: Routledge, 2001). Much of the funding for social-science research related to Cold War issues was funneled through agencies such as the CIA, as well as the short-lived Psychological Strategy Board and remains highly classified.

30 Vijay Prashad, "Mr. Kurtz! The horror! The horror!" *Asheville Global Report*, November 20–26, 2003.

31 Edgar H. Schein with Inge Schneier and Curtis H. Barker, *Coercive Persuasion: a Socio- psychological Analysis of the "Brainwashing" of American Civilian Prisoners by the Chinese Communists*, (New York: W. W. Norton, 1961).

32 George Orwell, "Politics and the English Language," in *Horizon* (London: 1946).

33 "Iraq Faces Massive U.S. Missile Barrage," CBS, January 24, 2003.

34 Lt. Gen. T. Michael Moseley, *Operation Iraqi Freedom by the Numbers*, USCENTAF, Assessment and Analysis Division, April 30, 2004, p.15.

35 "Nonlethal weapons should not be required to have a zero probability of producing fatalities or permanent injuries," DOD Directive 3000.3, Policy for Non-Lethal Weapons, July 9, 1996. See also, Council on Foreign Relations, Nonlethal Technologies: Progress and Prospects, Independent Task Force Report, Richard Garwin, Chairman, 1999, which states, "It is not the primary purpose of nonlethal weapons to prevent death or major injury." Nonlethal Weapons (NLW) "are intended to increase the lethality of force used against combatants, while reducing death and injury among noncombatant civilians" and are useful "in political terms," where "less violence equals greater acceptability." Jan Morris, a science-fiction writer, and coauthor with Colonel John Alexander and Richard Groller of *Warrior's Edge* (New York: Avon Books, 1992), is a major proponent of nonlethal weaponry, but even she admits that "casualties cannot be avoided."

36 David Barstow and Robin Stein, in "Under Bush, a New Age of Prepackaged TV News," *New York Times*, March 13, 2005, describe the use of video news releases by PR professionals released to news outlets and broadcast without attribution as though they were genuine news items.

37 Charlene Gubash, "Different shades of condemnation in Arab world to Berg killing," NBC, May 14, 2004.

38 David Thibault, "Berg's Killers Are Right about One Thing," CNS News, cnsnews.com, May 11, 2004.

39 Stephen Zak, "No More Apologies for Abu Ghraib," CNS News, cnsnews.com, May 5, 2004.

40 Meyrav Wurmser, "Moment of Truth: These are trying times for proponents of liberalism in the Middle East," *National Review Online,* May 24, 2004.

41 Edward Said, *Orientalism* (New York: Vintage, 1979).

42 Moseley, *Operation Iraqi Freedom by the Numbers.*

43 Human Rights Watch, "The War in Iraq and International Humanitarian Law FAQ," website.

44 Harlan K. Ullman and James P. Wade, *Shock and Awe: Achieving Rapid Dominance* (Washington, D.C.: NDU Press Book, December 1996).

45 Susan Martin, "No-fly' zone perils were for Iraqis, not allied pilots," *St. Petersburg Times*, October 29, 2004.

46 The Nazi bombing of Guernica was premised on continuous air attacks breaking the spirit of the population, erroneously, as it turned out in that case. See Gordon Thomas and Max Morgan Witts, *Guernica: The Crucible of World War II* (New York: Stein & Day, 1975); and Peter Watson, *War on the Mind: The Military Uses and Abuses of Psychology* (NewYork: Basic Books, 1978), pp. 217–19: "Everything that pertains to combatant trauma is intensified in the case of helpless civilian populations under direct attack. It has long been recognized that the most effective way to demoralize large civilian populations is through massive aerial bombardment. This was a primary motivation in the invention of aerial bombardment of open cities by the Nazis in the Spanish Civil War and World War II."

47 "Ex-U.S. Marine: I Killed Civilians in Iraq," DemocracyNow.com, May 24, 2004.

48 Irwin Arieff, "U.N. Sees 500,000 Iraqis Casualties at Start of War," Reuters, January 7, 2003.

49 Paul Richter, "U.S. Weighs Tactical Nuclear Strike on Iraq," *Los Angeles Times*, January 25, 2003.

50 Ken Coates, "Fallujah: Shock and Awe," CommonDreams.org, November 19, 2004.

51 AP, "US troops claim they have occupied whole of Fallujah," November 14, 2004.

52 Peter Linebaugh, "Torture and Neo-Liberalism with Sycorax in Iraq," Counterpunch.org, November 27, 2004.

53 AP, "Navy Probes New Iraq Prison Photos," December 3, 2004.

54 Jeffrey St. Clair, "Targeting Civilians in Fallujah," Counterpunch.org, October 6, 2004.

55 Proportionality is the underlying basis for humanitarian law pertaining both to *jus ad bellem* and *jus in bello*. See Roy Gutman and David Rieff, *Crimes of War: What the Public Should Know* (New York: W. W. Norton, 1999).

7. Ideology I: Prometheus

1 James Mann, *Rise of the Vulcans: The History of Bush's War Cabinet* (New York: Viking, 2004).

2 Catholic neoconservatives Michael Novak, George Weigel, and Robert Royal have published their own just war theories favoring the Iraq war in direct opposition to the Vatican. In his speech, "*'Just War' Theory and U.S. Policy in Iraq,*" delivered in Rome on February 10, 2003, Novak, who won the 1994 Templeton Prize for Progress in Religion, argued that just war theory had to accommodate the advent of asymmetrical warfare.

3 Peter Singer, *The President of Good and Evil: The Ethics of George W. Bush* (New York: E. P. Dutton, 2004).

4 Aziz al-Taee is associated with Clear Channel and the activist conservative group, Free Republic, among others. The *Chicago Tribune* reported on March 19, 2003, that the, "sponsorship of large rallies by Clear Channel stations is unique among major media companies." See also William Bunch, "Berg Met With Shady Iraqi," *Philadelphia Daily News,* May 17, 2004. Pictures of Taee speaking at a Patriots Rally on January 18, 2003 can be seen at many sites including http://community.webshots.com/photo/61282220/61285955AKXtsx. According to an article by Sherry Gossett on the conservative site World Net Daily, "Antiwar leaders charge Nazis rule White House," January 18, 2003, Free Republic activists and others organized the rally in response to

antiwar protests. Coincidentally, one of the reporters who "promoted" Taee's position (at a White House press conference on March 4, 2003) was none other than Jeff Guckert/Gannon, a male escort turned journalist who later became the center of a scandal over his access to the White House press room without journalistic credentials. Berg's Republican connections are said to have begun on a trip to Texas, where he learned tower climbing from a Republican businessman. He later worked at a Republican National Convention. See Jonathan Tuleya, "Prometheus Methods Tower Services Inc., the business that cost Nick Berg his life in Iraq, has no records with the Pennsylvania Department of State," *Daily Local News Online*, Philadelphia, May 14, 2004.

5 Michelle Goldberg, "The war over the peace," Salon.com, April 14, 2003.

6 Elise Labott, "Iraqi dissident meet with U.S. official," CNN, August 9, 2002.

7 Rebecca Traister, "Moore interviewed Berg for 'Fahrenheit,'" Salon.com, May 27, 2004.

8 Joel Berkofsky, "Videotaped execution of U.S. Jew raises questions about terror's targets," Jewish Telegraphic Agency, May 12, 2004.

9 "Nick Berg's Father and International A.N.S.W.E.R.," FreeRepublic.com thread, May 11, 2004.

10 Michael Manekin, "How pirate radio became legal … and why Northampton might benefit," *Valley Advocate,* 2001.

11 "Berg's encounter with "terrorist" revealed," LibertyPost.com thread, May 14, 2004.

12 Julie Rawe, "The Sad Tale of Nick Berg," *Time*, May 24, 2004; AP, "U.S. funds Iraqi television network," November 29, 2003.

13 Leon Worden, interview with Karpinski, *The Signal,* July 4, 2004.

14 Michael Powell and Michelle Garcia, "Nick Berg's Undying Spirit," *Washington Post,* May 14, 2004.

15 In the Norse shamanic tradition, Odin's ravens represent the powers of necromancy, clairvoyance and telepathy, and they were guides for the dead. Ralph Metzner, *The Well of Remembrance* (Boston: Shambala Press, 1994). But in Europe, at least from Christian times, ravens have several strikes against them: black is considered a negative color; ravens are carrion eaters; and they have a symbiotic relationship with man's oldest enemy, the wolf. In many western traditions raven represents darkness, destructiveness and evil. See also G. Ronald Murphy, *The Owl, the Raven, and the Dove* (New York: Oxford University Press, 2002).

16 Michel Foucault, *The History of Sexuality,* in 3 volumes (Harmondsworth, UK: Pelican, 1981).

17 ICRC Report, February 2004.

18 Farhad Manjoo, "Total Information Awareness: Down, But Not Out," Salon.com, January 28, 2003.

19 Brian Robinson, "Reenter the matrix," Federal Computer World, fcw.com, August 30, 2004.

20 Fox News, "'Patriot Act II' Irks Civil Libertarians," December 10, 2004.

21 "ACLU Disappointed with 'Intelligence Reform' Bill Passage," statement of the Director of the ACLU Washington Legislative Office, December 8, 2004, aclu.org. See also Robert O'Harrow Jr., "Senate Bill Proposes Anti-Terror Database," *Washington Post*, September 28, 2004.

22 Richard Benedetto, "Data Sought on Secret Spending," *USA Today,* February 2, 2004.

23 Website of Senator Leahy, "Senate Passes Feingold-Leahy Measure Making U.S. Agencies Accountable On Data Collection," September 16, 2004.

24 Interview with Dahr Jamail, "Violence Continues to Rock Iraq," DemocracyNow.com, December 6, 2004. Also see archives of DOD: DefenseLink: News Photos and Centcom Gallery Displayer for images.

25 Jean-Michel Stoullig, "Rumsfeld Commission Warns Against 'Space Pearl Harbor,'" AP, January 11, 2001. Under Rumsfeld there is now a highly -classified, very expensive program costing billions of dollars involving spy satellites which has been vehemently criticized by the senior Democrat on the Senate Intelligence Committee as likely to provoke the very attacks it is meant to

deter. See Douglas Jehl, "New Spy Plan Said to Involve Satellite System," *New York Times*, December 12, 2004.

26 Vladimir Maksimovskiy, "In Space over Kosovo, Satellites Gathering," Vremya-MN, April 13, 1999.

27 Michael Krepon and Christopher Clary, "Space Assets and the War in Iraq," Henry Stimson Center, 2004; "Space Role in Allied Force Extensive—Effective," United States Space Command, News Release no. 11-99, June 17, 1999.

28 William Bunch, "Berg Met with Shady Iraqi," *Philadelphia Daily News*, May 17, 2004.

29 Alexandra Starr, "Charlotte Beers' Toughest Sell," *Business Week Online,* December 17, 2001.

30 Sara Solovitch, "The American Dream," *Esquire*, January 2005.

31 Peter Finn, "A Lone Woman Testifies to Iraq's Order of Terror," *Washington Post*, July 21, 2003.

32 Mike Allen, "White House Angered at Plan for Pentagon Disinformation," *Washington Post,* February 25, 2002. SourceWatch.com, Center for Media and Democracy.

33 Michele Bond, "Public Diplomacy," National Defense University Archives, September 14, 1998.

34 Thom Shanker and Eric Schmitt, "Hearts and Minds," *New York Times*, December 13, 2004.

35 Thom Shanker and Eric Schmitt, "Pentagon Weighs Use of Deception in a Broad Arena," *New York Times*, December 13, 2004.

36 Mark Mazzetti, "PR Meets Psy-Ops in War on Terror," *Los Angeles Times*, December 1, 2004.

37 Ibid.

38 David Hughes, "Networking, Swarming and Warfighting," *Aviation Week and Space Technology*, September 29, 2003.

39 Joel Beinin, "Thought Control for Middle East Studies," Media Monitors Network, March 30, 2004.

40 BBC, "Fears over CIA 'university spies,'" June 2, 2005; and David Glenn, "Cloak and Classroom," The Chronicle of Higher Education, March 25, 2005. Also, Dave H. Price, "Exposing the Pat Roberts Intelligence Scholars Program—The CIA's Campus Spies," Counterpunch.org, March 12–13, 2005.

41 AFP, "Media watchdogs savage Pentagon: Planting of false stories," February 21, 2002.

42 Martin Aser, "A tale of two Iraqi schools," BBC, October 22, 2003. For a defense of de-Ba'athification, see Yuri Yarim-Agaev, "The Necessity of Destroying the Ba'ath Party," FrontPageMag.com, April 25, 2003.

43 Dorinda Elliott and John Barry, "A Subliminal Dr. Strangelove," *Newsweek,* August 22, 1994. Also see Douglas Pasternak, "Wonder Weapons," *US News & World Report,* July 7, 1997.

44 Jon Ronsom, *The Men Who Stare at Goats* (New York: Simon & Schuster, 2005). Ronson claims the secret unit spoke to him in retaliation against their detractors in the Agency.

45 N. Lewer and S. Schofield, *Nonlethal Technologies—a Fatal Attraction* (London: Zed Books, 1997).

46 Jurgen Altmann, "Acoustic Weapons," Research Paper, Experimentelle Physick, Universitat Dortmund, April 1998–1999. Although infrasound is used in riot control, accounts of physical trauma induced by it tend to be anecdotal. Researchers like Altmann argue that there is scant scientific evidence to conclude that it does significant physical damage, unlike high-pitched, extremely loud, or explosive sounds.

47 Certainly, even the most benign weapons technologies may create lethal effects under some conditions. It is the intent that separates this class of weapons from conventional munitions. Unintended lethal effects must be considered, and may modify, employment strategies and tactics. "Policy for Nonlethal Weapons," DOD Directive, July 9, 1996, cited in Col. Joseph Siniscalchi, USAF, "Non-lethal Technologies," Occasional Paper No. 3, March 1998, Center for Strategy and Technology, Air War College, Air University, Maxwell Airforce Base, Alabama.

48 A memorandum, written by no less than Paul Wolfowitz to Dick Cheney states: "A U.S. lead in nonlethal technologies will increase our options and reinforce our position in the post-Cold War world. Our Research and Development efforts must be increased." Paul Wolfowitz, Under Secretary of Defense for Policy, memorandum to the Secretary of Defense and the Deputy Secretary of Defense, subject: "Do We Need a Non-lethal Defense Initiative?" March 30, 1991.

49 Tom Loftus, "War games in a time of war," MSNBC, July 18, 2004.

50 Conn Hallinan, "Rumsfeld's New Model Army," ForeignPolicy-inFocus.com, November 4, 2003.

51 Irving Kristol, "The Neoconservative Persuasion: What It Was, And What It Is," *Weekly Standard,* August 25, 2003.

52 See Diana Johnstone, "Fools' Crusade: Yugoslavia, Nato, and Western Delusions," *Monthly Review*, November 2002.

53 Justin Raimondo, "Reclaiming the American Right: The Lost Legacy of the Conservative Movement," Center for Libertarian Studies, June 1, 1993.

54 Michael Lind, "A Tragedy of Errors," *The Nation,* February 23, 2004.

55 Jason Vest, "The Men from JINSA and CSO," *The Nation,* August 15, 2002.

56 Michael Lind, "Distorting US Foreign Policy: The Israel Lobby and American Power," *American Prospect,* April 2002.

57 Dana Priest and Barton Gellman, "U.S. Decries Abuse but Defends Interrogations," *Washington Post,* December 26, 2002.

58 Charles Hanley, "Prisoners describe brutality by troops," AP, November 2, 2003.

59 Ivan Eland, "Politics and the CIA," Antiwar.com, November 16, 2004.

60 Editorial, "Rumsfeld's Spy Game," *Toledo Blade,* January 31, 2005.

61 Ken Silverstein, "Military Lawyers Sought Outside Help on Interrogation Rules," *Los Angeles Times,* May 13, 2004.

62 Chalmers Johnson, "How the Bush Administration Is Subverting the CIA," History News Network, hnn.us, December 13, 2004. Johnson gives a lucid history of the misuse of the CIA's covert powers by the executive and terms the present intelligence agency the president's "Praetorian guard."

63 Zachary Coile, "9/11 panel dismayed by Bush's reaction," *San Francisco Chronicle*, Washington Bureau, Wednesday, August 4, 2004.

64 Haviland Smith, "Dubious Purge at the CIA," *Washington Post,* January 4, 2005.

65 Jim Lobe, "Pentagon's Feith Again at Center of Disaster," InterPress Service, May 19, 2004.

66 Michael Isikoff, Daniel Klaidman and Michael Hirsh, "Torture's Path," *Newsweek,* December 27–January 3, 2005.

67 "Bombing Anywhere on Earth in Less Than Two Hours," Space Daily, November 27, 2003. This is a slightly edited version of the initial introduction of a report by the U.S. government to explain the Falcon Project. The report is available for download directly from DARPA (Defense Advanced Research Projects Agency).

68 Jim Garamone, "Joint Vision 2020 Emphasizes Full-spectrum Dominance," American Forces Press Service, Washington, D.C., June 2, 2000. Joint Vision 2020 was released on May 30 and signed by the chairman of the Joint Chiefs of Staff, General Henry Shelton. See also "Rebuilding America's Defenses," PNAC website.

69 Zbigniew Brzezinksi, "Why Unity is Essential," *Washington Post*, February 19, 2003.

70 George Kennan, "The Sources of Soviet Conduct," *Foreign Affairs,* July 1947.

71 Michael Lind, "The Weird Men Behind George W. Bush's War," *New Statesman,* April 7, 2003. See also a partially convincing critique of the Trotskyite theory by Alan Wald, "Are Trotskyites

Running the Pentagon?" History News Network, hnn.us, June 23, 2003 and Lind's comeback on June 30, 2003, "I Was Smeared."

72 Samuel Huntington, "The Clash of Civilizations," *Foreign Affairs*, Summer 1993.

73 Bernard Lewis, "The Roots of Muslim Rage," *Atlantic Monthly,* September 1990.

74 Michael Hersh, "Bernard Lewis Revisited," *Washington Monthly,* November 2004.

75 Rafael Patai, *The Arab Mind* (Long Island City, NY: Hatherleigh Press, 1972/2002, rev. ed.)

76 Richard Bulliet *The Case for Islamo-Christian Civilization* (New York: Columbia University Press, 2004). See also Fawaz Gerges, *America and Political Islam: Clash of Cultures or Clash of Interests?* (Cambridge: Cambridge University Press, 1999).

77 Kristine MacNeill, "The War on Academic Freedom," *The Nation,* November 11, 2002.

78 "Return of Campus McCarthyism," *Berkshire Eagle,* February 16, 2004. Also see Martin Kramer, *Ivory Towers on Sand: The Failure of Middle Eastern Studies in America* (Washington, D.C.: Washington Institute for Near East Policy, 2001).

79 Edward Said, *Orientalism* (New York: Vintage, 1979).

80 The association of fascism with Islamism was first made by Christopher Hitchens, in "Against Rationalization," *The Nation,* September 20, 2001.

81 Fareed Zakaria, "Terrorists Don't Need States," *Newsweek,* April 5, 2004; and William Lind, "Understanding Fourth Generation War," LewRockwell.com, January 6, 2004. See also Part III of *The Power of Nightmares,* aired originally on BBC 2, November 3, 2004, written and produced by Adam Curtis.

82 Niall Ferguson, *Colossus: The Price of America's Empire* (New York: Penguin Press, 2004).

83 Sewell Chan, "Beheading victim loved 'adventure,'" *Washington Post,* May 14, 2004.

84 "So according to tradition, Nimrod was ruler of mankind at the time Abraham was born, which is about the year 1996 according to the Jewish count. Already Man had mastered the art of building, and so a project was embarked upon whereby Nimrod would prevent the human race from spreading too much and becoming decentralised. He envisaged a massive Tower, which would stamp Man's supremacy on the world and give him absolute leadership over people. So was built the Tower of Babel, a tower that could never really reach heaven, but could express Man's desire to compete with God. God was left with no option. His first choice, that there would be no nations but that the whole world would as a united front serve Him had failed. Now the only way back was to mix up the languages of humans and create the proliferation of nations that we know of today. The way back to God would now be easier because it would be much more difficult for one ruler to claim supremacy over the entire world." Parashat Noach from the Parsha archive of the Kingston Synagogue website.

85 Caroline Frost, "Saddam Hussein: Profile," BBC4, March 9, 2003.

86 Max Boot, "The Case for American Empire," *Weekly Standard,* October 15, 2001. See also Max Boot, *The Savage Wars of Peace: Small Wars and the Rise of American Power* (New York: Basic Books, 2003).

87 Robert Kaplan, "Supremacy by Stealth," *Atlantic Monthly,* July/August 2003. See also Robert Kaplan, *Warrior Politics: Why Leadership Demands a Pagan Ethics* (New York: Random House, 2001).

88 Robert D. Kaplan, "Indian Country: America's military faces the most thankless task in the history of warfare," Wall Street Journal Online, September 25, 2004.

89 Charles Krauthammer, "Victory Changes Everything," *Jewish World Review,* November 30, 2001.

90 Thomas P.M. Barnett, *The Pentagon's New Map: War and Peace in the Twenty-First Century* (New York: G. P. Putnum & Sons, April 2004).

91 James Webb, "Heading for Trouble: Do we really want to occupy Iraq for the next thirty years?" *Washington Post,* September 4, 2002.

92 Neil Swidey, "The Analyst," *Boston Globe*, May 18, 2003.

93 Lawrence J. Korb, "It's Time to Bench 'Team B," *Los Angeles Times*, August 8, 2004.

94 Nuclear Posture Review Report, submitted to Congress on December 31, 2001.

95 Michael E. O'Hanlon, in Brookings Institute policy brief #86, "Beyond Missile Defense: Countering Terrorism and Weapons of Mass Destruction," August 2001, estimates that based on Congressional Budget Office figures, the Global Protection Against Limited Strikes (GPALS) espoused by the previous Bush administration might cost $120 billion to $150 billion to develop and deploy—making for an average of $7 billion a year over a twenty-year period.

96 Peter Goodchild, *Edward Teller: The Real Dr. Strangelove* (Boston: Harvard University Press, 2004).

97 "The President's Real Goal in Iraq," Jay Bookman, *Atlanta Journal-Constitution*, September 29, 2002.

98 For an account of the psychological impact of war, see Richard Gabriel, *No More Heroes: Madness and Psychiatry in War* (New York: Hill and Wang, 1987). See also Peter Watson, *War on the Mind* (New York: Basic Books, 1978).

99 John Laughland, "Flirting with Fascism," *American Conservative Magazine*, June 30, 2003.

100 Martin Garbus, "A Hostile Takeover: How the Federalist Society Is Capturing the Federal Courts," *American Prospect*, March 1, 2003; Jamin Raskin, "Courts vs. Citizens," *American Prospect,* March 1, 2003.

8. Context III: Virtual Violence

1 Miles Moffeit, "Sex-assault cases from Iraq often stall," *Denver Post*, April 12, 2004.

2 Anna Cziezadlo, "For Iraqi women, Abu Ghraib's taint," *Christian Science Monitor*, May 28, 2004.

3 Nagem Salam, "Crimes in Iraq: A Tree with No Roots," Islam Online, June 14, 2004.

4 Rouba Kabbara, "Human rights groups: Iraqi women raped at Abu Ghraib jail," Middle East Online, May 29, 2004.

5 Seymour Hersh, "Torture at Abu Ghraib," *New Yorker,* May 10, 2004.

6 Cziezadlo, "For Iraqi women, Abu Ghraib's taint."

7 Ibid.

8 David Enders, "Women Prisoners in Iraq," Occupation Watch Center, December 12, 2003.

9 Rouba Kabbara, "Human rights groups: Iraqi women raped at Abu Ghraib jail," *Middle East Online,* May 29, 2004.

10 Iman Ahmed Khammas, "Iraqi Women in the Occupation Prisons as Material and Means of Violations," Occupation Watch Center, May 26, 2004.

11 "New Iraq's Prisoners, Unknown Numbers, Charges," *Al Zawra,* March 29, 2004. Also see Chris Shumway, "Pattern Emerges of Sexual Assault Against Women Held by U.S. Forces," *New Standard,* June 6, 2004.

12 Luke Harding, "Focus shifts to jail abuse of women," *Guardian,* May 12, 2004.

13 Luke Harding, "The Other Prisoners," *Guardian*, May 20, 2004.

14 Miles Moffeit, "Sex-assault cases from Iraq often stall," *Denver Post,* April 12, 2004.

15 AP, "Iraqi Children among Abused Prisoners at Abu Ghraib," May 7, 2004.

16 Andrew Miga, "Guards treated woman like donkey," *Boston Herald,* May 6, 2004.

17 Harding, "The Other Prisoners."

18 Orly Halpern, "Iraqi women stigmatized by prison: Once freed, they often disappear," *Globe and Mail*, July 21, 2004.

19 Harding, "The Other Prisoners."

20 "Rape of Iraqi/US Military Women," Lysistrata Project, May 26, 2004, http://www.lysistrataproject.org/WaronWomen.htm. This group and http://www.globalwomenstrike.net/ do not present documented evidence of rape but link to newspaper accounts containing allegations from detainees and others.

21 Houzan Mahmoud, "An empty sort of freedom," *Guardian,* March 8, 2004.

22 Robert Fisk, "Baghdad is a city that reeks with the stench of the dead," *Independent,* July 28, 2004.

23 AFP, "Iraqi Women Kidnapped, Raped," August 24, 2003.

24 Marie-Laura Colson, "Iraqi Women Have Lost the Post War," *La Liberation*, September 2, 2003.

25 For rape, the rate for 1998–2000 was 0.00 per 1,000 for Saudi Arabia, compared with 0.01 for Japan and 0.30 for the United States. *Seventh United Nations Survey of Crime Trends and Operation of Criminal Justice Systems* (U.N. Center for International Crime Reporting). See also, Haroon Siddiqui, "What Language is U.S. Speaking in Iraq?" *Toronto Star*, August 10, 2003.

26 Lauren Sandler, "Veiled and Worried in Baghdad," *New York Times*, September, 2003. See also, Susan Milligan, "Iraqi Women Recoiling in Fear of Crime," *Boston Globe*, August 3, 2003. Many families are afraid to send their daughters to school because people will kidnap them," said Saad Hashem, a 38-year-old father of four daughters. "Under Saddam, it was 100 percent safe. We could come home at 1 or 2 a.m.; police were everywhere." Colonel Guy Shields, spokesman for the coalition forces, said he had no information about reports of rapes and kidnappings. "The military is not keeping track of Iraqi criminal statistics," he said. L. Paul Bremer III, head of the civilian Coalition Provisional Authority, noted that Iraqi police had broken up two kidnapping rings, while a local women's group claimed that rapes and kidnappings occurred twenty times a day across the country because the harsh punishments meted out by Hussein's regime were no longer a deterrent. Finally, a Save the Children report in May showed that attendance at girls' schools had dropped by more than half, largely because parents didn't want to send their daughters out of the home.

27" Iraqi women shut out by fear," Radio Netherlands, July 2003.

28 AP, "Iraqis Concerned With Male Soldiers Frisking Women," June 18, 2003.

29 Howard Kurtz, "Anchors Try to Get Close to the Story In Baghdad," *Washington Post,* January 27, 2005.

30 Elizabeth Rubin,"Fern Holland's War," *The New York Times Magazine,* September 19, 2004.

31 Jeffrey Gettleman, "As U.S. Detains Iraqis, Families Plead For News," *New York Times,* March 7, 2004.

32 Peace Women, peacewomen.org.

33 Kim Ghattas, "Iraqi Women Struggle to be Heard," BBC, August 18, 2003. Also see Ghattas, "Iraqi Women Have Lost the Post War," and Ilene R. Prusher, "In freer Iraq, new curbs on women's wear," *Christian Science Monitor*, June 13, 2003.

34 Anna Cziezadlo, "For Iraqi women, Abu Ghraib's taint," *Christian Science Monitor*, May 28, 2004.

35 Charles Krauthammer, "Abu Ghraib As Symbol," *Washington Post,* May 7, 2004.

36 Vanessa Ho, "Airport pat-downs trigger alarm," *Seattle Post-Intelligencer,* November 25, 2004.

37 Peter Dale Scott, "Torture Photos, Videos, a Time-Honored CIA Tradition," Pacific News Service, May 14, 2004.

38 "Iraqi Woman Recalls Abu Ghraib Rape Ordeal," *Islam Online,* July 21, 2004.

39 Ariana Eunjung Cha, "The Cost of Liberty: In a Chaotic New Iraq, A Young Widow Turns to Prostitution," *Washington Post,* June 24, 2004.

40 Peter Finn, "A Lone Woman Testifies to Iraq's Order of Terror," *Washington Post,* July 21, 2003.

41 On May 1, the *Daily Mirror* (UK) carried pictures showing a hooded man being urinated on and assaulted with a rifle butt. The *Mirror* claimed it was given the photos by two anonymous soldiers. The following day, *The Sunday Telegraph* said six soldiers from the Queen's Lancashire Regiment were going to be arrested in connection with the apparent abuse. The *Mirror,* one of only two papers that opposed the war, had good reason to trust the photos, given the testimony of a number of soldiers, reports of abuse in the Independent, as well as earlier reports by Amnesty International and the International Red Cross. The Queen's Lancashire Regiment was also facing a charge of having murdered an Iraqi detainee. However, within a few days, there were charges that the pictures were hoaxed and a 25-member government investigation began. Rushing to judgment to preempt the charges against the QLR, the government found the pictures a hoax. Pressure from *Mirror*'s owners, Trinity Mirror, and several prominent U.S. corporations with shares in Trinity who had opposed the *Mirror*'s antiwar stance long before the photos were published led to the sacking of Piers Morgan, the *Mirror*'s editor, on May 14. The paper published an apology although it stood by its editorial decisions. The government never produced documentation to support its findings. See also Paul Wood, "Arab anger at Iraq torture photos," BBC, May 4, 2004.

42 Scott Shane, "The Web as al-Qaida's safety net," *Baltimore Sun*, April 2, 2003.

43 A well-known Iraqi-born Egyptian novelist, Buthaina Al-Nasiri, who refused to publish the photos believing them to be inauthentic and inflammatory, nevertheless affirms that they represent what really did take place at Abu Ghraib and elsewhere. Sherrie Gossett, "Fake Rape Photos Infuriate Arab World," WorldNetDaily.com, May 9, 2004.

44 Kelly O'Meara, "New DynCorps Contract Draws Scrutiny," Insightmag.com, 2003.

45 Sexinwar.com.

46 Timothy Egan, "Wall Street Meets Pornography," October 23, 2000. See also, "Dirty Business: Porn Profits Attract Blue-Chip Corporations," ABC News, March 25, 2002. General Motors' adult video trade is a bigger business than *Hustler*'s Larry Flynt, and EchoStar, backed largely by Rupert Murdoch, makes more money than the whole Playboy business.

47 Donna Hughes, "The Use of New Communication and Information Technologies for the Sexual Exploitation of Women and Children," *Hastings Women's Law Journal,* 2002; www.uri.edu/artsci/wms/hughes/demand.htm.

48 Karie Lyderson, "Rape Nation," Alternet.org, July 2, 2004.

49 Human Rights Watch, "Rape Crisis in U.S. Prisons: First-Ever National Survey Finds Widespread Abuse, Official Indifference," April 19, 2001. http://hrw.org/english/docs/2001/04/19/usdom168_txt.htm

50 "Citizens for a Free Kuwait also capitalized on the publication of a quickie 154-page book about Iraqi atrocities titled The Rape of Kuwait, copies of which were stuffed into media kits and then featured on TV talk shows and the *Wall Street Journal.* The Kuwaiti embassy also bought 200,000 copies of the book for distribution to American troops." John Stauber and Sheldon Rampton, "How PR Sold the War in the Persian Gulf," chap. 10 of *Toxic Sludge is Good for You: Lies, Damn Lies and the Public Relations Industry* (Monroe, Maine: Common Courage Press, 1995). See also Arthur E. Rowse, "Flacking for the Emir," *The Progressive,* May 1991; and Stan Goff, "Piss On My Leg: Perception Control and the Stage Management of War," Counterpunch.org, October 13, 2003.

51 UPI, "Saddam Worked For the CIA," April 11, 2003.

52 Lisa DePasquale, "Feminists Silent about Freedom for Iraqi Women," July 15, 2004.

53 Kay Hymowitz, "Why Feminism is AWOL on Islam," *City Journal,* Winter 2003.

54 Excerpts from Leila Ahmed, *Women and Gender in Islam: Historical Roots of a Modern Debate* (New Haven: Yale University Press, 1992).

55 "Can the Subaltern Speak?" in Cary Nelson and Lawrence Grossberg, ed., *Marxism and the Interpretation of Culture*, (Urbana: University of Illinois, 1988). Cited in Kay Hymowitz, "The Women Feminists Forgot," *Wall Street Journal*, March 7, 2003.

56 Cited in Hymowitz, "The Women Feminists Forgot."

57 See Chalmers Johnson, "Abolish the CIA!" TomDispatch.com, November 6, 2004, for a review of Steve Coll, *Ghost Wars: The Secret History of the CIA, Afghanistan and bin Laden, from the Soviet Invasion to 10 September 2001* (New York: Penguin, 2004).

58 Beatrice Hogan, "Women Winning: The new Iraqi constitution enshrines the rights of women. That's the good news. But will it deliver on its promise?" *American Prospect*, March 12, 2004.

59 Hannah Allan, "Muta'a temporary marriages appearing in Iraq," Knight-Ridder, August 26, 2003.

60 Yanar Mohammed, founder of Organization of Women's Freedom in Iraq, in "Iraq's Oppressed Majority," response to "Iraq's Hidden Treasure," by Raja Habib Khuzai and Songul Chapouk, women members of the Governing Council.

61 Lauren Sandler, "Veiled and Worried in Baghdad," *New York Times*, September, 2003.

62 Ahmed Janabi, Iraqi group claims over 37,000 civilian toll," Al Jazeera, July 31, 2004.

63 "Counting the Casualties," *The Economist*, November 4, 2004.

9. The Torture Trompe L'Oeil

1 AP, "Frederick gets 8 years in Iraq abuse case (Abu Ghraib)," October 21, 2004.

2 CNN, "ACLU: Records show Marines tortured Iraqi prisoners," December 15, 2004.

3 Seth Hettena, "130 troops punished or charged in abuse," AP, December 16, 2004.

4 AP, "Letter blasts Guantanamo techniques in 2002: FBI complaints lodged a year before Abu Ghraib scandal," December 7, 2004.

5 Amnesty International, "Iraq: Amnesty International reveals a pattern of torture and ill-treatment," http://web.amnesty.org/pages/irq-torture-eng.

6 Dahr Jamail, "Tell-tale Signs of Torture Lead Family to Demand Answers: Wife, Daughters Tell of Iraqi Man Discharged from U.S. Custody in Coma," *New Standard*, May 4, 2004.

7 Robert Fisk, "Who killed Baha Mousa?" *Independent*, December 15, 2004.

8 Amnesty International, "Iraq."

9 Joe Conason, "Torture begins at the top," Salon.com, December 17, 2004.

10 AP, "Reservist charged in Afghan prison abuse case," September 1, 2004.

11 James Hodge and Linda Cooper, "Roots of Abu Ghraib in CIA techniques," *National Catholic Reporter*, November 5, 2004.

12 Barbara Ehrenreich, "The Torture Files—Iraqi detainees allege mistreatment and abuse," *L.A. Weekly*, February 12, 2004.

13 Deborah Perlstein, "Ending Secret Detentions," Human Rights First Report, June 2004. Also, Isabel Hilton, "The 800-lb Gorilla in American Foreign Policy," *Guardian*, July 28, 2004.

14 AFP, "CIA Renditions of Terror Suspects Are 'Out of Control': Report," February 6, 2005.

15 Rajiv Chandrasekaran and Peter Finn, "U.S. Behind Secret Transfer of Terror Suspects," *Washington Post* Foreign Service, March 11, 2002.

16 "U.S. Decries Abuse but Defends Interrogations," *Washington Post*, December 26, 2002.

17 Dana Priest and Barton Gellman, "Ends, Means, and Barbarity: The use and abuse of torture," *The Economist*, January 11, 2003.

18 Eyal Press, "In torture we trust," *The Nation,* March 31, 2003.

19 *New York Times,* May 17, 2003; and *Los Angeles Times*, August 18, 2003.

20 Charles Hanley, AP, November 1, 2003.

21 Sherry Ricciardi, "Missed Signals," *American Journalism Review,* August–September 2004.

22 Joel Campagna and Hani Sabra, "Under Threat," CPJ, May 17, 2004; Howard Kurtz, "Anchors Try to Get Close to the Story In Baghdad," *Washington Post,* January 27, 2005.

23 Kurtz, "Anchors Try to Get Close to the Story in Baghdad."

24 Brig-Gen. Mary Anne Krusa-Dossin, "Embedding Media," Headquarters Marine Corps (HQMC) Public Affairs Brief, DOD, February 20, 2003.

25 Ricciardi, "Missed Signals."

26 Walter Jones (R-NC) in a letter to Defense Secretary Donald Rumsfeld on Nov. 29, 2004 cited in Rick Maze, "Lawmaker wants camera crews barred from combat theater," *Army Times,* Nov. 30, 2004.

27 "Mutilated body in Iraq not Margaret Hassan," AP/photo credit, Care Australia, December 1, 2004.

28 Jeffrey D. Sachs, "Iraq's civilian dead get no hearing in the United States," *Daily Star*, December 2, 2004.

29 Reed Brody, "Where's the Promised Accountability for U.S. Abuse of Prisoners in Iraq?" *St. Paul Pioneer Press*, August 5, 2004.

30 "Records Released in Response to Torture," FOIA request, released by the government 12/15/04, released by the ACLU 12/20/04, ACLU website, http://www.aclu.org/torturefoia/released/fbi.html

31 AP, "Navy documents detail abuse claims," December 15, 2004.

32 Jim Lobe, "Rummy Back on the Rocks," Inter Press Service, December 15, 2004.

33 New York Civil Liberties Union, "U.S. Soldiers Posed in Photos of Mock Executions of Detainees: More Cases of Abuse Revealed in Newly Released Documents," February 18, 2005. http://www.nyclu.org/torture_foia_pr_021805.html

34 James Taranto, "Why We Hate Them," *Opinion Journal*, September 9, 2002.

35 Christopher Schmitt and Edward Pound, "Keeping Secrets," *US News & World Report,* Decmber 22, 2003. See also Jennifer Van Bergen, "The Veil of Secrecy: The Bush Administration: a Closed Family System," Counterpunch.org, November 30, 2004.

36 PBS, "Judging Judges," February 15, 2005.

37 Jon Anderson, "Maj. Gen. Fast, former aide to Sanchez at Abu Ghraib, takes intelligence post," *Stars and Stripes,* March 15, 2005.

38 Rowan Scarborough, "Pentagon Analysts Hit Anti-U.S. Bias at Red Cross," *Washington Times*, December 1, 2004.

39 ABC News, "Soldier Alleges Abuse Cover Up," May 19, 2004.

40 Pam Zubeck, "Top Air Force lawyer punished for misconduct," *Air Force Academy Gazette*, December 23, 2004.

41 Eric Schmitt, "Abuse Inquiry Finds Flaws," *New York Times,* December 4, 2004.

42 Elise Ackerman, "Abu Ghraib Abuse More Wide Spread," Knight-Ridder, August 27, 2004.

43 Seth Hettena, "Navy Probes New Iraq Prison Photos," AP, December 4, 2004.

44 Seth Hettena, "Court-martial set for SEAL in abuse case," AP, March 21, 2005.

45 Douglas Jehl and Andrea Elliott, "Cuba Base Sent Its Interrogators to Iraqi Prison," *New York Times,* May 29, 2004.

46 Seth Hettena, "One SEAL cleared of detainee-abuse charges," AP, December 21, 2004.

47 Paisley Dodds, "Letter illustrates FBI concern about detainee treatment," AP, December 7, 2004; CBS/AP, "Prison Report Saw Int'l Law Risks," June 2, 2004.

48 Eric Schmitt, "Abuse Inquiry Finds Flaws," *New York Times,* December 4, 2004.

49 Josh White and Scott Higham, "Army Calls Abuses, 'Aberrations,'" *Washington Post,* July 23, 2004.

50 Physicians for Human Rights, "Schlesinger Panel's Report Inadequate: Not Strong Enough on Torture; Comprehensive Investigation Needed," August 24, 2004.

51 Jim Lobe, "Pentagon Finds Pentagon Innocent," Inter Press Service, March 12, 2005.

52 Human Rights First, "Getting to Ground Truth: Investigating U.S. Abuses in the "War on Terror," September, 2004. http://www.humanrightsfirst.org/us_law/detainees/getting_to_ground_truth.htm

53 Lobe, "Pentagon Finds Pentagon Innocent."

54 Dana Priest and Joe Priest, "Secret World of U.S. Interrogation," *Washington Post,* May 11, 2004.

55 ABC News, "Definitely a Cover-Up," May 18, 2004.

56 "Attacks on the Press 2003," Committee to Protect Journalists, cpj.org

57 Campbell Brown, "New Front in Iraq Detainee Abuse Scandal?" NBC, May 20, 2004.

58 Rick Rogers, "Marines admit abuse at second prison," *San Diego Union-Tribune*, May 22, 2004.

59 John Diamond, "Top commanders in Iraq allowed dogs to be used," *USA Today*, July 19, 2004.

60 Jake Tapper and Clayton Sandell, "Advice Rejected," ABC, May 16, 2004; Tom Regan, "Military lawyers advised Pentagon two years ago to protect prisoners," *Christian Science Monitor*, May 17, 2004.

61 John Barry, Michael Hirsh, and Michael Isikoff, "The Roots of Torture," *Newsweek*, May 24, 2004.

62 Carlotta Gall and David Rohde, "New Charges Raise Questions on Abuse at Afghan Prisons," *New York Times*, September 17, 2004.

63 Josh White and Thomas Ricks, "Iraqi Teens Abused at Abu Ghraib," *Washington Post,* August 24, 2004.

64 Jen Banbury, "Guantanamo on Steroids," Salon.com, March 3, 2004.

65 Ricciardi, "Missed Signals."

66 Ibid.

67 Ibid.

68 BBC, "Al Jazeera hit by 'missile,'" April 8, 2003.

69 Reporters Without Borders, "Two Murders and a Lie," January 15, 2004.

70 Naomi Klein "U.S. kills witnesses to its crimes,"*Guardian,* December 4, 2004.

71 Elizabeth Bumiller, Remarks at the Columbia University School of Journalism Convention, July 2004.

72 Ray McGovern, "All Mosquitos, No Swamp," TomPaine.org, December 3, 2004.

73 Ibid.

74 Neil Mackay, "Iraq's Child Prisoners," *Sunday Herald,* August 1, 2004.

75 Lisa Ashknaz Croke, "US Silent on Torture of Children," *New Standard*, August 16, 2004; Linda Wymore, "Sy Hersh at ACLU convention," *Mother Jones,* July 16, 2004.

76 Stephen Miles, "Abu Ghraib: Its Legacy for Military Medicine," *Lancet*, August 21, 2004.

77 "The CIA and the Media: How America's Most Powerful News Media Worked Hand in Glove with the Central Intelligence Agency and Why the Church Committee Covered it Up," *Rolling Stone*, October 20, 1977. Also see Loch K. Johnson, *America's Secret Power: the CIA in a*

Democratic Society (New York: Oxford University Press, 1989); "CIA in America," *CounterSpy,* Spring 1980; "Washington Post—Speaking for Whom?" *CounterSpy,* May-July 1981; "Loophole Revealed in Prohibition on CIA Use of Journalistic Cover," *New York Times,* February 16, 1996; "Making Intelligence Smarter," report of a task force of the Council on Foreign Relations, 1996; "Disinformation and Mass Deception: Democracy as a Cover Story," *Covert Action Information Bulletin,* Spring-Summer 1983; "The CIA's use of the press: A 'mighty Wurlitzer,' " *Columbia Journalism Review*, September/October 1974, p. 9-18.

78 Ricciardi, "Missed Signals."

79 R. Jeffrey Smith, "Knowledge of Abusive Tactics May Go Higher," *Washington Post,* May 16, 2004.

80 Jonathan Alter, "Time To Think About Torture," *Newsweek,* November 5, 2001.

81 Darius Rejali, "Of Human Bondage," Salon.com, June 18, 2004.

82 Darius Rejali, "A long-standing trick of the torturer's art," *Seattle Times*, May 14, 2004. See also Rejali, *Torture and Democracy* (Princeton, NJ: Princeton University Press, 2005).

83 Susan Sontag, "What Have We Done?" *Guardian*, May 24, 2004.

84 A. J. Langguth, "Torture's Teachers," *New York Times,* June 11, 1979. See also Langguth, *Hidden Terrors* (New York: Pantheon Books, 1978); William Blum, *The CIA: A Forgotten History* (London: Zed Books, 1986).

85 James V. McConnell, "Criminals Can Be Brainwashed," *Psychology Today*, April 1970. Schein's first book on the subject was *Coercive Persuasion* (New York: W. W. Norton, 1961). See also Harvard psychologist B.F. Skinner's *Beyond Freedom and Dignity* (New York: Alfred A. Knopf, 1971).

86 Mark Pinksy, "Alarms on the prison grapevine," *The Nation*, October 5, 1974.

87 Jessica Mitford, in *Kind and Usual Punishment: the Prison Business* (New York: Alfred. A. Knopf, 1973) quotes Bennett's book, *I Chose Prison* (New York: Alfred A. Knopf, 1970).

88 Malia Rulon, "CIA to release more data on Nazis it hired," AP, February 7, 2005. Also see, Philip Agee, *CIA Diary: Inside the Company* (Harmondworth, UK: Penguin Books, 1975).

89 Karin Goodwin, "Brainwash victims win cash claims," *Sunday Times* (U.K.), October 17, 2004; CBC News, "Woman awarded $100,000 for CIA-funded electroshock," June 10, 2004. See also Ann Collins, *In the Sleep Room: The Story of the CIA Brainwashing Experiments in Canada* (Toronto: Lester & Orpen Dennys, 1998); and Alexander Cockburn and Jeffrey St. Clair, "Ted K., the CIA & LSD," Counterpunch.org, July 15, 1999.

90 Testimony by Valerie Wolf, Claudia Mullen and Christine deNicola, Presidential Advisory Committee on Human Radiation Experiments, Washington, D.C., March 15, 1995. Published as *The Human Radiation Experiments: Final Report of the Advisory Committee on Human Radiation Experiments* (New York: Oxford University Press, 1996).

91 Colin A. Ross, M.D., *Bluebird: A Deliberate Creation of Multiple Personality by Psychiatrists* (Texas: Manitou Communication, 2000); also, George Andrew, *MK-Ultra: The CIA's Top Secret Program in Human Experimentation and Behavior Modification* (Winston-Salem, NC: Healthnet Press, 2001).

92 Nicholas Johnson, paper prepared for delivery at the Symposium on Ethics, "Retroactive Ethical Judgments and Human Subjects Research: The 1939 Tudor Study in Context"; and "The Tudor Study: Implications for Research in Stuttering," Ph.D. Program in Speech and Hearing Sciences, Graduate Center, City University of New York, December 13, 2002.

93 Seymour Hersh, "The Gray Zone," *New Yorker,* May 24, 2004.

94 AP, "White House Ducks Torture Proposal Queries," January 14, 2005.

95 Stephen Grey, "US accused of 'torture' flights," *Sunday Times*, November 14, 2004.

96 David Rose, "Revealed: The Full Story of the Guantanamo Britons," *Observer*, March 14, 2004.

97 Dana Priest, "Jet Is an Open Secret in Terror War," *Washington Post,* December 27, 2004.

98 Grey, "US accused of 'torture' flights."

99 BBC, "Uzbek 'torture' mother freed," February 24, 2004. See also Stephen Grey, "America's Gulag," *New Statesman,* April 30, 2004.

100 CBC News, "Maher Arar: Timeline," November 6, 2004.

101 Alexander Cockburn and Jeffrey St. Clair, "Torture: As American As Apple Pie," Counterpunch.org, August 5, 2004.

102 Norman Solomon, "From Attica to Abu Ghraib—and a Prison near you," MediaMonitors.net, August 6, 2004.

103 Rejali, "A long-standing trick of the torturer's art."

104 Richard Curtiss, "Rape, Torture, Massacres: The Israelis Did It All First," *Washington Report on Middle Eastern Affairs,* July–August, 2004.

105 Alfred McCoy, "The Hidden History of CIA Torture: America's Road to Abu Ghraib," TomDispatch.com, September 9, 2004. A fuller version of the article was published in *The New England Journal of Public Policy* 19, no. 2 (2004).

106 Peter Dale Scott, "Two Indonesias, Two Americas," Consortium for Independent Journalists, June 9, 2004.

107 Piyush Mathur, "Grim future for global foreign policies," *Asia Times,* April 15, 2004.

108 Linda Wymore, "The Good News about Abu Ghraib," *Mother Jones,* May 23, 2004.

109 McCoy, *The Hidden History of CIA Torture.*

110 Jewish Institute for National Security Affairs, "Israel Assists U.S. Forces, Shares Lessons Learned Fighting Terrorists," December 27, 2004.

111 Ibid.

112 John Stanton, "Kings of Pain: United Kingdom, United States and Israel," Counterpunch.org, May 15–16, 2004.

113 UPI, "Israel denies interrogation involvement," July 3, 2004; "U.S. Denies Israel Involvement in Iraq Involvement," Masnet & News Agencies, July 2004; "Israel denies Iraqi involvement," News24, April 7, 2004.

114 "There are no rules in such a game. Hitherto acceptable norms of human conduct do not apply. If the U.S. is to survive, long-standing American concepts of "fair play" must be reconsidered. We must develop effective espionage and counterespionage services. We must learn to subvert, sabotage and destroy our enemies by more clever, more sophisticated and more effective methods than those used against us. It may become necessary that the American people be acquainted with, understand and support this fundamentally repugnant philosophy." Report of the Second Commission on the Organization of the Executive Branch of the Government, chaired by former President Herbert Hoover, 1953–55 (1954).

115 McCoy, *The Hidden History of CIA Torture.*

116 Human Rights Watch, "Israel, the Occupied West Bank, Gaza Strip, and Palestinian Authority Territories," World Report, 2001, http://www.hrw.org/wr2k1/mideast/israel.html. Also, Steve Weizman, "Israel Uses Torture in Defiance of Court Ban," *Independent* (UK), November 12, 2001. See also "Torture in Palestine Territories," *World YWCA,* September 2001; Amnesty International, "Israel and the Occupied Territories," Report, 2001.

117 CNN, "FBI reports Guantanamo abuse," December 8, 2004.

118 Ibid.; Shankar Vedantam, "The Psychology of Torture," *Washington Post,* May 11, 2004; Thomas E. Ricks, "Abuse Inquiry Cites 26 Soldiers: 2 Deaths in Afghanistan Led to Army Probe," *Washington Post,* September 1, 2004.

119 "Lawyers cast light inside 'Gitmo,'" *Kansas City Star,* March 27, 2005.

120 Carol D. Leonnig, Dana Priest, "Pentagon Inquiry Said to Confirm Detainee's Allegations: Men Complained Female Interrogators Broke Sexual Taboos at Guantanamo Bay," *San Francisco Chronicle*, February 10, 2005.

121 Michael Isikoff and John Barry, "Gitmo: SouthCom Showdown," *Newsweek,* May 9, 2004.

10. Ideology II: The Tower of Babel

1 Lisa Myers, "Top terrorist hunter's divisive views," NBC, October 15, 2003.

2 Joel Bleifuss, "Rods from God," *In These Times,* September 3, 2003.

3 Danielle Haas, "U.S. Christians find cause to aid Israel: Evangelicals financing immigrants, settlements," *San Francisco Chronicle,* July 10, 2002.

4 Jeremy Leaming and Rob Boston, "Behind Closed Doors: Who Is The Council For National Policy And What Are They Up To? And Why Don't They Want You To Know?" Americans United for Separation of Church and State, October 2004.

5 Hal Lindsey, *The Late Great Planet Earth*, (Grand Rapids, MI: Zondervan Publishing, 1970).

6 According to popular Catholic critic Carl Olsen, "The real problem with dispensationalism is its understanding of the nature of the Church. It claims that Christianity has basically failed and that God is going to remove the Church, his heavenly people, and then deal with His earthly people, the Jews. John Nelson Darby, the ex-Anglican priest who created this belief system, believed that the Old Testament promises made to Israel were never fulfilled, but will be in the future, when he will establish an earthly, Jewish kingdom." Olsen, *Will Catholics Be Left Behind?* (Ignatius Press, 2003). For a scholarly view see Charles C. Ryrie, *Dispensationalism Revised and Updated* (Chicago: The Moody Bible Institute of Chicago, 1965).

7 Michelle Goldberg, "Fundamentally Unsound," Salon.com, July 29, 2002. For a larger overview, see Gershom Gorenberg, *The End of Days: Fundamentalism and the Struggle for the Temple Mount* (New York: Oxford University Press, 2002).

8 David Van Biema, "Missionaries Under Cover," *Time*, June 30, 2003.

9 Senator James Inhofe, "Israel's Right to the Land," Middle East Information Center, March 28, 2003.

10 Senator James Inhofe, Senate Armed Services Committee Hearing, May 11, 2004.

11 Brian Braiker, "The Persuader," *Newsweek,* Dec. 17, 2004.

12 Jerry Vines cited in Reed Irvine and Cliff Kincaid, "Another Pedophile Scandal," Accuracy in Media, July 11, 2002.

13 "Black October: Old Enemies at War Again," *Time*, October 15, 1973.

14 Sheldon Richman, "Zionism Mandates Official Discrimination Against Jews," *Washington Report on Middle East Affairs,* December–January, 1991.

15 Yigal Allon, "Israel: The Case for Defensible Borders," *Foreign Affairs*, October 1976. See also Tony Karon, "Reconciliation May Be the Only Road to Peace in 'Greater Israel,'" *Sunday Times* (South Africa), December 21, 2003.

16 Israel Shahak, *Jewish History, Jewish Religion: The Weight of Three Thousand Years*, (London and Boulder, CO: Pluto Press, 1994).

17 Michael Prior, ed., *Speaking the Truth about Zionism and Israel* (London: Melisende, 2004). Also see Donald E. Wagner, *Anxious for Armageddon* (Scottdale, PA: Herald Press, 1995). Wagner claims that the funding of the ICEJ is veiled in secrecy.

18 Edward Herman, "Anti-Semitism as a Tool of Israeli Ethnic Cleansing," *Swans,* November 25, 2002.

19 Joel Beinin, "Pro-Israel Hawks and the Second Gulf War," *Middle East Report,* April 6, 2003.

20 Michael Dobbs, "Harvard's Leader Keeps Up Push to Remake School for 21st Century," *Washington Post*, June 24, 2004.

21 Israel Shahak, "The Ideology Behind the Hebron Massacre," Middle East Institute, no. 471, March 18, 1994; and "The Background and Consequences of the Massacre in Hebron," Middle East Policy Council, 2002. Ian Lustick, "The Worldview of Jewish Fundamentalism: The Breadth of Consensus," in *For the Land and the Lord: Jewish Fundamentalism in Israel* (New York: Council on Foreign Relations, 1988). See also the chapter on nationalist Judaism in Yehoshafat Harkabi, *Israel's Fateful Decisions* (London: I. B.Tauris, 1988).

22 Israel Shahak and Norton Mezvinsky, *Jewish Fundamentalism in Israel* (London: Pluto Press).

23 See Nur Masalha, *Imperial Israel and the Palestinians: The Politics of Expansion* (London: Pluto Press, 2000).

24 "Rejecting the so-called right of return is nothing more than opposing any final settlement that results in flooding Israel with hostile Palestinians and thus eradicating the only Jewish state on the planet." Thus, negotiating with Palestinians becomes for the hysterical Krauthammer "this Nuremberg atmosphere." Charles Krauthammer, "The Real Mideast 'Poison,'" *Washington Post*, April 20, 2004.

25 "Who Needs a Jewish State?" *Los Angeles Times*, October 10, 2004.

26 Arjan El Fassed, "Imprisoned Decency," The Electronic Intifada, August 20, 2004. Between September 2000 and June 2003, approximately 2,000 Palestinian children were arrested and detained. Children as young as 13 were held in Israeli prisons with children aged 13 and 14 constituting approximately 10 percent of all child detainees. See also Sherri Muzher, "After High Court's Ruling Against Torture, Will Israel Stop Breaking Its Own Laws in the Name of Security?" *Washington Report on Middle East Affairs*, December 1999: "Israeli security forces forced 15 Palestinian women, ranging in age from 20 to 69, to undress from head to toe in the presence of women soldiers and/or policewomen. In two instances, women were required to undress in full view of a male police officer. Thirteen children, aged one month to 14 years old, were also undressed. In some cases women were compelled to undress in front of their relatives, their children and other children. Screams, curses, and beating accompanied the order to undress in several cases. (*Sexual Harassment in the Name of the Law: Violence and Degradation During Searches of Palestinian Homes in Hebron*, B'Tselem, December 1996.)"

27 In 1845, a democratic leader and editor, John L. O'Sullivan, gave the movement its name when he wrote: *"The right of our manifest destiny to over spread and to possess the whole of the continent which Providence has given us for the development of the great experiment of liberty and federative development of self government entrusted to us."* Alan Brinkley, *American History, A Survey*, vol.1 (New York: McGraw-Hill, 1995), p. 352.

28 Thus, for instance, "We Americans are the peculiar, chosen people—the Israel of our time; we bear the ark of the liberties of the world," Herman Melville, *White-Jacket* (1850), in *The Writings of Herman Melville*, vol. 5, ed. Harrison Hayford, Hershel Parker, and G. Thomas Tanselle (1969).

29 Ron Suskind, "Without a Doubt," *The New York Times Magazine*, October 17, 2004.

30 O. Palmer Robertson, *The Christ of the Covenants* (Phillipsburg, NJ: Presbyterian and Reformed, 1980).

31 Ronald S. Wallace, *Calvin's Doctrine of the Word and Sacrament* (Grand Rapids, MI: Wm. B. Eerdmans, 1957). See also A. A. Hodge, *Outlines of Theology* (New York: Carter & Brothers, 1860), chap. 5.

32 If, drunk with sight of power, we loose
Wild tongues that have not Thee in awe—
Such boasting as the Gentiles use
Or lesser breeds without the law—
Lord God of Hosts, be with us yet,
Lest we forget—lest we forget!
— Rudyard Kipling, "Recessional (A Victorian Ode)," 1897.

33 David Garland, "Penal Excess and Surplus Meaning: Public Torture Lynchings in 20th Century America," Working Papers, Yale Center for Cultural Sociology, March 2004.

34 Frederick Clarkson, "Theocratic Dominionism Gains Influence," *Public Eye Magazine* 8, nos. 1 & 2 (March/June 1994). See also Katherine Yurica, "The Despoiling of America: How George W. Bush became the head of the new American Dominionist Church/State," Yurica Report, February 11, 2004.

35 David Domke, *God Willing?: Political Fundamentalism in the White House, the 'War on Terror,' and the Echoing Press* (London: Pluto Press, August 2004). Steven Goldsmith, "Research details use of religion to help sell war on terror, Iraq," *University of Washington News*, August 10, 2004.

36 Max Boot, "What the Heck Is a 'Neocon'?" *Opinion Journal,* December 30, 2002. See also Claes G. Ryn, "The Ideology of American Empire," *Orbis* 47 (2003).

37 Rafael Patai, *The Arab Mind*, (1973). For a critique, see Ann Marlowe, "Sex, Violence, and the Arab Mind,'" Salon.com, June 8, 2004.

38 A professor at a U.S. military college, Brian Whitaker, writes in the *Guardian*, May 27, 2004, that in Patai's *The Arab Mind*, the reader is informed of "the Arab view that masturbation is far more shameful than visiting prostitutes." Whitaker says that opinions of Patai's book among Middle East experts at American universities "are almost universally scathing" and quotes one: "The best use for this volume, if any, is as a doorstop." However, after Patai's death in 1996, the book was reprinted by Hatherleigh Press in 2002 in time for the war in Iraq, with an enthusiastic introduction by Norvell "Tex" De Atkine, a former U.S. army colonel and the head of Middle East studies at Fort Bragg who called it "essential reading" and claimed that at Fort Bragg it "formed the basis of my cultural instruction."

39 Seymour Hersh, "Moving Targets," *New Yorker*, December 15, 2003.

40 Robert Collier, "Iraq: Global Security Firms Fill in as Private Armies," *San Francisco Chronicle*, March 28th, 2004.

41 William Arkin, "The Secret War," *Los Angeles Times,* October 27, 2002.

42 Megan K. Stack and Bob Drogin, "Detainee Says U.S. Handed Him Over for Torture," *Los Angeles Times,* December 13, 2005.

43 Alfred McCoy, "The Hidden History of CIA Torture: America's Road to Abu Ghraib," TomDispatch.com, September 9, 2004.

44 "To Hell and Back," *Essence*, March 2004.

45 Frances Stonor Saunders, *The Cultural Cold War: The CIA and the World of Arts and Letters* (New York: The New Press, 2000).

46 Burnham at least is candid enough to admit that the West's anti-Communism was often no more than anticolonialism by another name. See James Burnham, *The Suicide of the West: An Essay on the Meaning and Destiny of Liberalism* (Washington, D.C.: Regnery Gateway, 1985) in which Burnham identifies Communism as an anti-Western enterprise and liberalism (which he rejects, unlike most neoconservatives) as an acquiescence in the contraction of the West, that is, a rejection of Western hegemony.

47 Thomas More, *Utopia*, Book II, *Of their traffic.* 48 John B. Judis, *The Folly of Empire: What George W. Bush Could Learn from Theodore Roosevelt and Woodrow Wilson* (New York: Scribner, 2004). Judis argues that the neoconservatives also overlook Roosevelt's later reservations about expansion and renewed interest in multilateralism. See also Tom Barry, "Frontier Justice: From TR to Bush," Counterpunch.org, November 15, 2002.

49 In "Right man's burden: why empire enthusiast Niall Ferguson won't change his mind," *Washington Monthly,* June 2004, Benjamin Wallace-Wells argues that Ferguson provides "much of the theoretical ballast" for "British-inflected thinkers" like Max Boot and Marc Steyn, "who urged empire on a newly expansionist American regime, acting as a transatlantic goad, the collective ghost of pith helmets past." This Anglophile strain is noticeable especially among neoconservative immigrant writers like Indian-born Dinesh D'Souza.

50 For a critical view of this idolization see Michael Lind, "Neocons Should Hesitate before Embracing Winston Churchill," *The Spectator*, April 24, 2004.

51 Mihir Bose, "Tell us the truth of the Empire," *Observer*, October 6, 2002.

52 Colm O'Laithian, "Torture and Degradation in Iraq: Revenge American Style?" Counterpunch.org, May 13, 2004.

53 Anupama Rao, "Problems of Violence, States of Terror: Torture in Colonial India," *Journal of Postcolonial Studies* 3, no. 1 (2001).

54 Sven Lindquist, *A History of Bombing* (New York: W. W. Norton, 2003). Quoted in Tom Engelhardt, "Icarus (Armed with Vipers) Over Iraq: The Miracle of a Single Haasen Hand Grenade," TomDispatch.com, December 6, 2004.

55 Ibid.

56 Brian Ross, "Secret FBI Report Questions al Qaeda Capabilities," ABC News, March 9, 2005.

57 Philip Smucker, "How Bin Laden Got Away," *Christian Science Monitor,* March 4, 2002. Also, "Osama's Satellite Phone Switcheroo," CBS, January 21, 2003; "Bin Laden gives Pakistani troops the slip," AFP, March 07, 2004; Peter Bergen, "The Long Hunt for Osama," *Atlantic Monthly,* October 1, 2004.

58 "Osama may get away, Rumsfeld," *Rediff,* October 25, 2001.

59 Tom Engelhardt, "Which War Is This Again?" March 11, 2005. Engelhardt lists only 4 terrorist suspects—John Walker Lindh, Yasser Hamdi, Mullah Abdul Salam Zaeef, Khalid Sheikh Mohammed—who were apprehended by the United States alone; Abu Zubaydah was caught by a joint effort; and the other 35—Mullah Fazel Mazloom, Mullah Abdul Wakil Muttawakil, Ramzi Binalshibh, Yassir al-Jazeeri, Ibn Al-Shaykh al-Libi, James Ujaama, Richard Reid the "shoe bomber," Jose Padilla, Zacarias Moussaoui, Enaam M. Arnaout, Abd al-Rahim al- Nashiri, Mohammed Haydar Zammar, Abu Zubair al-Haili, Ali Abdul Rahman al Ghamdi, Ahmed Ibrahim Bilal, Abu Anas Al-Liby, Mohamedou Ould Slahi, Omar al-Faruq, Imam Samudra, Mohsen F, Najib Chaib-Mohamed, Atmane Resali, Ghasoub al-Abrash al-Ghalyoun, Abu Talha, Bassan Dalati Satut, Mounir al-Motassadek, Ibrahim Mohammed K, Yasser Abu S, Ahmed Ellattah, Tarek Maaroufi, Nizar Trabelsi, Djamel Beghal, Kamel Daoudi, Sulaiman Abu Ghaith—were arrested by local authorities in Malaysia, Indonesia, Kuwait, the UAE, Saudi Arabia, Sudan, Morocco, Mauritania, Pakistan, Iran, Spain, France, Belgium, and Germany. This is either a remarkable display of incompetence by the U.S. military or proof that terrorism is only a pretext for military interventions by their nature incapable of addressing the issue.

60 Karen J. Greenberg, "The Courts and the War on Terror," TomDispatch.com, March 14, 2005.

61 Engelhardt lists Spain (Madrid bombing, 191 dead); Turkey (synagogue and bank bombings, 29 dead); Lebanon (the Hariri assassination, at least 15 dead); Morocco (Jewish community center, Spanish restaurant and social club, hotel, and the Belgian consulate, 40 dead); Afghanistan (recent car bombings, 12 dead), Tunisia (synagogue, 19 people dead); Bali (nightclub bombings, 202 dead); Thailand (car bombing, five dead); Saudi Arabia (at least 35 dead in multiple attacks on housing projects and an oil facility); Pakistan (12 dead); Russia (330 dead in Beslan school attack, 89 on two sabotaged jetliners, and five more in a bombing near Kizlyar); the Philippines (coordinated bomb attacks, 11 dead).

Index